dynamic DALLAS

AN ILLUSTRATED HISTORY

DARWIN PAYNE, AUTHOR
MICHAEL V. HAZEL, PHOTO EDITOR

Published by
Heritage Media Corp.
Heritage Building
1954 Kellogg Avenue, Carlsbad, California 92008
www.heritagemedia.com
ISBN: 1-886483-72-8
Library of Congress Control Number: 2002113088

Darwin Payne *Author*
Michael V. Hazel *Photo Editor*
Charles E. Parks *CEO/Publisher*
Lori M. Parks *Editorial Director*
Stephen Hung *Executive Vice President*
Randall Peterson *CFO*

Design	**Editorial**
Gina Mancini *Art Director*	Betsy Baxter Blondin *Editor-in-Chief*
Robert Galmarini	Betsy Lelja *Softcover Managing Editor*
Chris Hamilton	Mary Campbell
Marianne Mackey	John Woodward
Charlie Silvia	**Staff Writers:**
	Gregory Lucas
	Julie Gengo
Administration	Victor Menaldo
Kelly Corcoran *Human Resources Manager*	
Lisa Barone	
Melissa Coffey	
Juan Diaz	**Production**
Cyndie Miller	Deborah Sherwood *IT/Production Manager*
Stephanie Stogiera	Dave Hermstad
Vicki Verne	Arturo Ramirez

Profile Writers
Tonie Auer
Becky Belew
Allen Gardiner
Nancy Reuben Greenfield
David Kirkpatrick
Jade Kurian
Anna Lazarus
Greg Lucas
Rex Oppenheimer

Published in Cooperation with Preservation Dallas
www.preservationdallas.org

First Edition
Copyright©2002 by Heritage Media Corporation
All rights reserved. No part of this book may be reproduced in any form or by any means, electronic or mechanical, including photocopying, without permission in writing from the publisher. All inquiries should be addressed to Heritage Media Corp.

The Dallas skyline looms over the flood plain of the Trinity River, the geographical feature that first attracted the city's founder, John Neely Bryan. *Carolyn Brown Photography*

CONTENTS

4	*Acknowledgments*
7	*Preface*
8	*Chapter One* AT THE THREE FORKS: A Wanderer from Tennessee Envisions a City
20	*Chapter Two* RAILROAD CROSSROADS: Perseverance and Ingenuity Pay Off
30	*Chapter Three* BOOMTOWN ON THE TRINITY: Becoming a Real City
46	*Chapter Four* A TIME TO BE THOUGHTFUL: Problems of a Growing City
64	*Chapter Five* GETTING MODERN: Time to Think Ahead
78	*Chapter Six* LOOKING INWARD: Ups and Downs in the 20s
90	*Chapter Seven* CAUSES FOR CELEBRATION: Progress on Many Fronts
102	*Chapter Eight* OVERCOMING TRAUMA: Dallas and the Assassination
110	*Chapter Nine* SUDDENLY DIFFERENT: Preparing for the New Century
120	*Partners in Dallas*
272	*Bibliography*
274	*Index*
279	*Index of Partners & Web Sites*

ACKNOWLEDGMENTS

We have been immeasurably assisted in obtaining information for the text of this illustrated work by a number of fine new books appearing that detail the historical background of Dallas and the North Central Texas area. We are indebted to the authors, who include but are not limited to Michael V. Hazel, Jacquelyn Masur McElhaney, Robert B. Fairbanks, Gerry Cristol, Elizabeth York Enstam, Susanne Starling, Rose G. Biderman, Alan B. Governar and Jay Brakefield.

Anyone who has done research in Dallas history invariably owes gratitude to Carol Roark of the J. Erik Jonsson Central Dallas Public Library. Carol and her always-helpful staff in the Texas/Dallas History and Archives Division were an invaluable resource for this work as well as for almost all research in Dallas history. Similarly, Rachel Roberts and Alan Olson of the Dallas Historical Society are the guardians of a valuable collection of documents, photographs and artifacts essential to anyone who seeks to understand or write about the history of the city, county and area.

Gary Smith of Old City Park: The Historical Village of Dallas was generous in providing historic images for the book, and Carolyn Brown, an accomplished photographer, generously provided her contemporary photographs for the final chapter.

In the bibliography are noted several term papers prepared under Darwin Payne's direction as part of a Dallas history graduate seminar he teaches at Southern Methodist University. The students in these courses continue to create new pathways toward understanding this city and the area's past.

Finally, of course, we are grateful to the good people at Heritage Media Corporation for permitting us to be involved in this project, especially Charles E. Parks, chief executive officer; Betsy Blondin, editor-in-chief; and John Woodward, coordinating editor.

— Darwin Payne and Michael V. Hazel

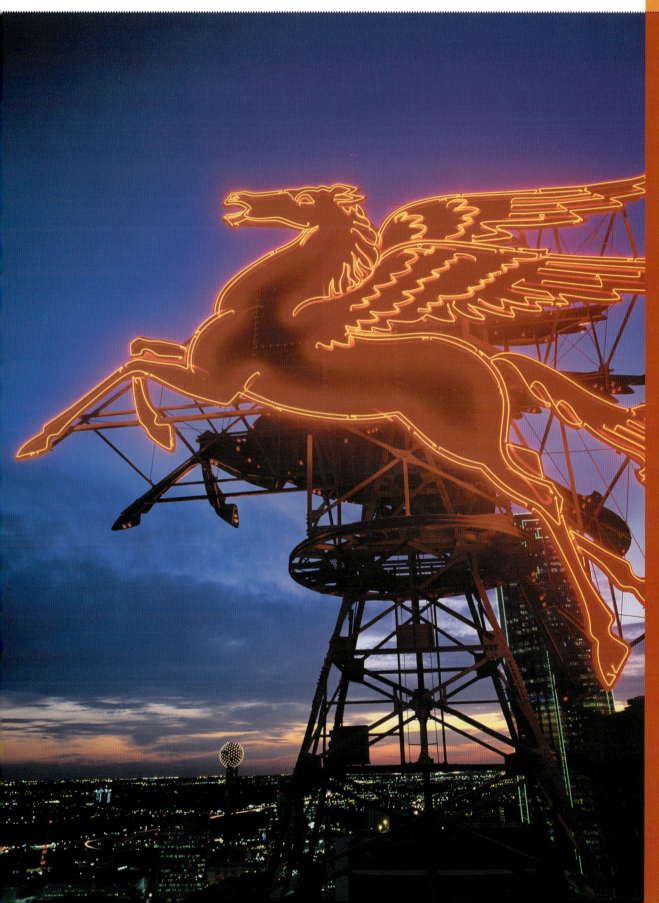

Pegasus was restored during 1999 and relit in ceremonies on New Year's Eve.
Carolyn Brown Photography

The skyline of downtown Dallas is only a mile from Fair Park, but viewed from the Hall of State across the Art Deco Esplanade it seems remote. Fair Park has been designated a National Historic Landmark.
Carolyn Brown Photography

PREFACE

How pleasant it has been for me as a writer to take this journey through the history of Dallas, a city whose very name conjures up certain images — unfortunately, not always favorable ones — throughout the world. As I trust the reader will find, this very modern city has a most intriguing and even surprising background that should alter stereotyped notions that are all too prevalent.

In the past several years a welcome surge of interest in Dallas history has occurred. More and more individuals are discovering and enjoying new considerations of the city's past. This has been manifested in many ways.

One has been the publication of a number of new books — this being, we trust, one of them — that offer increasingly detailed historical information about one of the nation's most dynamic cities. I have listed many of these books and extended my thanks to the authors in the acknowledgments and bibliography. Another indication of the city's growing awareness of its background is the continued success of the annual Dallas History Conference, an event founded by Michael V. Hazel, who served admirably as illustrations editor for this present volume.

Yet another manifestation of the city's interest in its past is the number of thriving organizations dedicated to preserving the city's heritage. One of them, Preservation Dallas, is the sponsor of this book. Others include especially the Dallas Historical Society, celebrating in 2002 its 80th year as an institution dedicated to the preservation and appreciation of Dallas and Texas history, an organization with which I am proud to have been affiliated. Another is the Dallas County Heritage Society, whose *Old City Park: The Historical Village of Dallas* provides a beautiful and authentic re-creation of Dallas history under the direction of Gary Smith. One of the institutions that specializes in a particular aspect of the city's history is the fine Sixth Floor Museum at Dealey Plaza, headed by Jeff West with the able assistance of archivist Gary Mack.

Soon arriving in Dallas will be a new museum dedicated to the city's history to be located in the historic Old Red Courthouse. Thomas H. Smith is project director for the museum, expected to open some time in the not-too-distant future as the Museum of Dallas History at the Old Red County Courthouse. Smith's work, as well as that of the team of Dallas historians he is leading in gathering new information about the city's past, was very useful to this author.

— Darwin Payne
August 2002

CHAPTER ONE

At the Three Forks

1   A WANDERER FROM TENNESSEE ENVISIONS A CITY

𝓘n the year 1836, when patriots were fighting heroically from behind the walls of the Alamo and on the battlefield of San Jacinto to win independence for Texas, the region of the Three Forks of the Trinity River — the place where Dallas would be founded — remained wild and devoid of civilization. In this unspoiled north central portion of Texas, a land overlooked by

When this map of Texas was published in 1840, there were no permanent settlements in the region of the Three Forks of the Trinity River.
Dallas Public Library

Spanish missionaries of the mid-1700s and Anglo settlers arriving later with Stephen F. Austin, the Republic of Texas saw an opportunity as the 1840s began to attract new settlers who could raise families and crops, establish communities, and help bring stability to the undeveloped and struggling republic.

Only a few scattered outposts dotted the broad expanses of this area. One gateway for American immigrants entering from the north existed at Holland Coffee's trading station on the Red River about 75 miles above the Three Forks area. About the same distance to the northeast was Fort Inglish, where a wooden blockhouse had been built in 1837 as a frontier outpost. Closer was a stockade known as Fort King or Kingsboro (present-day Kaufman), thrown up in 1840 about 30 miles southeast of the place that would become Dallas. More and bigger such settlements clearly were desired.

As an incentive to settlement, in 1840 the Republic of Texas Congress enacted the Military Road Act to establish a road extending from Austin through Waco and through the Three Forks area to Coffee's Station. Courageous surveyors, mindful of the possibility of Indian attack, entered the Three Forks area that same year.

Robert Sloan led one contingent of surveyors. At the juncture of White Rock Creek and the Trinity River, Indians in 1840 attacked and killed one of his men, Sam Club, the first such death in what would become Dallas County. Col. William G. Cooke, a veteran of the San Jacinto campaign, led another survey party into the area and in early 1841 established the temporary Cedar Springs post only a couple of miles from what one day would become downtown Dallas. Cedar Springs was an inviting environment for new settlers, and while Cooke's post was not a permanent one, the area developed not much later into a community of its own. Still another surveyor, Warren Ferris, worked out of Kingsboro. A former mountain man of the Rockies, Ferris was the official surveyor for Nacogdoches County, but he accepted a special assignment from the well-to-do speculator who had established Kingsboro — Dr. Henry King — to find the precise location of the Three Forks of the Trinity and to lay out a site for a town to be known as Warwick. Ferris struggled in vain to find it, but there was no such place. The three forks of the river — the West Fork, the Elm Fork and the East Fork — did not come together at a single location. All such plans stopped anyway with Dr. King's death in September 1841. Ferris, however, would become the principal surveyor for the area in the years ahead.

Always, there was the fear of Indians, not just by the surveyors, but especially by prospective settlers. It made them reluctant to move into the unprotected area. A major Indian settlement along Village Creek, some 25 miles west of where Dallas would be founded, was a special deterrent. At Village Creek contingents of the Caddos, Wacos, Cherokees, Seminoles, Kickapoos and Shawnees lived together in harmony. Their success at growing crops gave evidence that the land could be especially attractive for pioneer homesteaders. But to prospective settlers, the existence of such an accumulation of Indians seemed menacing.

To eliminate this concern, in the spring of 1841 Gen. Edward H. Tarrant sent out a call for volunteer soldiers. He assembled them at Coffee's Station, marched them southward and on May 22, 1841, attacked the Village Creek settlement. Soldiers killed 12 Indians, destroyed their habitats, burned their crops and caused the survivors to flee, never to return. One Texan, John B. Denton, was killed in the battle. Denton County, just to the north, would be named in his honor. The commanding officer would be remembered, too, for Tarrant County, eventually encompassing the battle site, would be named for him.

To instill an added element of comfort for those settlers willing to move into the area, Gen. Tarrant commissioned one of his soldiers, Maj. Jonathan Bird, to construct a fort. In October 1840 Bird led 36 men from Fort Inglish to a site on the West Fork of the Trinity (mid-way between the downtown areas of present-day Fort Worth and Dallas). The men built a blockhouse and at least two other wooden structures and surrounded them with picket walls. The soldiers, encouraged by the possibilities of homesteading in the area, returned in November 1841 to Fort Inglish, gathered their families and brought them back to the place they now called Bird's Fort.

It was about this same time that John Neely Bryan, a Tennesseean trained as a lawyer in his native state but struck with wanderlust, located a fine-looking bluff on the banks of the Trinity about 15 miles downstream from Bird's Fort. Bryan, a single man 30 years of age, had migrated to Texas a few years earlier, having paused for a while in Arkansas after leaving Tennessee, then working at Holland Coffee's station as a clerk. From this location on the Red River he occasionally made forays into North Central Texas to trade with Indians.

Having arrived in November 1841 at the site where he would found a city destined to become one of the

John Neely Bryan, the founder of Dallas, married Margaret Beeman, daughter of another pioneer family, in 1843.
Dallas Historical Society

Chapter 1

nation's largest, one can surmise that Bryan already knew several things. At this location the floodplain of the Trinity narrowed. Underlying the river's muddy waters at this place was a solid limestone bottom, making it a natural crossing, one already used by Indians and buffalo. The surrounding land, Bryan knew from his knowledge of the Indians with whom he traded, was fertile. The Republic of Texas, he surely knew, recently had authorized construction of the military road to the Red River, and likely it would take advantage of this very crossing. Finally, in this day when waterways offered the quickest and most efficient means of travel, Bryan calculated that the Trinity eventually could be navigated from Galveston Bay to just about this spot and no farther. (Indeed, five years earlier—and Bryan may have known this, too — a steamer called the *Scioto Belle* had attempted to navigate the entire river. It may have reached as far north as the Three Forks region.) This very point, Bryan believed, was the logical place for a port city, where the agricultural riches to be produced on these fertile black prairie lands could be loaded onto boats going to Galveston Bay.

Here then, at the place one day to be known the world over as Dealey Plaza, the place where the 35th president of the United States would be slain, Bryan dreamed of the future and busied himself by making a campsite with brush, poles and dirt. This was where he would make a claim and found a town.

Not far away were those first settlers at Bird's Fort, recently arrived themselves but already not faring well. When the soldiers had returned with their families it had been too late to plant crops. Subsistence was to come from occasional supply wagons. In late December, with food running short, the pioneer settlers were worried about a supply wagon now overdue from Fort Inglish. On Christmas Day, with snow on the ground, three men from Bird's Fort set out toward the Elm Fork of the Trinity to cut a new road through the woods and to assist the wagon in its passage. In the snow they found bear tracks, followed them to a big tree and began chopping at the trunk, thinking the bear was after honey. Suddenly three shots rang out, presumably from nearby Indians in hiding. One of the men, Wade (Hamp) Rattan, fell dead. The other two, their horses having fled, hid in the woods until dusk, then walked back in bitter cold to the fort, some 15 miles away. One of the two, Solomon Silkwood, died a few days later from exposure. Rattan's body was retrieved several days later, his faithful dog "Watch" still at his side. He was buried at Bird's Fort. The gloom there deepened.

Meanwhile, other meaningful events were occurring that would be important to Bryan's dreams and demoralizing to those at Bird's Fort. The Republic of Texas, eager to speed up the process of settling this North Central Texas area, already had entered into the first of several contracts with a company formed in Louisville, Kentucky. The company, the Texas Emigration and Land Co., (soon to be known simply as the Peters Colony after its primary organizer, William C. Peters), was given authority and inducements to colonize a large section of this area, including the Bird's Fort area. The families at Bird's Fort, already disillusioned, now

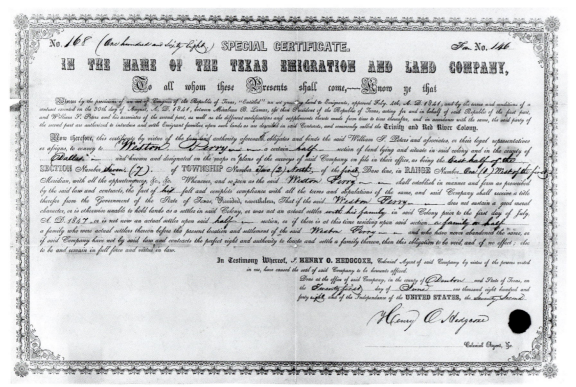

The Texan Land and Emigration Company — commonly called the Peters Company — offered 640 acres of land to any head of a family who would settle within its colony in North Central Texas.
Dallas Historical Society

became alarmed that they might not be able to get title to the nearby lands that they intended to settle.

It was in this state of uncertainty in January 1842 that the Bird's Fort settlers listened carefully to a visitor many of them already knew — John Neely Bryan. In October Bryan had been one of those who helped build the fort, having come down from Coffee's Station. He had a proposition for the families. The place he had settled on the bluff of the Trinity and that he already was calling "Dallas" was surrounded by land he described as far superior to that around Bird's Fort. They might want to move there. Why not come and examine the area themselves?

Intrigued, a former steamboat captain named Mabel Gilbert and a man from Illinois, John Beeman, followed Bryan downstream to his rude encampment. "So well pleased" with the land were they that they decided to move there. Gilbert returned to Bird's Fort to fetch his wife and their pet parrot Jackoo and then floated downstream to "Dallas" on canoes made from two big cottonwood trees. A few weeks later on about April 1, 1842, Beeman and a larger contingent of disillusioned Bird's Fort settlers came by land. After four days of hard travel they settled at places up and down the White Rock Creek bottoms about five miles beyond Bryan's place. Among their numbers were three Beeman families with numerous children, the Landen Walker family and four single men. The Beemans in particular would become permanent and stable yeoman farmers in the area.

Bird's Fort was destined to wither away. Dallas, under the aggressive campaigning of its founder Bryan, and the Three Forks area in general — by virtue of Peters Colony advertisements — soon gained a reputation that they were much larger than they really were.

A pioneer identified only as "W.A.F." visited sometime before May 1842. He already knew of Dallas, but he was surprised to find it so small—only "one solitary log cabin" and four or five people. A few months later a pioneer named John B. Billingsley passed through. "We had heard a great deal about the Three Forks of the Trinity and the town of Dallas... We heard of it often, yes, the place, but the town where was it? Two small log cabins, the logs just as nature found them... This was the town of Dallas and two families, ten or twelve souls were its population."

In August 1842 the venerable Sam Houston, president of the Republic of Texas, hero of San Jacinto, and famed friend of Andrew Jackson, came through Dallas on his way to Bird's Fort to sign a treaty with numerous Indian tribes in the North Central Texas area. Traveling with him was an Englishman named E. Parkinson who spent two nights at the "projected site for a town called Dallas." Encountering Bryan, Parkinson found him to be a "hardy backwoodsman, and a sensible, industrious, ingenious and hospitable man" with a vision of creating at this point on the Trinity River a navigable port. From the looks of the sluggish, muddy river, this seemed improbable to Parkinson.

More and more immigrants from the United States were entering Texas. By 1843 some 25 families had settled in the area between Bird's Fort and Dallas. Many of these were along Mustang Branch (today's Farmers Branch), where Peters Colony had set up an office. Even Bryan's town fell within the boundaries of Peters

Sam Houston, president of the Republic of Texas, passed through Dallas in 1842 on his way to sign a treaty with Indians in the region.
Dallas Historical Society

John C. McCoy, subagent and surveyor for the Peters Colony, quit the company and settled in Dallas to become the town's first practicing attorney.
Dallas Historical Society

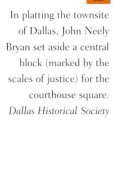

Dallas County was named for George Mifflin Dallas, elected vice president of the United States in 1844 on a ticket with James K. Polk.
Dallas Historical Society

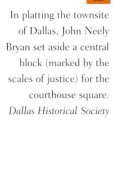

In platting the townsite of Dallas, John Neely Bryan set aside a central block (marked by the scales of justice) for the courthouse square.
Dallas Historical Society

Colony and he had no trouble with his land claim, but the company's difficulties in accommodating arriving settlers caused Bryan and others to complain bitterly.

Likely it was the overwhelming demands of the office that caused the Peters Colony agent, a young lawyer from Indiana named John Calvin McCoy, to quit the company in 1846 as its sub-agent and surveyor. He wanted to stay in the area, though, and he became Dallas' first practicing attorney. (Bryan, of course, was a lawyer, and he was admitted to practice in Texas, but he seemed to take little interest in the profession.) In 1849 McCoy built the first frame building in town as his office, located on the east side of the new log-cabin courthouse. McCoy would become one of Dallas' outstanding early citizens. By the time he died in 1887 he had served his adopted town in many leadership roles — he helped Bryan organize Dallas County in 1846 after Texas was admitted into the United States; he served as the county's first district clerk; he was a founder of the Tannehill Masonic Lodge (still in existence in 2002); he became the first district attorney of the 16th Judicial District of the state; and he served two terms in the Texas Legislature.

Texas' annexation by the United States had little impact on the people of Dallas, for the presence of government authorities was hardly noticeable in its remote setting. But it no doubt had been Bryan's own energy that was largely the reason Dallas was chosen as the temporary county seat for the new Dallas County. Designation as the county seat, if only temporary, gave the small town a head start in its competition with other settlements such as Farmers Branch, Cedar Springs, Hord's Ridge, Lancaster and a few others. Like Dallas, all these were growing as new settlers continued to pour in.

The city of Dallas and Dallas County bore the same name — not an unusual thing. But years later questions arose. Were they named for the same man? When Texas came into the union in 1846 the newly organized county definitely was named for George Mifflin Dallas, vice president at the time under James K. Polk, the president most responsible for annexing the state. But Bryan had named the town three or four years earlier when George Mifflin Dallas was a little-known Pennsylvanian politician with no conceivable ties to Bryan in his native Tennessee or in far-away Texas. In later years it would be speculated that Bryan may have had someone else or something else

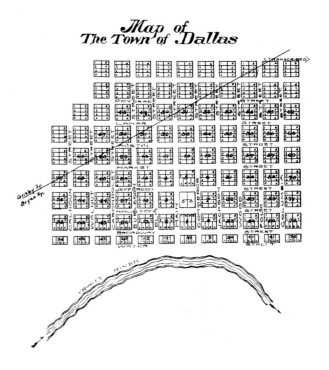

Dynamic Dallas: An Illustrated History

in mind. Perhaps he named it for Commodore James Alexander Dallas; perhaps he accepted the name suggested by Mabel Gilbert's wife, Charity. Other remote possibilities existed, but no one would know for certain.

A tiny log cabin courthouse, 16 by 16 feet, was erected on the lot Bryan designated for that purpose. The cabin was situated on the corner of the lot rather than the middle so Bryan's corn crop would not be disturbed. Inside the primitive building were split-log seats and a large fireplace and chimney. When the state's new 6th Judicial District held its first session in Dallas on December 7, 1846, Judge William Beck Ochiltree chose to preside not in the courthouse but in the town saloon. Presumably, that structure had more space.

Among those citizens being added to the area's population were two lawyers destined to play huge roles in Dallas' future. One was John M. Crockett, who arrived in the spring of 1848 with his wife and moved into a log cabin that doubled as office and home. Crockett would become the town's second mayor, a representative to the state Legislature and the Smithsonian Institution's meteorological observer for Dallas. The second was Nathaniel M. Burford, who came the same year from Tennessee and in 1850 was elected the county's first district attorney. He would become a member of the Texas Legislature (where he was elected speaker of the house) and then serve for years as a judge.

In 1850, with 163 residents living in Dallas and an additional 2,600 or so scattered throughout the county, the Texas Legislature ordered an election to determine the permanent county seat. As temporary county seat, Dallas had an advantage, but no guarantee that it would be chosen. In the first balloting Dallas led with 191 votes, followed by 178 for Hord's Ridge (located on the other side of the Trinity) and 101 for Cedar Springs. A runoff was required. Those who had favored Cedar Springs threw their support to Dallas, preferring that the county seat remain on their side of the river. In the August runoff Dallas defeated Hord's Ridge, 244 to 216. Thus was Dallas assured pre-eminency in the county, an early important step in its development.

Lawyers, merchants, doctors, carpenters and others whose professions or trades flourished only in a town now had reason to choose Dallas rather than other settlements in the county. Some residents in nearby towns decided to relocate to Dallas to participate in the economic boom that occurred after its designation. A new and more proper courthouse was constructed, once again a log cabin but this one larger, 16 feet wide by 32 feet long. The courtroom was used when the far-flung 6th Judicial District occasionally held sessions in town. The district clerk and county clerk had offices with fireplaces and bookshelves.

The town was growing, and plenty of people other than Bryan thought it had a future. A newspaper, the *Cedar Snag*, began publication in 1848 at a time when Dallas had fewer than 50 residents. Its publisher and editor was James Wellington Latimer, who brought his printing press and type to town on a wagon. In the years ahead the newspaper would become the *Dallas Herald*, a periodical that would last for almost four decades. Among the town's population of 160, including 37 slaves, in 1850 were seven lawyers, three doctors, five

John M. Crockett served as Dallas' second mayor and as a representative in the State Legislature. *Dallas Historical Society*

James Wellington Latimer hauled his press and type from Paris, Texas, to Dallas in 1849 to start the town's first newspaper. *Dallas Historical Society*

The *Dallas Herald* appeared weekly, advertising local merchandise and services as well as providing national news to Dallas-area residents. *Dallas County Heritage Society*

After buying John Neely Bryan's remaining interest in Dallas for $7,000, Alexander Cockrell built a sawmill and a toll bridge. Immediately after his death in 1858, his widow summoned a photographer to take this, the only known photograph of him. *Dallas County Heritage Society*

carpenters, two tailors, a cabinetmaker and a stonemason. Three dry-goods stores, two groceries, two blacksmith shops and one drugstore existed. It was a respectable town indeed.

Although Dallas seemed to be doing quite well, for some reason its founder was discouraged. Bryan was said to be drinking excessively, and he even left Dallas in the mid-1850s after he shot and wounded a man whom he believed had insulted his wife. Margaret, his wife, was the daughter of John Beeman, one of those Bird's Fort settlers Bryan had enticed to come to his area.

Before going away, Bryan had befriended a man who would succeed him as the most important individual in town. This was Alexander Cockrell, a veteran of the recent war with Mexico. Cockrell had settled in the hills southwest of Dallas after the war, where he met and married Sarah Horton. He put to good use his experience as an Army teamster by sending ox-drawn wagons, laden with goods, from Dallas on round-trip destinations to Jefferson in East Texas, Houston and Shreveport. He prospered greatly in this endeavor. Bryan, who had had the vision to found Dallas but seemed unable to capitalize on its growth, offered to sell Cockrell his remaining properties in town. In 1853 Cockrell paid Bryan $7,000 for those properties and became the town's foremost citizen.

Described by a contemporary as a man of "tireless energy," Cockrell launched an energetic program to invigorate the town that was now largely his. First, he built a circular sawmill at the foot of Commerce Street and erected a covered wooden toll bridge over the Trinity to replace Bryan's ferry and to connect the town to settlers in Hord's Ridge. That done, he relocated the sawmill just south of town and opened it to customers as an important boon to builders, contractors and architects. On the southeast corner of the downtown square he constructed a two-story brick building and leased it out. A myriad of his other commercial activities brought a faster tempo to the streets.

The town's incorporation came soon afterwards in 1856 by an act of the Texas Legislature. An election was held in 1856 in which voters chose as their first mayor Dr. Samuel Pryor, a physician who supplemented his income by operating the drug store. In the following year a new two-story brick courthouse replaced the primitive log structure.

Incorporated or not, the streets of Dallas could be wild and woolly. Bryan had been right about the natural crossing at the river, and in the 1850s cowboys driving cattle bound for markets in Missouri and other places north of Texas crossed the Trinity within sight of the courthouse. Naturally, the herds often paused outside of Dallas so that the thirsty cowboys could come into town. On occasion the *Dallas Herald* reported cattle stampeding through town. Dallas was on the Shawnee Trail, a branch of the better known Chisholm Trail, and cattle raisers in South Texas were finding better prices in the northern markets a decade before the more famous post-Civil War drives to Kansas.

While the periodic appearance of cowboys lent a festive air to town, the appearance of another group in 1855 — far more disparate in nature — gave the townspeople much more to talk about. Some 200 idealistic Europeans, about half the population of Dallas, arrived to establish a utopian settlement called La Reunion on a limestone bluff overlooking the valley of the Trinity just three miles west of town. They were followers of the French socialist philosopher, Charles Fourier, who believed it possible to achieve a perfect community when organized according to a "realistic" acceptance of human nature.

As was true with other such utopian communities, this experiment was doomed to failure, but while it lasted the residents of Dallas could look upon it with curiosity and wonder. In the community were artists, musicians, weavers, jewelers, artisans and others who were inexperienced at what they perhaps most needed to know — how to grow crops from the land. The utopians fared miserably, and by 1858 the community largely had collapsed. Its legacy, however, was the injection into Dallas life a cosmopolitan, European flavor that was unique for any pioneer settlement. One of its settlers, Ben Long, moved into Dallas and twice was elected mayor.

While the town's founder, Bryan, was away in the west between 1855 and 1861 during his self-imposed exile, his successor as Dallas' leading

Cockrell's valuable holdings bordering the Trinity River made him the town's most important citizen. *Dallas Historical Society*

Dr. Samuel Pryor, a physician who supplemented his income by operating a drug store, was elected the first mayor of Dallas in 1856.
Dallas Historical Society

After the collapse of the utopian La Reunion colony, Swiss-born Ben Long settled in Dallas and eventually served two terms as mayor.
Dallas Historical Society

Because her husband was illiterate, Sarah Horton Cockrell handled all the paperwork associated with their businesses. After his death, she continued to manage the family's enterprises, becoming Dallas' wealthiest citizen.
Dallas Historical Society

The Cockrells' own home was a two-story frame house on Commerce, on the bluff above the Trinity River. The woman sitting on the upstairs porch in this photograph is thought to be Sarah Cockrell.
Dallas Historical Society

citizen, Cockrell, met with tragedy. On April 3, 1858, having feuded with the newly elected city marshall, Andrew M. Moore, Cockrell was shot to death in an altercation with Moore less than a block from the courthouse. A murder trial ensued, the most sensational yet seen in the city. After three days of testimony, a jury rendered a verdict of not guilty. Cockrell's widow, Sarah, took over her husband's many interests. A year after her husband's death she opened the finest inn in town, the St. Nicholas, which far overshadowed the reliable old Crutchfield House. Soon she would engage herself in other entrepreneurial activities, becoming over the next decades one of Dallas' outstanding citizens.

ST. NICHOLAS BALL.
DALLAS, TEXAS.

You are respectfully invited to a Ball, to be given at the ST. NICHOLAS HOTEL, in Dallas, on Thursday evening, the 27th inst., the last day of the Fair, at 6 o'clock, P. M.

MANAGERS:

JNO. W. SWINDELLS, Dallas — L. A. YOUNG, Lancaster.
J. M. PATTERSON, " — NAT TERRY, Ft. Worth.
T. C. HAWPE, " — W. C. SWEATT, Waxahachie.
WM. B. MILLER, " — S. O. GIBBS, Kaufman.
JOHN W. LANE, " — J. K. P. RECORD, McKinney.
A. C. HALLECK, Grape Vine. — GUSTAVE BUREAU, Reunion.
THOS. J. JOHNSON, Johnson's Station.

N. H. DARNELL, Proprietor.

Many of Dallas' leading citizens served as "Managers" for a grand ball celebrating the opening of Sarah Cockrell's elegant St. Nicholas Hotel in 1859.
Dallas County Heritage Society

CHAPTER TWO

Railroad Crossroads

2 PERSEVERANCE AND INGENUITY PAY OFF

Less than two decades after John Neely Bryan selected his site on the Trinity, the little town he envisioned had grown to a population of about 500. In 1860 it must have seemed bigger to the area homesteaders and their wives, for to them it was a bright beacon of civilization. Here a woman could find a broad range of items needed to make her farm home

Following two log structures, the third Dallas County courthouse was a two-story, red-brick building costing $7,400, completed in 1856. It survived the fire of 1860 but was torn down in 1871 and the materials sold for $465.
Dallas Historical Society

The Crutchfield House opened in 1852 on Main Street, between Houston and the Trinity River, charging $12.50 to $15 a month for room and board. The original structure burned in the fire of 1860 but the hotel was rebuilt on the same site and survived until 1888.
Dallas Historical Society

comfortable — plates, silverware, lanterns, cloth, thread and more. The farmer could buy harnesses for his horses and mules, plows, seed, buckets, hand tools and other essentials needed for growing crops on a bountiful land. Such goods arrived in Dallas from Shreveport or Jefferson or Houston on heavily laden wagons pulled by five or six yokes of strong oxen — the kind of freight wagons that Alexander Cockrell had been so good at managing.

At the center of town stood a new, two-story courthouse — already the third on the site — made, as specified by attorney John J. Good, from the "best brick that could be manufactured in the county." Around and near the square were two hotels, saloons, a sawmill, doctors, lawyers, two drugstores, a newspaper, livery stables, brickyards, blacksmith shops, a jeweler, a milliner and a barbershop. There was even a fine carriage-maker in town, widely recognized for the high quality of his work. He was a Frenchman, Maxime Guillot, who had stopped in Dallas en route to California in 1852 to become the town's first manufacturer.

Stagecoach lines radiated from all directions to nearby towns such as Kaufman or Fort Worth or farther away to Austin, San Antonio and Houston. Travelers could ride on a bumpy coach pulled by a four-horse team, transferring farther along the way to stagecoaches going to St. Louis or Little Rock or even Santa Fe. Average traveling cost was about 15 cents a mile.

Folks were very much aware that a railroad might one day pass through town and end Dallas' isolation, connecting it perhaps to Galveston or Houston. The Houston and Texas Central Railroad had acquired a state charter in 1848 to build a line from Galveston Bay all the way to the Red River. Such a possibility was tantalizing. The *Dallas Herald* newspaper regularly touted the benefits of rail and urged the H&TC to hasten its way towards Dallas.

On any particular day one could find travelers on stopovers wandering around the courthouse square or lounging in the Crutchfield House or Sarah Cockrell's new St. Nicholas Hotel. Many were headed west; some were returning home back east. They had "seen the elephant." When the circuit judge made his scheduled visits to hold court, visiting lawyers from nearby areas added a fresh buzz of excitement to town.

By far the majority of settlers in Dallas County were farmers working small plots of land, most between 50 and 100 acres in size. The farmers grew a wide variety of crops such as wheat, sweet and Irish potatoes, flax, corn, peas and beans, wheat and cotton. A few farmers owned slaves, rarely more than two or three. Of the 228 slaveholders, 56 of them possessed only a single slave. Nobody in the county had as many as 30. Of the county's 8,665 residents, 1,074 were slaves.

This wagonload of people in front of the Crutchfield House appears to be headed for an outing.
Dallas Historical Society

In the county and city were large numbers of immigrants from Tennessee and Kentucky, others from the lower South and a good number from the Midwest. Besides the Europeans who had come to La Reunion, there were foreign-born residents from England, Switzerland, Scotland, Belgium, Sweden, Norway, Poland and Germany's various states.

Despite such diversity, Dallas undeniably identified itself as a part of the South. This was evident as tensions heightened between the North and South in the 1850s. Each issue of the *Herald* displayed on its front page a flag with the slogan, "States Rights."

News frequently was disturbing. Stories told of growing unrest among the slaves, of planned slave insurrections and of trouble-making abolitionists. Readers of the *Herald* were warned to be in a state of "watchfulness," to be suspicious of unknown visitors and to demand that strangers give "a reasonable account of themselves." In nearby Fannin County a "Committee of Expulsion" forced the departure of visiting Northern Methodist ministers whose words and actions had caused North Texas slaves to become "sullen and disobedient."

Such was the climate in Dallas in the summer of 1860, and on the hot Sunday afternoon of July 8 it seemed that the worst fears materialized. A fire erupted in a box of wood shavings in front of the W.W. Peak & Brothers Drug Store on the west side of the courthouse square. Flames spread quickly from one frame building to another, and within two hours virtually every building on the western and northern sides of the square was destroyed — practically the entire business district. "TERRIBLE CONFLAGRATION! THE TOWN OF DALLAS IN ASHES! EVERY STORE AND HOTEL BURNED. LOSS $300,000." This was the headline in the *Telegraph of Houston*. The *Dallas Herald*, its office

The *Dallas Herald* displayed its political sentiments in 1860 with a "States Rights" flag above its masthead.
Dallas Historical Society

Chapter 2

and presses destroyed, could not publish news of this disastrous event. The new brick courthouse, located in the center of the square, was spared, but the heat was so intense that curtains inside the windows were said to have burst into flames. Young trees recently planted around the building perished.

Judge Nat Burford, holding court in Waxahachie when the fire occurred, returned the next day to find just one solitary brick building still standing and the ruins still smoking. Small groups of people talked in whispers. This disaster, they believed, had been no accident. It must have been deliberately set, for other mysterious fires had broken out in Pilot Point, Milford, Honey Grove, Black Jack Grove, Millwood, Jefferson and Austin. Two days later the houses of J.J. Eakins and Silas Leonard outside of town were destroyed by fire, and two days after that Crill Miller's house burned. Suspected in this latter fire was one of Miller's own slaves.

A vigilante committee made up of 52 of "the most respectable and responsible gentlemen of this county" organized, and extra-legal committees also formed in other affected towns. In Dallas the vigilantes interrogated nearly 100 slaves. Fifteen days after the fire occurred, the vigilante committee, ignoring Judge Burford's pleas to act within the law, concluded that area slaves had been aided and abetted by visiting abolitionists. Three slaves were identified as ringleaders, and they were condemned to die. The next day the three accused men were taken under armed escort to the banks of the Trinity at Main Street, then hanged. Two visiting abolitionist preachers, Blunt and McKinney, were jailed, then publicly whipped and ordered out of the county.

For years thereafter the great fire of 1860 would be debated. Could there actually have been a diabolical plot of such dimensions? Did the imaginations and prejudices of vigilante committees in Dallas and elsewhere overwhelm their better judgments? Were the confessions genuine? Did the simultaneous fires start because the extreme heat wave caused batches of the new "prairie match" to ignite? Nobody knew for certain, nor do they know today. The origin of the fire of 1860 remains one of Dallas' great mysteries.

There was no alternative but to rebuild. In October 1860 the *Herald* reported that the "sound of the hammer" could be heard from morning until night. Many of the structures, this time, were of brick rather than frame. "Scores of industrious, active and competent mechanics" could be seen on all sides of the courthouse as they went about their tasks.

A few months later came the awful calamity of the Civil War. When the question of secession was placed before Dallas voters, the tally was 741 for secession and 237 against. But with the decision made, all joined wholeheartedly in the Confederate cause. In that spring of 1861 the town reveled along with other Southern states in a keen sense of excitement — parades, artillery and festive illuminations. Companies and regiments of cavalry and artillery organized in town under such names as "Texas Hunters," "Lone Star Defenders" and "Dead Shot Rangers." They

Judge Nat Burford tried to maintain justice following the devastating fire of July 1860.
Dallas Historical Society

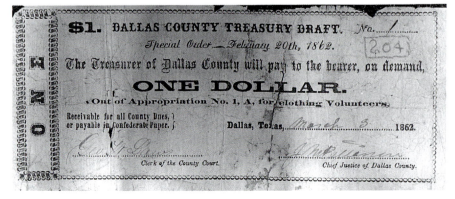

The Dallas County Treasurer issued warrants, redeemable in Confederate currency, for items such as military uniforms.
Dallas Historical Society

In 1844 Anthony Banning Norton pledged never to shave until Henry Clay was elected president of the United States, a pledge he maintained for the rest of his life. A staunch Unionist, he was appointed a district judge in 1868.
Dallas Historical Society

After leading "Good's Battery" for the Confederacy, John J. Good was easily elected a district judge following the war, only to be removed in 1867 by the Reconstruction government.
Dallas Historical Society

Henry C. Ervay successfully defied the efforts of Governor E. J. Davis to remove him as mayor of Dallas in 1872, helping lead to the downfall of the carpetbagger regime in Texas.
Dallas Historical Society

marched eastward to the battlefronts, where their boyish exuberance was soon whittled down by the harsh realities of war. The Confederacy designated Dallas as a general quartermaster and commissary headquarters. Pistols for the war effort were manufactured in Lancaster.

As the conflict raged from 1861 to 1865, Dallas and the surrounding area were spared scenes of battle, but of course the impact of those huge armies clashing elsewhere clearly could be felt. Imported articles of food

After leaving the bench, A. B. Norton practiced law, supported the Republican Party and published *Norton's Union Intelligencer* in Dallas until his death in 1893. *Dallas Historical Society*

and manufactured goods became scarce. Shoes often were made from cloth or from the sides of old saddles. The *Herald* reduced its size because of the scarcity of newsprint and ceased publication for a while. Women took over much of the work formerly done by men, now absent. Of a county population of more than 8,665 at the beginning of the war, more than 1,300 men served — about one out of every three males of all ages. So many women and children were left without husbands and fathers that they had difficulty caring for themselves. The *Herald* urged creation of an organized effort to assist them through the lean war years.

The surrender at Appomattox and the fall of the Confederacy did not precipitate in Dallas any signs of unusual mourning. A number of Southern planters in other states, believing that the cultivation of cotton without the benefit of slave labor would be impossible, moved to the Dallas area where wheat was being produced in huge quantities. Lawyers, merchants and entrepreneurs came, too, and the *Herald*'s editor, John W. Swindells, urged residents to cooperate with the new guidelines imposed upon them in Reconstruction. Register to vote and concentrate on building the community — that was his advice. By November 1865, a total of 1,260 citizens in Dallas County had taken the amnesty oath from an authorized board that was also visiting such towns as Lancaster, Cedar Hill, Scyene and Farmers Branch for that purpose.

Voters in Dallas County and others within the 16th District had the opportunity in June 1866 to elect a new judge. John J. Good, recently returned from Confederate duties in the war, easily won. But when the Radicals in Congress seized the initiation from President Andrew Johnson, the Texas commander for Reconstruction removed Good and other ex-Confederates from office, replacing Good with a series of judges who — interestingly enough — were well received in Dallas. One of them, Andrew Banning Norton, became one of Dallas' leading and most fascinating citizens over the next years as both a public official and publisher of a newspaper, *Norton's Union Intelligencer*.

The last gasp of Reconstruction rule in Dallas came in 1872. Radical Gov. E.J. Davis pre-emptorily ordered Mayor Henry S. Ervay and City Attorney John M. McCoy replaced with his own appointees. Ervay refused to yield his office or surrender the city's records, and he was jailed. The venerable John C. McCoy (John M. McCoy's uncle) traveled to Austin and obtained a writ of habeas corpus to free the mayor from jail. When the state attorney general ruled that Gov. Davis no longer had the power to remove city officials from office, the carpet-bagger regime in the entire state soon ended.

Despite the turbulence of war and Reconstruction, the 1860s were not unkind to the city and county. Dallas County's population jumped during the decade from 8,665 to 13,314, and the population of Dallas itself soared from 678 to nearly 3,000. By 1870 Dallas had 18 stores, two hotels, two flouring mills, four grocery stories, a billiard saloon and an assortment of other businesses. "We have a thrifty, law-abiding, enterprising population," declared Sarah Horton Cockrell.

Yet more was wanted. The Trinity River remained unnavigable. There were no rail connections — the H&TC during the war had ceased its northward march to the Red River. Freight wagon trains were struggling to bring in sufficient goods needed for a thriving community. The town still felt isolated.

The best possibility for connecting Dallas to the rest of the world seemed to be via the Trinity. A $15,000 prize was offered to Captain James H. McGarvey and Dick Dowling if they would guide a boat upstream from Galveston Bay to Dallas. McGarvey accepted the challenge, and in May 1867 he departed from Galveston Bay onto the mouth of the Trinity on a 60-foot long steamwheeler, *Job Boat No. 1*. Seven months later as the new year commenced, McGarvey was nowhere near Dallas. He had been laboriously clearing the river as he moved upstream. Finally, a year and four days after it had begun its journey, *Job Boat No. 1* docked on the riverbank below the courthouse in Dallas.

The *Herald* proclaimed McGarvey's arrival as "the greatest event that will ever occur in the history of Dallas." Dallas businessmen, inspired, now raised enough money to build their own steamboat, which they anointed the *Sallie Haynes* in honor of a local merchant's daughter. Soon after its completion in December 1868, the boat departed from Dallas for Galveston Bay amidst great huzzahs. Alas, when the *Sallie Haynes* reached Trinidad in Henderson County, it met another boat. They could not pass. After exchanging cargoes, they each managed to reverse directions. The *Sallie Haynes* retreated to Dallas. In the coming months the *Sallie Haynes* made several voyages up and down the upper reaches of the Trinity, but it never got anywhere close to Galveston. Eventually, it struck a stump and sank.

Better outlets were desperately needed if Dallas was to reach its potential. The main road to the east led to Jefferson, 150

The arrival of the first train in July 1872 began the transformation of Dallas into a boomtown. *Dallas Historical Society*

John Henry Brown, formerly mayor of Galveston and soon to be mayor of Dallas, presided at ceremonies welcoming the railroad to Dallas in 1872. *Dallas Historical Society*

miles away, which had a water outlet to the Red River to the Mississippi to New Orleans and thence to the Gulf of Mexico. Wagons headed east for Jefferson carried meat, wool, buffalo hides and other goods; on the return trip the same wagons brought back to Dallas merchandise and staples. The journey to Jefferson took about four weeks using a team of horses; ox-drawn wagons were slower. Bad weather always caused delays.

Most of the Southern states were linked by rail, but not Texas. Now, with the end of the war, the H&TC once again was moving, its precise northern pathway still uncertain. The railroad's charter required only that its terminus be located on the Red River between Coffee's Station and the eastern boundary of the state, an expanse of some 200 miles. Dallas teetered on the western edge. Some towns didn't want the railroad. Waxahachie in Ellis County feared that the railroad would introduce undesirable elements. Dallas, though, saw the railroad as an essential element for its future. Strategy sessions at community meetings explored ways to ensure its passage through Dallas. Pressured no doubt by intense Dallas lobbying, in 1870 the Texas Legislature set down guidelines requiring the H&TC to cross the Trinity River in Dallas County. But when the railroad surveyors laid out a path well within the county but eight miles east of the courthouse, despair once again reigned. A five-man committee of leading citizens approached railroad officials. What could be done to move the railroad's path westward through Dallas?

The answer: A cash grant of $5,000, free right-of-way, and donation of depot grounds. Dallas voters approved the inducements, 167 to 11. This brought the H&TC track seven miles to the west of its original plan, one mile east of the Dallas County courthouse and cause enough for celebration.

On July 16, 1872, with the population of Dallas hardly more than 3,000, a crowd of about twice that size size gathered for their first glimpse of a special H&TC train due to arrive from Corsicana. Its steam engine pulled freight cars bearing lumber and merchandise and a single passenger car filled with important guests. As the distant train grew near, the clanging of the bell by the engineer set off a wild celebration. A young attorney, Robert Seay, wrote in his diary, "Men whooped, women screamed or even sobbed, and children yelped in fright and amazement."

A celebratory barbecue was held at noon on the fairgrounds, open and free to all citizens. A brass band played "Dixie," and one of Dallas' leading citizens, John Henry Brown, paid homage to all who had worked to bring the railroad to Dallas. On the speakers' stand was none other than John Neely Bryan. Revelers at some 500 tables enjoyed a meal of barbecued buffalo sent from Col. Charles Goodnight's ranch out west. That evening, most of the people congregated at the new H&TC depot to watch the train depart on its return run to Houston.

Amidst all the anticipation for the H&TC, another tantalizing prize had emerged — the possibility of being on the route of an east-west railroad line that would cross the nation through Texas and link the East Coast with the Pacific Ocean. If this new railroad — soon to be called the Texas & Pacific — could cross the H&TC at Dallas, the city's pre-eminence as the leading city of North Texas would be assured.

The effort to secure this east-west railroad for Dallas succeeded in a fashion that would become a legendary example of how civic ingeniousness played such an important part in the city's development. John W. Lane, the owner and editor of the *Dallas Herald*, who was also

The arrival of the east-west Texas & Pacific Railroad in 1873 made Dallas the first rail crossroads in Texas and ensured its position as the commercial center of North Texas.
Dallas Public Library

fortunately a state representative at the time, inserted a rider to legislation related to the name change for the railroad. It required the T&P to "cross the Central [H&TC] Railroad within one mile of Browder Springs. The Legislature was rapidly approaching adjournment, and no one knew or seemed troubled about determining the location of Browder Springs. As Lane well knew, Browder Springs was less than a mile south of the Dallas courthouse. Unmindful of this, the Legislature adjourned, not to meet again until the next session.

When they learned of this requirement, T&P railroad officials were so disgusted that they determined to build the line as far away from Dallas as they could, one mile south of Browder Springs. This would place the line two miles away, too far from town. Once again, the city's leaders acted decisively with a generous offer to T&P that voters approved. If it would come through the heart of town the railroad would receive $100,000 in bonds, two acres of land as a site for the general office building, and another 25 acres. The offer was accepted, and the T&P line was laid along Burleson Avenue, one block south of Elm Street. A grateful Dallas promptly renamed Burleson as Pacific Avenue.

Completion of the T&P track in 1873 brought the first direct connection between North Texas and the East. Dallas had become the crossing point for the two railroads in North Central Texas. The boom that started with the arrival of the H&TC continued.

CHAPTER THREE

Boomtown on the Trinity

3 BECOMING A REAL CITY

The railroads, overnight, transformed Dallas. The pace of daily life quickened. An influx of ambitious and entrepreneurial-minded settlers poured into town — merchants, shopkeepers, saloonkeepers, lawyers, doctors, mechanics, blacksmiths, carpenters — and floaters and gamblers, too. Within a few months the population more than doubled, jumping from 3,000 in early 1872 to more

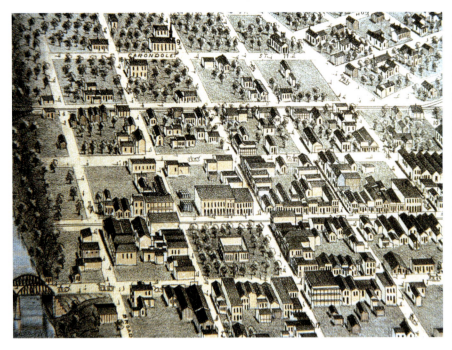

This detail from a bird's-eye view of Dallas, produced as the first railroad arrived in 1872, shows the Cockrell iron bridge across the Trinity River at the left, a block and a half from the courthouse square. *Dallas Historical Society*

In less than two years the boom saw 1,660 new structures erected in town, 33 of them boardinghouses to accommodate the large number of newly arrived men eager to make their fortunes before sending back home for their families. Societies and churches were founded; a volunteer fire department was organized; an opera house was built; private schools were started; and a new limestone courthouse replaced the old brick one.

A town such as this needed a city directory. The first one, issued in 1873, described the resurgence in activity as bringing in "over fifty large two and three-story brick houses for business — some with iron fronts, some with stone; also numerous stone and concrete houses, and several hundred frame buildings of every description from palatial residences down to shanties."

than 7,000 in September of that year. Still the people continued to come, and by 1880 the population reached 10,358, more than tripling the 1870 figure.

"All Dallas has gone wild," Catharine Coit wrote to her relatives in South Carolina. "There is such a rush to get rich that everybody is trying to do something to get money to invest in lots before it is too late."

Besides the benefits brought so dramatically by the H&TC and the T&P, a new bridge spanning the Trinity brought additional ones. Alex Cockrell's widow, Sarah, had sponsored it by organizing the Dallas Wire Suspension Bridge Company and building it at a cost of $65,000. The bridge extended with its two arches from the foot of Commerce Street to the other side of the river, a distance of 300 feet. It opened as a toll bridge on March 2, 1872, providing a convenient link between Dallas and area farmers and communities on the other side of the river. It was imposing, too, prompting the 1873 Dallas City Directory to call it "the most magnificent [bridge]... in the frontier states."

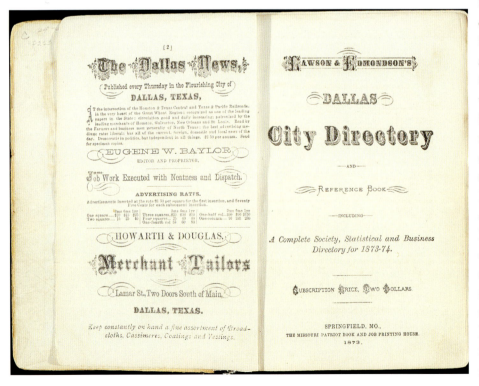

The first City Directory for Dallas was published in 1873. *Dallas Historical Society*

With ironwork manufactured in St. Louis, this bridge across the Trinity River measured 300 feet in length. Originally a privately owned toll bridge, it was purchased by the city in 1882 and opened free to the public.
Dallas Historical Society

Sometimes overlooked in the excitement of the day were the new telegraph lines. They had had been built by the railroads as an essential part of their own communications system. Time not required for railroad use was available to Dallas residents, bringing to them the miracle of instant electronic communications to friends and relatives in distant states.

In a rapidly developing community such as this, lawyers were needed to bring a sense of order. There seemed to be no shortage of them in Dallas. They organized the "Legal Association" in September 1872 and a year later created the "Bar Association of Dallas." In one of his earliest acts, the first president, John J. Good, requested District Judge Hardin Hart in the spring of 1873 to excuse "jurors, parties and witnesses" for two weeks in June because the county's wheat crop needed to be gathered.

Because the H&TC terminal was a mile east of the courthouse, the town grew in that direction along Elm, Main and Commerce streets. To make the trip faster and easier, a

By the time this photograph was taken in the 1880s, Sarah Cockrell had become the wealthiest citizen in Dallas.
Dallas Historical Society

Chapter 3

Physician, Confederate general, rancher and minister, Richard M. Gano was among the prominent Dallas citizens who bought shares in the iron bridge. *Dallas County Heritage Society*

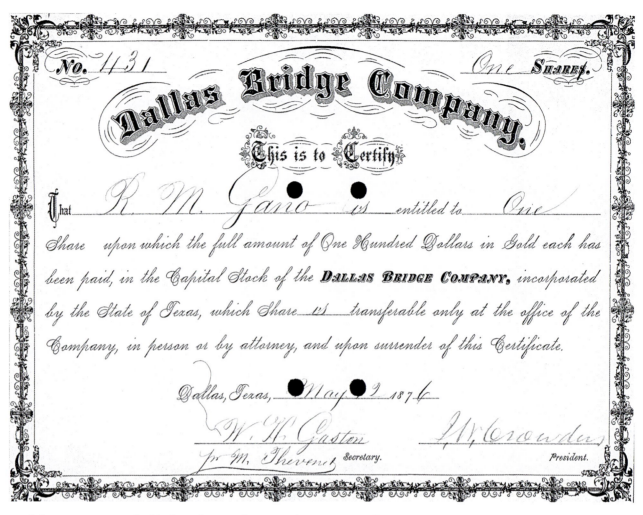

track for streetcars was laid linking the courthouse to the terminal. These first streetcars were pulled by mules as they would continue to be for many years. The courthouse square continued to attract business activity and remained the focus of town, but inevitably, shops began springing up around the railroad terminal, too.

The economic panic of 1873 that stalled the nation may have been actually helpful to Dallas. Because of financial problems, the T&P Railroad stopped construction in nearby Eagle Ford, just west of town. Eagle Ford enjoyed a temporary prominence, but for all practical purposes Dallas was the railroad's western terminus, a status it held for three years. Fort Worth, 30 miles to the west and eager for the T&P's arrival, stewed with impatience, chafed at the lack of progress, suffered some economic distress because some businesses had expanded in anticipation and eyed Dallas' prosperity with a degree of resentment. A rivalry between the two sister cities was born.

Dallas, enjoying its advantages, served as the nearest rail connection for buffalo hunters in West Texas to ship their hides back East. By 1875 the city had become the largest market in the world for buffalo hides. When the T&P finally reached Fort Worth in 1876, that city's nearer proximity to the West Texas buffaloes saw it replace Dallas as the world's largest buffalo hide market.

Especially prominent among the newcomers to Dallas were a number of merchants who for years to come would provide civic leadership and set a pattern for others who followed. They included especially the Sanger brothers, who had been founding dry goods stores at terminus locations as the H&TC moved north but found their best and most lasting success in Dallas. Their store, Sanger Brothers, became the first retail outlet in Texas to maintain a buying office in New York. Before the 1870s ended, the store's innovations included imposing a departmental system in which each department maintained separate records and establishing free home delivery for

Men unafraid of heights were in great demand to string telegraph and telephone lines in the rapidly growing city.
Dallas Historical Society

Seen from the Trinity River bottomlands, Dallas County's fifth courthouse was erected in 1880 using the walls of its predecessor, which had burned. James Flanders, Dallas' most important 19th-century architect, designed the French-inspired, Second Empire building.
Dallas Historical Society

Wagons loaded with cotton lined Elm Street as farmers brought their bales to Dallas to ship out on the railroads.
Dallas County Heritage Society

Mule-drawn trolleys connected the courthouse square with the new railroad depot a mile east.
Dallas Public Library

Dallas customers. Alex Sanger's acceptance by the community was instant — a year after his 1872 arrival he was elected to the city's board of aldermen. This would not be so unusual. In 1880 five of the city's eight aldermen were "northerners," elected, as early historian Philip Lindsley recorded, "without regard to party, politics, or nativity." Other new "terminus merchants" who lent special leadership and infused a spirit of commercialism in town were E.M. Kahn, a clothier, and hardware store owners Huey and Philp.

Of course, there were other newcomers to the city who spent their time in less-seemly pursuits. One was a dentist named John Henry (Doc) Holliday, who had left his home state of Georgia for Dallas because as a tubercular he needed a climate more conducive to recovery. Soon after arriving, he and his new dental partner, Dr. John A. Seegar, won three prizes at the county fair for their dental work: the best set of teeth in gold, the

Dynamic Dallas: An Illustrated History

best set in vulcanized rubber, and the best set of artificial teeth and dental ware. Holliday began spending too much of his time in the new gambling saloons. He was good at counting cards and figuring the best odds for his bets. On May 12, 1874, he was arrested with 12 others for gambling illegally. Not much later, he exchanged gunshots with a saloon keeper, an event preceding his departure for points farther west, where the "Gunfight at the O.K. Corral" awaited his participation.

There were others in town who could relate well to Holliday. Belle Starr, whose real name was Myra Belle Shirley, grew up in the settlement of Scyene, just east of Dallas (later well within Dallas city limits) and began associating with frequent visitors such as the Younger brothers and James brothers. It was at Scyene in 1871 that John Younger shot and killed a deputy sheriff, Charles H. Nichols, who had been sent from town to arrest him. Younger fled on horseback, eluding the posse that followed him.

Sam Bass of Denton terrified the Dallas area in 1878 when he robbed four trains within 25 miles of the city. At the last one, in Mesquite, he engaged in a wild exchange of gunfire. He fled into Central Texas with the Texas Rangers in pursuit. Finally, near Round Rock in Central Texas, they caught up with Bass and shot and killed him.

By 1880 Dallas had a population of 10,358; the county had 33,488. On a brief walk along the city streets one would have heard a surprisingly large number of foreign accents and foreign languages. Germans, Italians, French, Swiss, Swedes and Norwegians were a few of the nationalities represented in the county's 2,201 foreign-born.

By this time, John Neely Bryan was no longer alive. His mental faculties had wandered in his last years, and in February 1877 his family committed him to the state mental hospital in Austin. He died there on September 14, 1877, an incident which seemed to pass unnoticed in the city he had founded and which clearly was living up to the promise he had envisioned for it.

Dallas' sophistication was marked in 1881 when one of the Sanger brothers, Philip, installed telephones to link his home in the new development of the Cedars, just south of town, with the department store. Some said it was the first telephone in the entire state. It followed Alexander Graham Bell's invention of the telephone by only five years.

A year later Sanger Bros. shared with Mayer's Garden, a popular saloon, the honor of becoming the first establishments in town to have electric lights. Crowds flocked to see this miracle.

Philip Sanger's house was so magnificent that 50 years after it had been built, the writer Edna Ferber said it was "worth a trip to Texas" to see. Indeed, many of the "terminus" merchants had settled in this fashionable area, so named because of a natural thicket of cedar trees blocking out the growing noise and confusion of the city.

Sanger Brothers was the first true department store in Dallas, offering a wide variety of goods at fixed prices.
Dallas Historical Society

One of five brothers who immigrated to the United States from Germany and opened retail outlets, Alexander Sanger became active in Dallas civic affairs.
Dallas Historical Society

This highly fictionalized life of Belle Starr established her image as the "Bandit Queen." *Dallas Public Library*

(Far right) Philip Sanger installed a telephone — possibly the first in Texas — in his elegant home in "The Cedars" in 1881; it connected to his store downtown. *Dallas Historical Society*

John Neely Bryan, the founder of Dallas, lived long enough to witness the arrival of the first railroad, but he died not long afterward in the state mental hospital. *DeGolyer Library, Southern Methodist University*

A.H. Belo, owner of the *Galveston News*, wrote to a man who knew the area well, a vice president of the Texas & Pacific Railway named Frank S. Bond, to ask his advice as to the best location for such an endeavor. Bond did not hesitate to recommend Dallas. In the years ahead, Bond wrote to Belo in February 1881, it surely would maintain its position as the most important city in Northern Texas. "It is the center of a rich agricultural country, and the lines of road constructed, will always secure to it cheap freights and make it a central distributing point for business of all kinds." Nearby Fort Worth had certain advantages, Bond said, being located nearer to a coal supply and having a better water supply and drainage, but he doubted that it would ever overtake Dallas.

The Cedars had made the city's residents aware, for the first time, of class distinctions. On the north edge of town another fine residential street, Ross Avenue, offered large houses occupied by prominent citizens.

Down in historic Galveston, these years the largest city in the state, the owner of the *Galveston News* was casting curious glances toward the state's north central area. The *News*' own publication, the *Texas Almanac*, had predicted as early as 1872 that "northern Texas shall in the course of time contain the largest population of any equal extent of territory in the State, and... is destined from this time forward to be the seat of wealth and the center of the popular power in Texas." An idea occurred — why not establish a branch newspaper in this area?

Not until more than a year later did Belo call a trusted young employee, George Bannerman Dealey, into his office, and give him the assignment to scout the North Central Texas area and find the best location for a new newspaper in the area bounded roughly by Arkansas on the east, Oklahoma on the north, Waco on the south, and Abilene on the west. Dallas had been recommended enthusiastically, but Belo's mind was open.

For the next several months Dealey, a native of England who had joined the *News* as a clerk in the mailing room at the age of 19, traveled over the area — Fort Worth, Waco, Denton, Texarkana, Lewisville, Hillsboro, Mineola, Jefferson, Sherman and countless

In the 1890s Ross Avenue became the "silk stocking" district of Dallas, lined with beautiful homes.
Dallas County Heritage Society

Col. Alfred H. Belo, publisher of the *Galveston News*, decided to launch a sister paper in Dallas and moved to the city in 1885 to signal his confidence in the venture.
Belo Archives

As general manager of *The Dallas Morning News*, 26-year-old George Bannerman Dealey was responsible for starting up the paper in 1885. He later bought a controlling interest and headed the paper until his death in 1946.
Belo Archives

others. He finished his assignment in January 1883 and prepared a lengthy memo for Col. Belo, outlining pros and cons for the places he had visited but recommending Dallas as the best place.

Two and a half years later, on October 1, 1885, the first edition of *The Dallas Morning News* appeared on the city streets. It was issued from a modern three-story brick building on Commerce Street and produced on the most modern equipment available. George Bannerman Dealey was the general manager. He would never leave his adopted city. By the time of his death in 1946, Dealey had inspired and watched over Dallas' progress over a period touching, quite incredibly, seven decades.

Unbridled enthusiasm seemed to permeate the city in those days. The year 1886 provided good examples of Dallas' civic energy as it beckoned to become the leading town in Texas. In this year the 50th anniversary of the most momentous event in Texas history, the victory over Santa Anna at the San Jacinto battlefield, was observed. And where should this semi-centennial celebration be held but Dallas? No matter that the city had not even existed in 1836. On the streets of Dallas marched 143 veterans of that epochal battle, including Col. John S. "Rip" Ford and Capt. W.A.A. "Big Foot" Wallace. Some 2,000 schoolchildren watched in awe.

That same year the idea of hosting a state fair was conceived. Dallas had held its first county fair in 1859, but now civic leaders such as Alex Sanger, W.H. Gaston, Thomas L. Marsalis, Sydney Smith, E.M. Reardon and Col. J.B. Simpson decided to sponsor a state fair that would impress the entire state with "the greatness of Dallas as a market."

Two possible sites emerged. One was J.H. Cole's land north of town (present site of North Dallas High School and Cole Park), and the other was W.H. Gaston's 80-acre site on the south side of the T&P tracks in East Dallas.

The board of directors chose Gaston's land, but their decision was not unanimously accepted. "The ground selected for the fair is the worst kind of a hog wallow," complained C.A. Keating, a leading farm implement dealer. It would not be appropriate for displaying agricultural implements. The warring factions rejected the *News*' appeal for "calm and dispassionate reasoning." Led by Keating, the farm implement men formed a rival association and made plans for their own fair.

Thus, in late October 1886, Dallas played host to two separate and competing state fairs, one on the Gaston property lasting two weeks and the other held for a single week on Cole's land. Both were well organized with spectacular exhibitions, unusual attractions such as fireworks and balloon ascensions, various buildings, race tracks with grandstands, stables and more. Both were successful, both attracted thousands of fair-goers and both achieved financial gains.

Afterward, *The Dallas Morning News* repeated its insistence that the two factions must unify for the good of the town. With such encouragement, common sense prevailed. Agreement to combine the activities came in February 1887. The Gaston site would be enlarged by 25 acres and be the permanent site. Thus was born the Texas State Fair and Exposition, an event that would become one of the annual hallmarks of Dallas and bring millions and millions of visitors to the fairgrounds over many years to follow.

Actually, the site for the Texas State Fair and Exposition was not in Dallas proper but in East Dallas, a separate town with its own municipal government, school system, water supply and other accouterments. East Dallas' origin was tied to developments that had sprung up naturally around the H&TC terminal because it was, after all, a mile from the courthouse square. Residents in the area such as W.H. Gaston,

Dynamic Dallas: An Illustrated History

G. B. Dealey and associates proudly gathered around the press following publication of the first issue of *The Dallas Morning News* on October 1, 1885. *Belo Archives*

(Far left) William H. Gaston provided land in East Dallas for the Texas State Fairgrounds. *Dallas Historical Society*

Cecil A. Keating, a farm implement dealer, supported the State Fair, Trinity River navigation and the Board of Trade. He even appeared as King in a Mardi Gras-type carnival in 1901, designed to encourage tourism. *Dallas Historical Society*

Chapter 3

Within only a few years, the State Fair had become a major annual event, offering large prizes and attracting thousands of people to Dallas each fall.
Dallas Historical Society

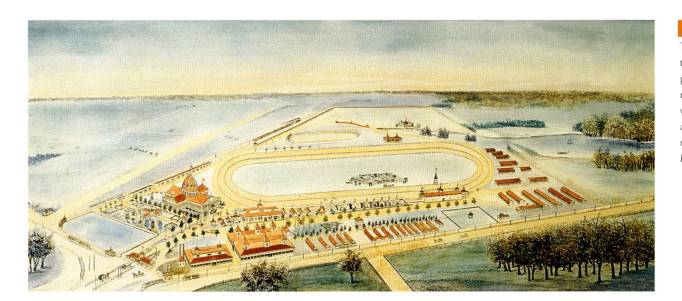

The original sketch for the fairgrounds gave a prominent position to the racetrack. Horse racing was to be the principal attraction for the next 25 years.
Dallas Historical Society

Jefferson Peak, John C. McCoy, Col. C.C. Slaughter and John L. Henry had led the drive to incorporate the area as a separate city. Residents approved incorporation in September 1882. Because of the prominence of W.H. Gaston, local residents for a while persisted in calling the town "Gaston," but this soon gave way to the official name of East Dallas, suggested by the settler who had lived there the longest, Jefferson Peak.

East Dallas' lifetime would be short. Its ties to Dallas proper were intimate, and it was generally acknowledged that the two towns should merge into one. In 1889 the Texas Legislature, by request, withdrew the charter for East Dallas so that all its holdings — streets and public buildings — as well as its debts, were transferred to the city of Dallas on January 1, 1890. As Mayor George W. Crutcher said in his closing report, the merger with Dallas

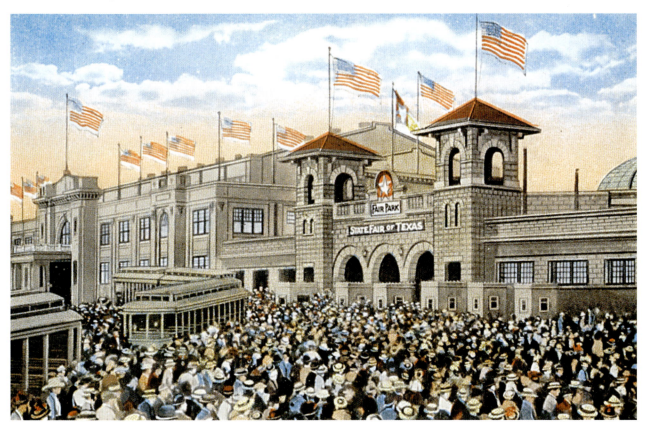

Special streetcars delivered crowds of visitors to the State Fair each October.
Dallas County Heritage Society

Chapter 3

While the Trinity River still marked the western boundary of Dallas in 1890, the town had spread rapidly north and east during the past decade.
Dallas Historical Society

(Below) This promotional drawing for Oak Cliff depicted residences rising on the hills beyond the Trinity River, with a train providing transportation from downtown Dallas.
Dallas Historical Society

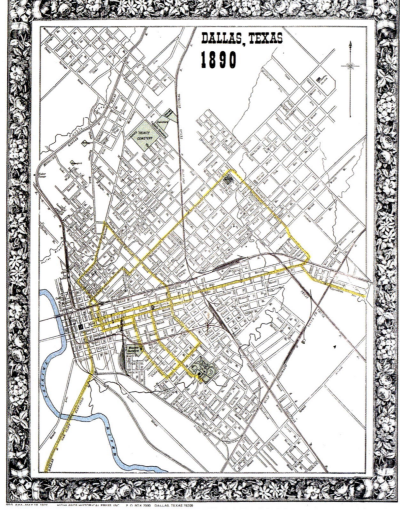

would no doubt add to "the prestige of Dallas, the metropolis of the great Southwest."

Just on the other side of the Trinity River a separate community with an entirely different set of circumstances emerged. Two Dallas wholesale grocers, Thomas L. Marsalis and his, partner, John S. Armstrong, purchased some 2,000 acres to build a beautiful planned development. It would encompass the old community known as Hord's Ridge, which had languished after Dallas had defeated it in 1850 in the election to be county seat. Armstrong soon pulled out of the partnership, leaving Marsalis as the sole visionary of a development he named Oak Cliff. For this new development he chartered the Oak Cliff Water Supply Co., set aside 150 acres for Oak Cliff Park and laid out a site with large lots, broad streets and wide alleys. More spectacularly, he constructed a railroad line to downtown Dallas to provide an easy commute. In October 1887 Marsalis placed advertisements in *The Dallas Morning News* announcing the auction of lots the following week.

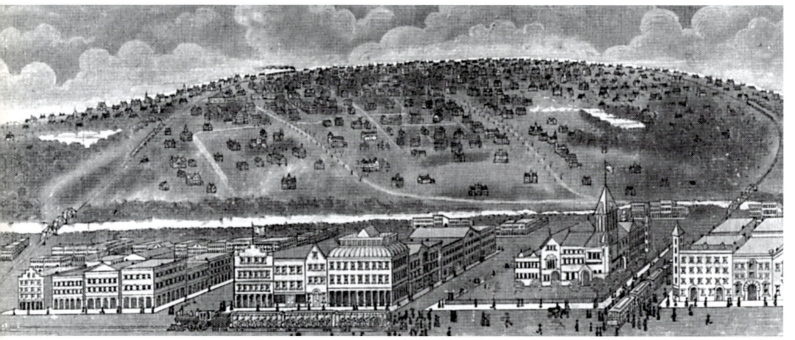

Dynamic Dallas: An Illustrated History

In the following days, the curious — numbering, it was claimed, several thousand a day — descended upon Oak Cliff to view the available lots. *The Dallas Daily Herald* proclaimed that the name of Oak Cliff had gone abroad "in every direction, and visitors are simply amazed that this magnificent site has been so long overlooked."

On the first day of the auction, Tuesday, November 1, 1887, some 600 people arrived by train and another 150 by buggies and carriages. The highest bidder would have his choice of lots, and that honor was claimed by F.N. Oliver, a newspaperman from Pilot Point, Texas, who paid $1,250. Oliver, who would become Oak Cliff's mayor, chose the lot at the northwest corner of Tenth Street and Grand (later renamed Marsalis). By noon, after only two hours, $23,000 worth of property had been sold.

A few years later Oak Cliff was described as a "beautiful residence city" presenting the "most charming and varied scenes of beauty over the sweeping prairies and the cross timbers that cluster on the banks of the Trinity." Some of the lovely homes erected on the spacious lots cost as much as $50,000, and they were occupied by "some of the most prominent and wealthy men of Dallas and the state."

Like East Dallas, Oak Cliff was a separate city with its own school system and municipal government. Also like East Dallas, it was destined to become a part of Dallas proper, too, its annexation being delayed though until 1903.

Meanwhile, the 1890 census figures proved that those who had prophesied a glorious future for Dallas had been correct. With a population of 67,003, Dallas County was the state's most populous county, and Dallas, with 38,067 residents, was the biggest city in Texas.

The W. A. Bonner home was one of many beautiful residences constructed in Oak Cliff during the 1890s.
Dallas County Heritage Society

Chapter 3

CHAPTER FOUR

A Time to be Thoughtful

4 PROBLEMS OF A GROWING CITY

Dallas exuded energy and optimism, and why not? The future seemed boundless. A mere child in age compared to other leading cities in Texas, Dallas was bigger than Galveston with its busy port, bigger than Houston and bigger than San Antonio with its distinctive heritage. On a typical day pedestrians of all sorts walked briskly up and down crowded

Main Street was the center of business activity in Dallas in the late 19th century. *Dallas County Heritage Society*

Streetcars provided easy access to offices and stores along Main Street as well as the rest of downtown Dallas at the turn of the century. *Dallas County Heritage Society*

downtown streets. Horse-drawn carriages and buggies clattered noisily. Tall poles with stacks of crossties bore the weight of sagging electric and telephone wires. Streetcars carried loads of passengers. Contrasting sharply with the city's salesmen, shopkeepers, newsboys, bankers, office workers, lawyers and laborers were farmers regularly arriving daily in wagons pulled by horses or mules and filled with vegetables and fruits.

A few women were entering the work force. Some worked in offices as "typewriters," or clerks and bookkeepers; others were dressmakers and milliners; a large number operated boarding houses; many taught school; some were cashiers in retail shops. Many also worked as laundresses or chambermaids. The majority, of course, did not hold jobs, and many of the leading women organized into literary and study clubs, benevolence societies and musical groups.

A major new building started going up in late 1890 that would give Dallas a semblance of a skyline. It was a new courthouse, replacing the previous one destroyed by fire. It was the sixth one to be built at the site specified for that purpose by John Neely Bryan. When finished in December 1892, the building that would become known fondly many years later as the "Old Red Courthouse" was said to be "unsurpassed in the grandeur of its architecture, the magnificence of its proportions and the elegance of its finish and appointments" by any other courthouse in the South.

Among the county's population there continued to be a growing number of foreign-born. More of them were from Germany than from any other nation. England, Scotland and Wales were well represented, too, and so were Switzerland, Sweden, Austria, Russia, France, Sweden, Italy, China, Denmark, Poland and others. Before the decade would end, a German-language publication, *Feld und Flur*, would be published in the city; the Italians would organize a mutual aid society called Societa Roma Mutuo Soccorso (and in 1913 their own newspaper, *La Tribuna Italiana*); and the Swiss would form a singing society, Schweitzer Maennerchor.

A larger minority group — about 20 percent of the population — were African-Americans, who, having emerged from slavery, struggled quietly to achieve a semblance of equality. Black men tended to work in agriculture or as laborers; black women found work most often as laundresses or domestic servants. Some black professionals were visible, though, even before the turn of the century — lawyers and doctors and teachers. Bluitt's Sanitarium offered patients "the most scientific operations" at reasonable prices. An African-American attorney named Sam H. Scott practiced law in the city in 1881. Scott evidently was accepted without question, but he departed for Arkansas after less than a year in Dallas. *The Dallas Herald* wrote that he had conducted himself with "propriety and discretion" and he left with the "good will" of all with whom he had come in contact.

The second African-American attorney in town, Joseph E. Wiley, stayed longer and made more significant contributions. Arriving in 1885, he made a name for himself as an aggressive entrepreneur. In 1901 he organized the Colored Fair and Tri-Centennial Exposition, a three-month-long event that attracted thousands of visitors to Dallas. At the same time, Wiley raised $10,000 from both white and black investors to found his New Century Cotton Mill Co. As *The Dallas Morning News* wrote, the cotton mill afforded "the first opportunity to Afro-Americans in the southwest to demonstrate that they can manufacture into the finished product the staple which they have so long cultivated successfully."

"The Queen City of the Southwest," as some called their town, abounded in citizens with schemes as big or bigger than Wiley's. One of the biggest and most long-awaited goals of all — navigation on the Trinity from Dallas to Galveston Bay — was revived in the 1890s. Besides the glory of it, there was an economic motive. Savings on freight charges alone, especially for shipping

Dallas women found a new employment opportunity as telephone switchboard operators in the early 1900s.
Dallas Historical Society

The telephone company offered special training classes for its new women employees.
Dallas Historical Society

The new Dallas County Courthouse, designed by M. A. Orlopp of Arkansas, was the most imposing structure in town when it opened in 1893. Its bell could be heard for miles around.
Dallas County Heritage Society

cotton, were calculated to be enormous. To work toward this goal, a number of leading businessmen organized in 1891 the Trinity River Navigation Company. By 1892 they had raised $62,500. Their backers included 192 businessmen and every bank in the city.

To clear the more difficult upper stretches of the Trinity for navigation, the company commissioned the building of a 64-foot stern wheeler named *Snag Boat Dallas*. A crowd of 13,000 showed up for the boat's launching, after which the crew immediately went to work. Meanwhile, a much bigger boat for actually navigating the river, a 113-foot steamboat named the *H.A. Harvey Jr.*, was purchased. It departed for Dallas from Galveston in March 1893, and after two laborious months making its way up the river it finally arrived — such a day for Dallas. The celebration exceeded even that which had greeted the first train in 1872. A gigantic parade was held, artillery salutes sounded, lunch was served at the riverbank, grand orations about the future were made and *The Dallas Morning News* printed pages in red ink to note that on this day the feasibility of navigating the Trinity had been "proved" and was "no longer a dream."

Unfortunately, such was not the case. The upper reaches of the river — narrow and winding, often shallow, and obstructed with debris — simply were not conducive to navigation. A temporary earthen dam at McCommas Bluff, 13 miles downstream, kept the water high enough

Dr. Benjamin Bluitt opened the first sanitarium for African Americans in 1905 in a building that still stands on Commerce Street.
Dallas Historical Society

Citizens of Dallas greeted the arrival of steamboats on the Trinity River in 1893 with great fanfare, but attempts to make the river navigable all the way to the Gulf of Mexico proved impractical.
Dallas County Heritage Society

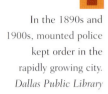

In the 1890s and 1900s, mounted police kept order in the rapidly growing city. *Dallas Public Library*

Members of the Commercial Club (forerunner of the Chamber of Commerce) traveled to small towns throughout the region to encourage business with Dallas. *Belo Archives*

to permit daily excursions for partygoers aboard the *Harvey* for a few years, but little more. The excitement faded away; the *Harvey* was idled; and in 1898 it was sold to new owners in Louisiana. Disappointed but not undaunted, the Trinity River Navigation Company continued its efforts to secure state and federal appropriations to make the river truly navigable. A few small locks and dams were constructed toward that purpose. By 1909 the company had spent $165,000 on river improvements, and through 1915 the federal government spent another $2.1 million. But work on the river ended with World War I. In the decades to come, lasting as late as the 1970s, the dream occasionally surfaced. But it was hopeless. Regular navigation on the Trinity never occurred.

By the turn of the century Dallas led the world in the manufacture and sale of saddlery, and it was the leading market for cotton gin machinery. The city had recovered nicely from the economic "panic of 1893," a difficult time that saw five local banks fail and brought a momentary decline in population. The 1900 census, however, found Dallas no longer the largest city in Texas. That honor had been assumed by San Antonio. Worse, as far as the city leaders were concerned, Dallas was not second either, that honor going to Houston. Dallas had a population of 42,639, only about 4,000 more than in 1890.

The organization most mindful of the city's economic development was the Commercial Club (soon to become the Chamber of Commerce), a group of civic-minded businessmen always alert to possibilities for growth. In February 1901, Captain D.E. Grove spoke at the Commercial Club's quarterly meeting on the topic, "Outside Capital and Texas Investments: How to Bring Them Together." Inspired by this talk, an "excursion committee" was created immediately to bring added wholesale business in a rather unique but direct way — by making personal calls via rail to areas on all sides of Dallas. On the evening of May 19, 1901, a special train carrying 36 of Dallas' leading businessmen departed for a grand tour with stops at small towns throughout North Texas, Oklahoma and the Indian Territory, with frequent stops at small towns along the way for speech-making and festivities. Elegant badges adorned with white ribbons were distributed. A handsome booklet that included pictures of the courthouse, a scene at the fair grounds, views of the busy streets and profiles of prominent businesses, described the benefits of trading in Dallas. Those taking this first seven-day trip were the most outstanding men of the city: Alex Sanger, William O. Connor, A.P. Tenison, G.H. Schoellkopf, Tom Padgitt, James A. Dorsey, C. Weichsel, W.A. Green, A. Harris, J.B. Adoue and many more.

Prominent Dallas architects Lang and Witchell designed this 10-story building for Sanger Brothers in 1910, helping the firm remain the leading department store in Dallas.
Dallas County Heritage Society

The Commercial Club excursions even included a small printing press on a train car, with which the members printed daily bulletins.
Belo Archives

Chapter 4

Shoppers flocked to the opening of Titche-Goettinger, another department store, in 1903.
Dallas Historical Society

By the time this advertisement for Neiman-Marcus appeared in 1923, the women's clothing store had achieved a national reputation for haute couture.
Dallas Historical Society

after the turn of the century established department stores that would become prominent, familiar fixtures in downtown Dallas for years to come. They included, among others, Adolph Harris, Max Goettinger, Edward Titche and Sol Dreyfuss.

The store destined to last longer than any of these under its original name and to gain attention far exceeding the boundaries of Dallas and even the nation, Neiman-Marcus, was a relative late-comer, being founded in 1907. Its founders had gained their knowledge of the retail trade business through their employment with two of the existing stores, Sanger Bros. and A. Harris. Herbert Marcus started his career in 1897 as a shoe salesman for Sanger Bros. His sister, Carrie, began work in the ladies' blouse department at A. Harris & Co., and in 1904 met and married Al Neiman of Fort Worth after a whirlwind romance of only four months. When Herbert Marcus' wife, Minnie, became pregnant in 1905 and Sanger Bros. declined to give him a large enough raise despite years of what he believed was dedicated service, the two couples moved to Atlanta, Georgia, and opened a sales promotion business. After two years marked by considerable success, they entertained two offers to buy their business. One was for $25,000 in cash; the other was the franchise for either Missouri or Kansas for a new soft drink known as Coca-Cola. Spurning the soft drink possibility, they took the cash and returned home to open an exclusive, high-fashion store where ready-made ladies' wear could be bought. From its first days in September 1907, Neiman-Marcus impressed its customers with its inventory of finest-quality merchandise, with its attentive and knowledgeable sales staff and with its stated conviction that there was never a good sale for the store unless it was a good buy for the customer. The store's leadership in fashion would help Dallas gain the reputation it enjoyed by mid-20th century as having the best-dressed women in the nation.

Some of the new buildings rising at the turn of the century were truly magnificent. The ornate Wilson Building, opened in 1904, was proclaimed the finest

The excursions, intended in large part to compete with St. Louis as the major trade center for a broad area, became an annual tradition, each one more elaborate than the previous, ultimately including even a band to serenade the audiences and a printing press to prepare specific handouts. Each year the men spread goodwill and solicited business at countless towns in all directions — to New Mexico, East Texas, West Texas, South Texas and Central Texas. Their success seemed reflected in the growth of the city's wholesale business. It jumped from $54 million in 1900 to $125 million a decade later, exceeding the goal by $25 million.

Businessmen such as Alex and Philip Sanger and E.M. Kahn, who had arrived coincidentally with the railroads to establish prominent retail stores, were followed by a number of other Jewish merchants who before and

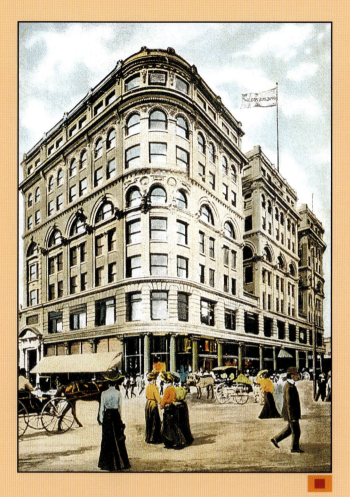

Designed by the Fort Worth architectural firm of Sanguinet and Staats and inspired by the Grand Opera House in Paris, the Wilson Building was the first eight-story building in Texas when it opened in 1903.
Dallas County Heritage Society

At 14 stories, the Praetorian Building was Dallas' first true skyscraper when it opened in 1909.
Dallas County Heritage Society

Religion was an important part of life in Dallas from the community's earliest days, and by 1900 the city boasted many impressive houses of worship. *Dallas Public Library*

office building south of St. Louis. The 14-story Praetorian Building, arising in 1909 as the city's first true skyscraper, offered a grand view of the surrounding area from the top floor for 25 cents. Churches such as the First Baptist Church, First Presbyterian, Cathedral of the Sacred Heart and Gaston Avenue Baptist provided awe-inspiring temples for worship. Temple Emanu-El's synagogue on South Ervay Street, constructed in 1898, was that congregation's second fine home.

It was through the good work of such faiths that several private hospitals were started, especially St. Paul's Sanitarium and the Texas Baptist Memorial Sanitarium (later Baylor Hospital).

Despite the fine work of religious institutions, and because of the city's preoccupation with growth and new businesses, some of the institutions necessary for the good health and welfare of a municipality had been neglected. For instance, there was the failure to have a free public library. Even the Commercial Club, the businessmen's organization so concerned with growth, soon realized this omission. In an 1898 resolution the club declared sadly that there was "no other city of the size of Dallas in the United States which does not have at least one good public library."

It fell to the clubwomen of Dallas — inspired by *Dallas Morning News* columnist Pauline Periwinkle — to remedy this deficiency. They were led especially by May Dickson Exall. Through Mrs. Exall's leadership, the several women's clubs came together in late 1898 to organize the Dallas Federation of Women's Clubs, and they agreed that their first project would be to secure a public library. Hearty editorial support came from *The Dallas Morning News* and the *Daily Times Herald*. The city of Dallas promised to provide $2,000 a year to maintain a library, but not the money to build one. Major financial contributions for that purpose came from Col. Alfred H. Belo of *The Dallas Morning News*, John S. Armstrong, Col. W.E. Hughes, Alex and Philip Sanger

 The Sisters of St. Vincent de Paul opened St. Paul's Sanitarium, later renamed St. Paul's Hospital, in 1898. It was Dallas' first "modern" hospital, with electricity and hot and cold running water.
Dallas County Heritage Society

 Texas Baptist Memorial Sanitarium, which later became Baylor Hospital, opened in 1909 with 250 beds.
Dallas County Heritage Society

Chapter 4

As president of the Dallas Library Association, May Dickson Exall headed
the movement that built and opened a free public library in Dallas in 1901.
Dallas Public Library

and Col. C.C. Slaughter. With $11,000 in hand plus the guaranteed support of city hall, Mrs. Exall approached steel magnate and philanthropist Andrew Carnegie, who recently had funded a public library for Fort Worth. Yes, he replied, "surely I shall do for Dallas what I did for Fort Worth, especially since your Library Association has succeeded in raising $11,000." But there was a caveat. The $2,000 a month from the city of Dallas was not, in his opinion, sufficient. That amount must be raised to $4,000 a month. The stipulation was agreed upon, and in October 1901, thanks largely to Mr. Carnegie, a new $50,000 library opened at Harwood and Commerce streets. The handsome, red-brick structure was, a newspaper reporter wrote, "probably the most beautiful library building in the South."

An important component of the library had been suggested by influential Dallas artist Frank Reaugh, who suggested that one room be designated as a place for viewing art. The women instantly agreed. The art room proved so popular that in 1903 Mrs. Exall, now president of the library's board of trustees, successfully recommended creation of the Dallas Art Association. This organization immediately began pursuing a program of art education and purchasing works of art for a permanent collection. Eventually, these activities evolved into the Dallas Museum of Fine Arts (later Dallas Museum of Art).

The library and the art museum were just the beginning of many accomplishments by Dallas' organized clubwomen. In the next years they used their boundless

Constructed with $50,000 donated by Andrew Carnegie, the Dallas Public Library opened at the corner of Commerce and Harwood in 1901 with nearly 10,000 books.
Dallas County Heritage Society

The Public Art Gallery on the second floor of the Carnegie Library was the forerunner of the Dallas Museum of Art.
Dallas Public Library

(Above) The Dallas Federation of Women's Clubs sponsored Trinity Play Park, which opened in 1909 with playground equipment and a paid supervisor.
Dallas County Heritage Society

The flood of the Trinity River in April 1908 was the most devastating in Dallas' history.
Dallas Historical Society

energies and money-raising abilities to establish free nurseries in working-class neighborhoods, build playgrounds for children, cause the water to be purified, lobby the city council to pass a pure food and drug ordinance, promote a clean-up movement and get two of their leaders elected to the school board (the first women elected to public office in Dallas). Their passion for the public welfare and their ability to put muscle into their causes prompted in Dallas a municipal government that for the first time began to consider and to act upon its social responsibilities to all its citizens.

Through their good work the clubwomen of Dallas re-emphasized the need to examine the overall health of a city and especially a need for planning. Dallas, "in exaggerated form," wrote city planner George Kessler, displayed all the difficulties attendant upon the sudden expansion of a village as a temporary railroad terminus into a great city — with "no apparent thought having been given in the interim to the needs of the increasing population."

A disastrous event in 1908 forcefully reminded the city's leaders of this. A deluge of rainfall in the spring caused the usually sluggish Trinity River to rise to a depth of 52.6 feet, overflowing its banks and sending water into areas never known to have been touched by floods. As many as 4,000 people were left homeless. The long wooden bridge connecting Dallas to Oak Cliff collapsed under the pressure of the surging waters, isolating the two sections. The Texas & Pacific railroad trestle was washed away. All rail service to and from town was discontinued. Telegraph and telephone lines fell down. The electric power plant failed, an event that halted streetcar service. The water pumping station at Turtle Creek was flooded, leaving the city without a water supply. This disastrous condition lasted for days and telegraphed a clear message: something must be done.

As a start, the Trinity River must be tamed. George B. Dealey led the charge, presenting a paper to a group of influential leaders in the Critic Club on the virtues of city planning and followed it with a series of editorials and articles forcefully advocating a comprehensive city plan. The Dallas City Plan and Improvement League was formed as an adjunct to the Chamber of Commerce to achieve this goal. The organization hired an expert from St. Louis, George Kessler, to draw up a city plan.

In 1912 Kessler presented a bold, thoughtful scheme that would take years to fulfill. *The Dallas Morning News* was so pleased that it called his plan an "epochal event" in the city's history. Central was a bold recommendation to move the Trinity River away from downtown and into the center of its flood plain, where it would be enclosed by levees. Kessler recommended boulevards and parks to make the city beautiful. He urged the construction of a central railroad passenger terminal to replace the five inconvenient existing ones. He advocated construction of a civic center. He recommended straightening streets that made odd turns in the middle of town, and widening and extending others. He wanted the Texas & Pacific Railway tracks — so coveted

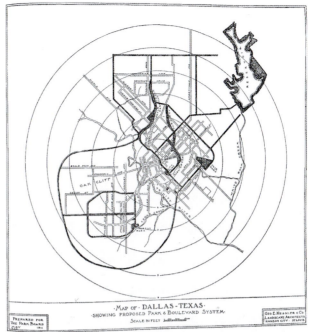

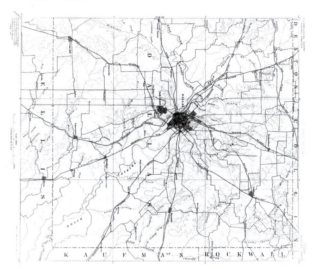

(Far left)
Among George Kessler's proposals was a park and boulevard plan. *Dallas Historical Society*

George Kessler's City Plan for Dallas, published in 1912, recommended a series of civic improvement projects. *Dallas Historical Society*

By the 1910s, Dallas was the hub of a network of railroad lines, linking the city with all parts of the nation. *Dallas Historical Society*

less than four decades before — removed from Pacific Avenue to eliminate what had become a hazard and an impediment to development. And he also saw a need to remove the tracks of the H&TC Railroad, using its right-of-way to build a central boulevard to unify northern and southern parts of town.

Kessler's plan was an inspiration, but it was so big that it was frightening. Certainly, it could not be achieved immediately. But it was there as a guideline for years to come — a blueprint to lift Dallas beyond any impression that it had grown with "no apparent thought."

Even before Kessler revealed his plan, a major step to correct a past problem already had been initiated as a result of the flood of 1908. This was the construction of a huge, all-weather viaduct across the Trinity River that would defy the greatest of floods. The Oak Cliff viaduct, built at a cost of $650,000, opened in 1912 before some 58,000 spectators. Later to be known as the Houston Street viaduct, it was thought to be the longest reinforced concrete structure in the world.

The first major implementation of the Kessler Plan came in 1916 with construction of a central railroad passenger terminal on Houston Street, the handsome new Union Terminal building, costing $1.5 million. Rail lines were re-routed to this structure so that those passengers arriving in Dallas intending to transfer to another line could do so without even leaving the terminal. Five years later, the T&P tracks down Pacific Avenue were removed and re-routed, resulting in a revitalization of that thoroughfare and a boost to downtown Dallas. There had been considerable anguish and debate over this move, for a number of old-timers could remember the excitement surrounding the tracks' arrival in 1873. Removal of the other tracks that had helped Dallas realize its dream, the H&TC tracks, would wait until Central Expressway was built after World War II.

Dallas boosters proudly advertised the Oak Cliff Viaduct as "the longest concrete bridge in the world" when it opened in 1912.
Dallas County Heritage Society

The Oak Cliff Viaduct provided an attractive as well as a flood-proof access from the west side of the Trinity River to downtown Dallas.
Dallas County Heritage Society

Chicago architect Jarvis Hunt designed Union Terminal, which opened in 1916 in ceremonies attended by the Governor of Texas. It consolidated the passenger services of nine different railroads.
Dallas County Heritage Society

CHAPTER FIVE

Getting Modern

5 TIME TO THINK AHEAD

$\mathcal{A}$s the 20th century moved ahead, Dallas continued to feel a sense of isolation and more than a little insecurity. It was a major city in Texas, but to the rest of the nation hardly known at all. By rail it was days away from the populated cities of the East Coast. Its ranking in 1900 as the 86th-largest city in the United States provided little reason for many outside of Texas to pay much attention to it.

While Dallas continued to spread north and east in the years before World War I, the area west of the Trinity River also developed after Dallas annexed Oak Cliff in 1903.
Dallas Historical Society

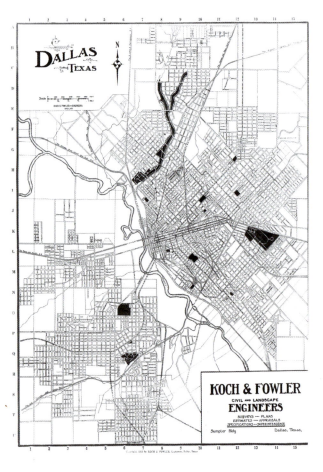

Civic boosters even composed a song, "Meet Me in Dallas," as they campaigned to attract conventioneers to Dallas in 1916.
Dallas Historical Society

Electricity also powered a regional rail transportation system, the "interurban," which began developing in 1902. The network started with service to Fort Worth, then expanded over the next years to such towns as Denison, Terrell, Waco, Ennis and points in between. Interurban cars traveled either singly or in multiple units as fast as 60 miles per hour. Some were "limited" with only a few stops; others were "local" cars with stops at each small town along the way. By 1925 six lines offered more than 350 miles of track. From its peak in the 1920s the system experienced a slow decline until it faded away entirely in the 1940s. What caused the demise of this remarkable, inexpensive mode of travel? The growing popularity and availability of the automobile.

An eccentric multimillionaire railroad tycoon, E.H.R. (Ned) Green, introduced self-propelled vehicles — horseless carriages — to the city and to the entire state on October 5, 1899, when he and his driver, George P. Dorris, (chief engineer of the company that manufactured the automobile) drove his two-cylinder, two-seat vehicle to Dallas from Terrell, where it had arrived by train. The journey, only 30 miles long but replete with sensational anecdotes, took five hours to complete. Advance word of

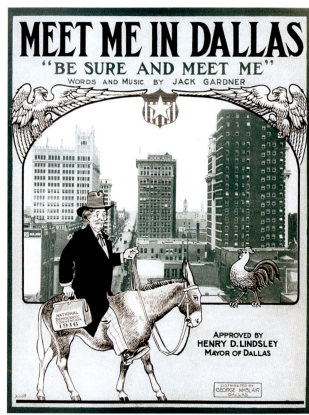

Perhaps it was natural that Dallasites — or Dallasans, as a few called themselves — were concerned with ease of movement, both within the city as well as to other parts of the state and nation. Such a concern was destined to serve them well in this new century.

The old mule-drawn streetcars that had been in use since 1872 started being replaced in 1887 by steam-powered streetcars, and then, after just four years, the "steam age" was overtaken by electrically powered streetcars. Electrical power shortages sometimes caused problems, and at these moments it was fortunate that some mule-drawn streetcars were still in service. Not until after the turn of the century were the faithful mules completely replaced by electrical cars.

Almost everyone rode the streetcar, as ridership figures for 1925 showed. Some 65 million passengers boarded streetcars that year. Four different street railway companies with tracks extending in all directions served riders. By 1928 those tracks covered 119 miles. (In 1956 all streetcars would be removed from Dallas streets as an impediment to automobile traffic.)

Dynamic Dallas: An Illustrated History

the men's progress spread throughout Dallas, and by the time Green and Dorris reached the city streets, huge, curious crowds had gathered. The men sought to satisfy the onlookers by riding up and down Main Street at 15 miles an hour. "Nothing that has passed along the streets of Dallas since the parade of the Kaliphs has attracted greater attention," *The Dallas Morning News* wrote on the next day.

Dallas residents readily took to the automobile. Four years later in 1903 nearly 40 vehicles — electric, steam and gasoline — could be seen on the city streets. In the following year a group of car enthusiasts headed by Col. Green himself founded the Dallas Automobile Club. In 1905 the city hosted the first 100-mile automobile race ever held in the United States. Five cars raced around the track at Fair Park for that distance. The winner was none other than Col. Green's Pope-Toledo, driven by his chauffeur, Ollie Savin. By the end of 1908, 446 cars were listed in The Register of Motor Vehicles and Machines in the city of Dallas. A new business, believed to be the first drive-in gasoline station in the nation, opened at the corner of Commerce and Prather. "Hurry back," the attendant would tell his customers, using a phrase that soon would be copyrighted by an oil company and used as a national slogan.

In 1910 the city directory listed 37 automobile dealerships, the preponderance of them along Commerce Street between Lamar and Ervay. In this same year the State Fair of Texas began its first annual automobile show, destined to be one of its greatest yearly attractions from that point forward. In 1911 *The Dallas Morning News* began printing the first of its regular automobile sections. In 1914 Ford Motor Co. constructed an assembly plant at Canton and Henry streets where more than 5,000 cars a year soon would be produced.

By 1920 Dallas could comfortably call itself the automobile distributing center of the Southwest. The wholesale business reached $200 million or one-third of the total wholesale business in the city for the entire year. Dallas truly warmly embraced this new marvel of

Mule-drawn trolleys were a curiosity by World War I when electric streetcars dominated the transportation network. *Dallas Public Library*

(Above) The interurban rail system provided rapid transportation between Dallas and neighboring cities.
Dallas County Heritage Society

Because financier Ned Green had a wooden leg, he depended on a chauffeur to pilot his horseless carriage through the streets of Dallas.
Dallas Historical Society

(Far right) By 1910, the City Directory included an entire section devoted to automobile dealerships and services.
Dallas Historical Society

came to town for a three-day program, March 4-6, 1910, amid great fanfare. As he assembled his Curtiss biplane on the eve of his first show he announced a show that would include swallow swoops, figure eights, dips, rapid curves, fast descents and attempts to set world records in speed and altitude. Hampered by high and irregular gusts of wind, Brodie struggled in vain to get into the air before thousands of spectators at Fair Park. On Saturday he managed to get no higher than 35 feet before smashing into the ground, bloodying his nose and mouth, and ending the exhibition. Spectators were refunded their admission fees of $1 each, and the Chamber of Commerce issued an apology for Brodie's failure. But the fact that 20,000 enthusiastic spectators had paid money to see Brodie gave strong indication that they wanted more.

This they got in January 1911, when the Chamber brought to town the famous International Aviators, featuring more than half a dozen pilots from throughout the world who were touring the nation's cities and giving dazzling

technology and daily life that would revolutionize the entire nation and world.

Hardly more than a decade after Col. Green brought the first automobile to Dallas, still another wonder of the new age appeared — the airplane. The city's early fascination with and recognition of the future possibilities of aviation would bring great dividends.

After the first international air meet was held in Los Angeles in January 1910, the Dallas Chamber of Commerce immediately arranged for what its members believed would be the first exhibition in Texas of "heavier-than-air" flying machines. A solitary flyer, Otto Brodie,

Dynamic Dallas: An Illustrated History

displays of height, speed and dives. Dallas Mayor Stephen J. Hay was invited to take a "complimentary ascension" in one of the airplanes, being assured that the flight would be at least 2,000 feet high so that if an accident should occur "a gradual descent may be made and a suitable spot selected to alight in order that the machine may not be injured." The mayor declined.

At Fair Park crowds numbering up to 20,000 gathered to see the "birdmen," and as many as 30,000 others were thought to be on the city streets looking up into the air to get a glimpse of their antics. So well received was the five-day event that the Chamber of Commerce persuaded the aviators to extend their meet for another three days.

Inspired by the aviators' show, some Dallas residents began experimenting with their own aircraft. Harry L. Peyton, a 19-year-old youth, built his own flying machine and got it into the air in March 1912. He and another man, Steve "Texas" Hicks, an expert rifle shot, formed a partnership and began putting on air shows in different towns — Peyton flying and Hicks shooting at targets on the ground and at odd objects Peyton threw from the airplane.

Another Dallasite, Lestere Miller, made his first solo flight in a plane he constructed with a motorcycle engine. At a landing field in East Dallas he began teaching others to fly at his Texas School of Aviation, which he operated between 1914 and 1917. In that latter year the *Daily Times Herald* arranged for Miller to fly all the way to Fort Worth. He made his first attempt on January 1, 1917, climbing from his sick bed, mounting his aircraft in East Dallas, flying to a site at the Oak Cliff Viaduct and entertaining a crowd of 15,000 with aerial acrobats. After landing to prepare for his takeoff to Fort Worth, it required 20 hard-working policemen to move the crowd away for him to get aloft again. Engine trouble at Cement City just west of town caused Miller to return. A week later, departing again from his East Dallas field near the Lakewood Country Club, he managed to reach his destination, delivering gifts and letters of greetings. Fort Worth, thrilled at Miller's arrival, sent greetings and gifts with him back to Dallas. Miller's return trip from took only 21 minutes. For the first time, Dallas and Fort Worth had been connected by air. It was not yet a partnership, but one day it would be.

With U.S. entry into the World War I that same year, the War Department immediately saw aviation as an important new aspect of combat. Training fields to teach military pilots became a priority. Texas seemed to be an ideal site because of its climate and terrain.

Ford Motor Co. constructed an assembly plant on the edge of downtown Dallas in 1914 and was soon producing 5,000 cars a year there. *Dallas Public Library*

Stunt pilot Otto Brodie attracted many admirers to a three-day exposition in 1910.
Dallas Public Library

Teamwork was essential to launching early aircraft, as participants in a 1911 aviation meet at Fair Park demonstrated.
Dallas Public Library

Leading businessmen, working through the Chamber of Commerce, sent a delegation headed by Mayor Joe E. Lawther to Washington, D.C., in mid-1917 to secure an aviation school for Dallas. On faith, the Dallas men assured officials that they could find a suitable site, and they soon did. Using both purchases and leases, they secured an open space adjacent to Bachman Lake at Maple Avenue and Denton Drive.

The War Department agreed that the land was very acceptable, and by November 1917 the Army had constructed a first-rate facility on the property that included hangars, repair shops, tents and a landing field. A name was given to the new military aviation school — Love Field — named for Lt. Moss L. Love, an aviator killed in a training flight in San Diego, California, in 1913. First flights from Love Field were made on November 23, with the new camp commandant, Maj. Douglas B. Netherwood, taking to the air in a machine assembled on the grounds. As young cadets underwent training, crowds of local residents began to congregate near the Lemmon Avenue entrance to Love Field to watch landings and take-offs. A newspaper reporter counted between 12 and 18 airplanes in the air at one time.

Yet another Army training facility was located at Fair Park in East Dallas. Known as Camp Dick, it was established as a cadet gunnery school. Dallas residents took kindly to the military men in their city. On Thanksgiving Day, 1917, every military man was invited to private homes for a meal.

Maj. Netherwood of Love Field and Fort Worth's aviation military commander, assisted by the chambers of commerce of Dallas and Fort Worth, began in mid-December to map out aviation routes to surrounding cities in all directions so that cross-country flights could become daily occurrences. This entailed identifying and marking large, open and well-drained sites every 25 miles for emergency landings and repairs.

A year after Love Field was opened, the war ended and the Army halted its military flight training. The Dallas Chamber of Commerce found itself holding a beautiful facility with no activity, but faith in the future of aviation prompted it to hold onto the property to develop it as a civilian field. By the mid-1920s Love Field could boast of 11 modern hangars offering complete flying services. Col. Billy Mitchell visited in 1925 and declared Love Field to be one of the "best flying fields in the country." In 1926 air mail delivery with connections to New York City and San Francisco began — the first in Texas — and in 1927 passenger service to Chicago commenced. By 1930 the Chamber of Commerce reported — perhaps with some exaggeration — that Dallas Love Field was the third-busiest airport in the nation in regards to passenger service. Whatever the accuracy of that assessment, Dallas had committed itself to being a leader in aviation.

After World War I, the Dallas Chamber of Commerce took over Love Field and leased the hangars to a variety of aviation entrepreneurs.
Dallas Public Library

Dallas Mayor Joe E. Lawther headed a delegation to Washington, D.C., in 1917 to secure an aviation school for Dallas.
Dallas Historical Society

By 1926 the Chamber of Commerce was promoting Dallas as an aviation center, as this cover from its monthly magazine indicates.
Dallas Historical Society

As the first president of Southern Methodist University, Dr. Robert S. Hyer planned the curriculum, hired the faculty and selected the school colors — Harvard Crimson and Yale Blue.
Dallas Historical Society

Just as the city had been late in providing a public library for its citizens, it similarly lagged in another important intellectual endeavor. As Dallas entered the second decade of the 20th century, it lacked a first-class institution of higher learning. Others had noticed this omission. In 1910 the secretary of the General Education Board of New York proclaimed Dallas to be the best unoccupied college site in the nation.

Inspired perhaps by this remark, civic leaders made overtures to Southwestern University, an established Methodist college in Georgetown, Texas, to move its campus to Dallas. Southwestern's president, Robert Stewart Hyer, had favored such a move for several years, believing that the institution could prosper best by moving away from its rural environment to a more urbanized part of the state with a heavy Methodist population. As an enticement to Southwestern, citizens of Dallas raised $400,000 and offered a 50-acre site. Georgetown's trustees in 1910 declined the offer by a 21 to 13 vote.

Thus came a decision by the Methodist governing bodies in 1911 to found in an entirely new Dallas university, accepting the city's offer of $300,000 and a site of 666.5 acres donated primarily by William W. Caruth and the widow of John S. Armstrong. Hyer himself agreed to leave Southwestern and move to Dallas as the founding president of the new Southern Methodist University. In the fall of 1915 classes met for the first time on the campus in the new suburb of University Park, adjacent to Highland Park. The surprisingly large entering class of 456 freshman, included Umphrey Lee, elected president of the student body and later president of the institution itself. The centerpiece of the campus, Dallas Hall, was built with the $300,000 raised by Dallas citizens and named in their behalf. A handsome Georgian revival structure with a copper dome and Corinthian columns, it remained the pivotal building on campus into the 21st century.

As the city began to achieve a degree of sophistication through such things as a library, art museum, university and symphony orchestra, a resident still could go just a few miles outside town and encounter the crop that had funded so much of its growth — cotton. Within a 150-mile radius farmers were growing one-sixth of the world's cotton crop on the black waxy soil. Dallas had become the staging area for marketing and distributing this cotton, and it was the world's leader in the manufacture of cotton gin machinery. Cotton merchants from throughout the world lived in Dallas to be close to the Cotton Exchange so they could buy the staple in huge quantities for their textile mills.

Dynamic Dallas: An Illustrated History

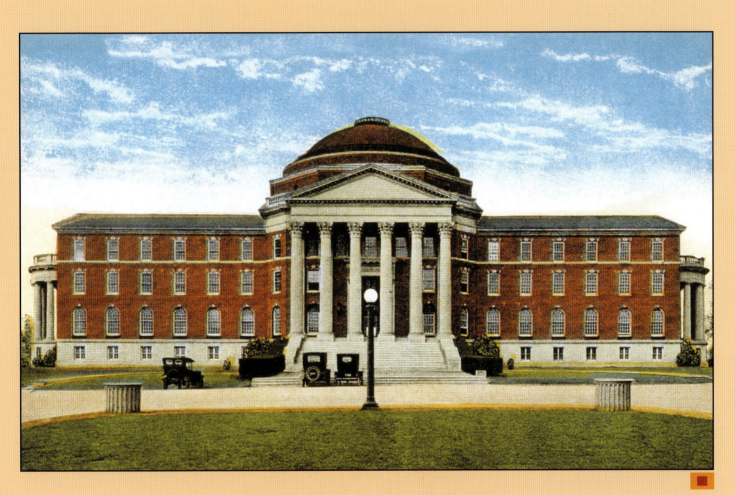

The centerpiece of the new SMU campus was named Dallas Hall in
honor of the local citizens who contributed $300,000 to construct it.
Dallas County Heritage Society

Farmers on the rich agricultural land surrounding Dallas depended on the city as a market for their crops.
Dallas County Heritage Society

In 1926 the Dallas Cotton Exchange erected a 17-story building designed by prominent local architects Lang and Witchell in downtown Dallas. It contained 220,000 square feet of floor space and housed cotton brokers from throughout the world.
Dallas County Heritage Society

Local banks had shared in the prosperity of the area cotton farmers, for they readily extended loans based on expected profits from cotton fields yet to be planted. Banking was an important industry in itself in Dallas, especially after 1914 when the city had won the honor of becoming one of 12 regional headquarters for the new Federal Reserve Bank.

While cotton was king in Texas and in Dallas, as early as 1921 there was evidence that a new industry might be the wave of the future. The evidence was a new skyscraper towering over the city's skyline — the Magnolia Petroleum Building. Twenty-nine floors high, it was the tallest building in the state. While no oil had been discovered in Dallas County, Dallas was in the center of a region of oilfields on all sides and a favorite location for oil companies such as Magnolia. In 1922 *Dallas* magazine declared that thousands of new organizations based in the city were prospecting for oil or gas. The Sunday newspapers carried huge advertisements by these wildcatters seeking venture capital with bold claims about their prospects:

Dynamic Dallas: An Illustrated History

The Federal Reserve Bank retained a firm of Chicago architects to design its Dallas headquarters, which opened in 1921 at Akard and Wood streets downtown.
Dallas County Heritage Society

Designed by noted British architect Sir Alfred C. Bossom, the 29-story Magnolia Building was one of the four tallest buildings outside New York City when it opened in 1922 and the tallest in Dallas for 20 years. *Dallas County Heritage Society*

"This is not a gamble, but a business proposition," Mason Refining Co. said in its advertisement. "All the undesirable elements of speculation are gone and yet the dividends will be large enough for the spectator." Another advertisement promised "quick action and large returns," and many others carried similar messages.

At least one of these wildcatters lived up to these extravagant claims. Columbus Marion (Dad) Joiner, 70 years of age and working out of an office on N. Akard Street, defied experts who had said there was no oil in East Texas when he made a sensational find in Rusk County in 1930 with his Daisy Bradford No. 3 well. The area turned out to be the biggest, most prolific oil field in the world over the next two decades. The ensuing rush to East Texas created a tremendous boom. The effect was especially keen in Dallas, which became a convenient headquarters for even more independent producers, corporations, wildcatters, promoters, investors, pipeline operators, oil-well scouts, lease hounds and drilling contractors. By 1931 the Chamber of Commerce declared that Dallas had "definitely become the most important oil city in the world," and in 1932 a total of 787 companies in the city were dedicated to the petroleum business. In 1934 the American Petroleum Institute held its annual convention in Dallas, and for that occasion the Magnolia Petroleum Building added to its rooftop a revolving, double-sided flying red horse, "Pegasus." It would become a lasting and colorful icon for the city itself for the rest of the century and into the next one.

Placed atop the Magnolia Building in 1934, Pegasus, "the flying red horse," quickly became Dallas' most famous landmark. *Dallas County Heritage Society*

Chapter 5

CHAPTER SIX

Looking Inward

6 UPS AND DOWNS IN THE 20s

The "modern" age for Americans began, it often has been observed with the "Roaring Twenties," a time of flappers and short skirts, bobbed hair, Prohibition, speakeasies, Babe Ruth, flagpole sitters and a rising stock market ending in a spectacular crash.

For Dallas, it was a decade of change. The city's population increased by more than 100,000, or about 60 percent. Construction

By 1920 the downtown Dallas skyline was impressively urban.
Dallas County Heritage Society

Beer baron Adolphus Busch commissioned St. Louis architect Tom Barnett to design a luxury hotel for Dallas, inspired by the Plaza Hotel in New York.
Dallas County Heritage Society

The Fair Park Auditorium provided a comfortable venue for the performing arts in Dallas.
Dallas County Heritage Society

could be seen everywhere — office buildings, housing developments, schools, churches and movie theaters. Dallas consistently ranked high in the nation in the number of building permits issued. Residents were proud of their soaring skyline. By mid-decade more than 100 structures stood between five and 29 floors high. Continuing to tower over all was the Magnolia Petroleum Building, followed by the 22-story Adolphus Hotel. The Adolphus had been constructed in 1912 as the city's finest hotel, and it was located just across the street from the Magnolia. These two major buildings made this intersection of Commerce and Akard the recognized center of town, a fact made even more pronounced in 1925 with the opening of the $5.5 million Baker Hotel directly across Commerce from the Magnolia Building.

Dallas had become enthralled with the telephone. It was said to have more of them — 50,000 in early 1924 — than any other city in the South. One calculation showed the city to have more telephones per capita than any city in the world!

In 1925 the cornerstone was laid for a handsome new auditorium at the southwest corner of Fair Park with a seating capacity of 5,200 and to be built a cost of $575,000. Fair Park Auditorium, later called the State Fair Music Hall, would be the future home of countless

Dynamic Dallas: An Illustrated History

cultural events — concerts, operas, dramatic productions, musical comedies and more. Just a couple of hundred yards away, a new circular municipal swimming pool opened on the fair grounds.

The city's growth had surpassed its water supply. White Rock Lake, thought in 1912 to satisfy the municipal water needs for many years, was supplemented in 1927 by a huge new reservoir, Lake Dallas in Denton County. It held enough water, it was believed, to serve a city with 750,000 to a million residents.

Dallas had advanced to the point where a single high school no longer could handle the demands of its rapidly growing school population. Since the public school system's founding in 1879, the district had grown such that by the end of the 1920s Dallas could boast of six high schools serving a population on all sides of town. The original high school, Central, was renamed Bryan High in 1917 in honor of the city's founder and in observance of the street on which it was located.

African-American students attended the Dallas Colored High School, established in 1892 at Hall and Cochran streets, but moving to a new building in 1922 with a new name, Booker T. Washington High School. (Booker T. Washington's daughter, Portia Washington Pittman, began teaching music at this school in 1925.)

The city's expansion to the south and beyond the Cedars residential area along Park Row, South Boulevard and Forest Avenue prompted the building in 1915 of Forest Avenue High School to serve that population. A year later the new Oak Cliff High School (later renamed W.H. Adamson in honor of its first principal) opened on the other side of the Trinity, its first senior class of 32 students graduating two years later. In 1922 the new North Dallas High School opened its doors, and three years later Oak

The pump station at White Rock Lake was an important component of the city's water services.
Dallas County Heritage Society

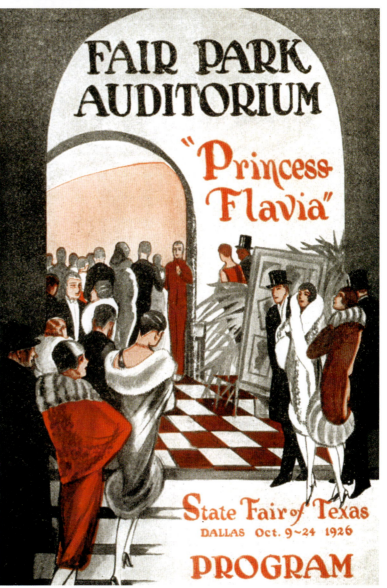

Sigmund Romberg's operetta, *Princess Flavia*, drew crowds to the Fair Park Auditorium during the State Fair of Texas in 1926.
Dallas Historical Society

Chapter 6

The city's public high schools were a source of pride to Dallas residents in the 1920s.
Dallas County Heritage Society

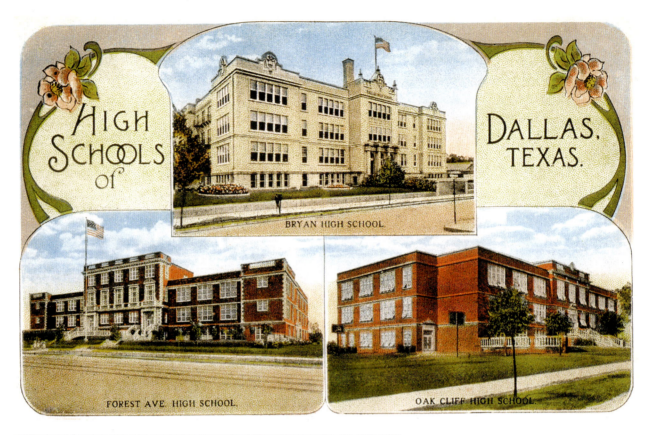

Until 1939, Booker T. Washington High School served all African American secondary school students in Dallas County.
Dallas Historical Society

Cliff's growing population required a second school for that area, Sunset High School. In 1928 a school opened for East Dallas — Woodrow Wilson High, the last new white school for 17 years.

Of course, there were problems in the city, as certainly had to be true for any fast-growing metropolis. No more than 10 percent of the Kessler Plan had been completed, a distressing fact that prompted organization in 1924 of the Kessler Plan Association to push the program through. The next year Dallas Mayor Louis Blaylock appointed a five-man committee headed by Charles E. Ulrickson to see what could be done to accelerate the process. A visiting city planner in 1925 told the Kiwanis Club that the city faced one of the most serious traffic problems in the nation unless something were done about the narrow downtown cross streets, the disjointed arrangement of outlying sections of town and the continuing barrier presented by the Trinity River.

The prosperity of the day, in retrospect, surely did not make life that much easier for certain citizens. Those on the police force, about 150 men, worked eight hours a day, seven days a week, and every day in the month except for one. A patrolman earned $1,680 annually. Elementary school teachers earned in some instances even less, their salaries ranging from

$1,266 to $1,700. High school teachers did better, being paid from $1,400 to $2,400 a year.

A perplexing and troubling aspect of the decade saw the sudden rise of a new organization, the Ku Klux Klan, which overnight became a powerful force in Dallas and much of the nation as it dramatically espoused the supremacy of native-born Americanism, patriotism, fundamentalist Protestantism, the sanctity of womanhood and a strict moral code. Such an agenda appealed to many citizens in this fast-paced era in which old-fashioned and treasured virtues seemed to be disappearing.

The secret organization made its presence known in Dallas in a sensational manner in April 1921 when its members kidnapped an African-American hotel elevator operator because of an alleged liaison with a white woman, drove him to a field six miles south of town, whipped him, painted the initials "KKK" on his forehead in acid, and upon returning to Dallas dumped him in front of the Adolphus where the alleged misdeed had taken place. Law enforcement officials on the next day refused to condemn the action. "Maybe it will be a lesson," said a judge.

Six weeks later on a Saturday night more than 750 Klan marchers in white gowns and hoods paraded on the downtown streets behind an American flag and a flaming cross. The city's streetlights conveniently went off to heighten the effect of the march. Every twentieth marcher carried a sign with a message. "We Stand for White Supremacy," "Gamblers Go," "Thieves Go," "Pure Womanhood" and "Grafters Go" were a few of them.

Some of the city's leading ministers were quoted favorably in the next day's newspapers. "The hand of God may be working through the Ku Klux Klan," said a Presbyterian minister. "If the situation is such that a Ku Klux Klan is justified in Dallas, then it is a good thing," said the pastor of the First Methodist Church. In the months ahead, many of the leading citizens of Dallas joined and supported the Klan. These included the sheriff, district attorney (who soon resigned in disgust over the Klan's lawlessness), some judges, doctors, lawyers and businessmen. Dallas Klan No. 66, growing rapidly to 13,000 secret members, claimed to be the largest chapter in the nation. In the spring of 1922, after a series of Klan whippings publicized in the newspaper, one unidentified Klansman said the organization's disguised members had "punished" at least 63 persons in the city and county for their transgressions. At the same time the Klan sought to identify and carry out its own punishments for wrong-doers, it occasionally would send a hooded member to a Sunday morning church service bearing a handsome monetary donation.

Some prominent persons in Dallas, however, believed members of the "Invisible Empire," as it was called, were entirely wrong in their extra-legal methods. *The Dallas Morning News* was especially outspoken against the Klan. Finally, a particularly egregious acquittal of a police officer who had been positively identified as one of several who had kidnapped a Jewish picture framer, beaten him and ordered him to leave town, inspired Klan opponents to launch their own organization, the Dallas County Citizens League. Among the anti-Klan leaders were Martin M. Crane, the former lieutenant governor and attorney general; O.B. Colquitt, former governor; Alex Sanger of Sanger Bros.; Mrs. E.P. Turner, a noted clubwoman; and Karl Hoblitzelle, owner of a chain of movie and vaudeville houses.

Dallas Klan No. 66 Drum and Bugle Corps, a 75-piece group, posed inside a square made up of Klansmen at the initiation of 5,631 new members at the State Fair in 1923. *Dallas Public Library*

The Dallas Morning News courageously attacked the Ku Klux Klan, risking the papers existence. Dallas Public Library

The first city council elected under the new Council-Manager system was composed of prominent businessmen. George T. Lee

A fierce struggle between these organizations ensued in the spring of 1922, but the Democratic primary showed that the Citizens League was no match for the Klan. Three admitted Klansmen captured top offices at the courthouse — the sheriff, a district judge and the district attorney, and Klan-supported candidates won every other race. The courthouse was under Klan domination. In the spring 1923 municipal elections, Klan-supported candidates also took control of city hall. The man who had been highly responsible for the Klan's success in Dallas, a dentist named Hiram Wesley Evans, moved to Atlanta, Georgia, where the national Klan was headquartered, and took over the entire organization.

Emboldened by its growing power, the Klan launched an aggressive boycott against *The Dallas Morning News* (a "dirty, slimy, Catholic-owned sheet") that included its afternoon paper, the *Journal*, and another small but feisty daily, the *Dallas Dispatch*. By the end of 1922 the *News*' circulation had declined by 3,000 and its cash surplus was depleted. The Klan boasted, erroneously, that the *News* soon would be bankrupt.

The influence of the Klan again was demonstrated in October 1923, when the State Fair of Texas held a special KKK Day. Approximately 160,000 people attended that day, among the highest weekday total in the Fair's history. That night, some 25,000 gathered to witness a mass Klan initiation of 5,631 new members.

Just when it seemed that the Klan would take control of all of Dallas and of Texas, too, the power of the "Invisible Empire" began in 1924 to decline almost as rapidly as it had emerged. The reasons were many. Perhaps the first was the failure of Dallas' Ku Klux Klan district judge, Felix Robertson, in his loss to Miriam Ferguson in the Texas gubernatorial campaign. Many Klansmen had preferred another candidate. Growing documentation of Klan abuses throughout the nation also helped reverse its popularity, as did *The Dallas Morning News*' campaign. By 1926 Dallas' Klan No. 66 membership rolls had declined from its high of 13,000 to 1,200.

One of the legacies of the Klan's short-lived reign at city hall was the demise of an organization called the Citizens Association, which had controlled municipal government since 1907. After the defeat of the Association's slate of municipal candidates in 1923, the organization never recovered, and affairs at city hall deteriorated through the rest of the decade. Demands arose to abandon the commission format, adopted in 1907, in favor of a more businesslike structure designed to remove politics from city administration. The *News* led the campaign to adopt the council-manager format, publishing in 1927 a series of articles that pointed out the inadequacies of Dallas' municipal government. R.E. Burt, elected soon after as mayor, appointed a committee to study the adoption of the council-manager plan, laying the groundwork for a new city charter that would be adopted by voters in October 1930.

The council-manager form of municipal government would last the city of Dallas from 1931 into the 21st century, providing a stable, efficient form of government that would see the city win countless plaudits for efficiency and good management. Under its scheme, elected council members hired a professional city manager as the city's chief administrative officer. Council members set policy only, removing political considerations from daily administration of the city. The plan's approval by voters followed a massive campaign organized by the city's business and civic leaders, who had formed a new group called the Citizens Charter Association (CCA). Having achieved its original purpose, the CCA became a permanent organization to insure that the work it had done would not be lost by turning the government over to politicians. For the next 40 years the CCA would select slates of business-minded candidates, bankroll their campaigns, promote their election and dominate city hall, bringing to Dallas a widespread reputation as a city where civic-minded businessmen were in control.

Already under way by this time was a renewed effort to implement major portions of Kessler's neglected city plan. In 1925 Mayor Louis Blaylock appointed a five-man committee headed by Charles E. Ulrickson to study ways in which some of Kessler's plans could be financed and implemented. Mayor Burt reappointed the committee, and in its 50-page report the Ulrickson Committee recommended in 1928 a $23.9 million capital improvement program — "Forward Dallas!" — that included among many other things the long-delayed move of the Trinity River into the middle of its floodplain, construction of levees on both sides for flood control, new viaducts to span the river and allocation of $450,000 toward the construction of a "Central Boulevard." Voters approved the 15 separate bond proposals and 32 necessary amendments to the city charter by a handsome majority.

"Forward Dallas!" changed the face of Dallas, fulfilling in many respects the specific projects put forth by George Kessler in 1911. Not until 1935 would the levee system be completed, and not until 1949 would the first stage of the "Central Boulevard," by then known as Central Expressway, be finished.

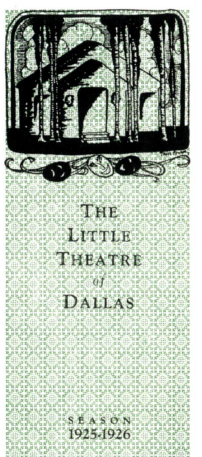

In the same mid-1920s period in which Dallas was enjoying an upward burst in population, debating the merits of the KKK, making aviation at Love Field a success and beginning efforts to implement important aspects of the Kessler Plan, a group of theatrical-minded residents were bringing national acclaim to the city in another way. A number of amateur thespians who in 1920 had organized as the Little Theatre of Dallas, achieved unusual success.

In 1924 the group entered a competition in Broadway by presenting a one-act play written by one of its own members, John William Rogers Jr., entitled *Judge Lynch*. The troupe finished first among 16 entrants, winning the Belasco Cup Trophy named for theatrical personality David Belasco. Returning to Dallas, the actors presented the play for 10 sold-out performances at Karl Hoblitzelle's new Majestic Theater, attracting audiences of more than 23,000.

The productions of the Dallas Little Theatre won national acclaim in the 1920s.
Dallas Historical Society

The next year the actors returned to New York City. This time they performed a portrayal of Negro life in the South in *No 'Count Boy*, a play by Paul Green. Quite remarkably, the group once again captured first place. Then in 1926 the Little Theatre of Dallas once again entered the competition and incredibly won first place for the third consecutive year. The actors had understood that with three consecutive wins, the Belasco Cup

Trophy would become their permanent possession, and they were disappointed to find this not to be the case. Thus disgruntled, they decided not to return to New York City for a fourth competition.

However, the dramatic arts in Dallas had received a major boost. A new theatre on Maple Street was built for the Little Theatre at a cost of $110,000, and the city was well en route to a reputation as a hospitable home for drama. Margo Jones, an impressionable girl from Denton, 30 miles north of Dallas, became a frequent patron of the Little Theatre. Inspired by what she saw, she entered the theatrical profession herself. Two decades later, just after World War II, she would bring even greater theatrical acclaim to Dallas through her own company, producing world premieres of such plays as Tennessee Williams' *Summer and Smoke,* William Inge's *The Dark at the Top of the Stairs* and the Jerome Lawrence/Robert E. Lee play, *Inherit the Wind*.

The arts were flourishing elsewhere in the city. At about this same time a group of young artists began gathering at the Dallas Art Institute, founded by Olin Travis in 1926 on the second and third floors of a building on Main Street. Among the students were Jerry Bywaters, who soon joined the faculty himself, Alexandre Hogue and a woman sculptor, Allie Tennant. In 1932 they and others formed the Dallas Artists League, dedicating themselves to stimulate "individual and collective effort" in all the arts through exhibitions, recitals, dramatic presentations, dance, literature and any other creative endeavor. As they worked and theorized about their art they began to be identified as proponents of "regionalism," a point of view holding that art should be a reflection of the area from which it evolved. In 1934 *Time* magazine heralded regionalism as the coming movement in the international art world. Bywaters became the leader of the group, ultimately serving as director of the Dallas Art Museum, chairman of the Art Department at Southern Methodist University, art critic of *The Dallas Morning News*, and being an accomplished artist himself.

Perhaps the most colorful part of Dallas was an area not recognized until later for the contributions it was making to the nation's musical culture. This was "Deep Ellum," the area stretching along Elm Street to the east of the H&TC tracks and the adjacent Central Avenue. Deep Ellum was a district of owner-operated retail shops, pawn shops, cafes, nightclubs, furniture stores and grocery shops, an area where the Jewish and black cultures intermixed. In the evening Deep Ellum became a place where music, gambling, nightlife and prostitution flourished.

The Majestic Theater anchored "theater row" along Elm Street where audiences could select from dozens of vaudeville and moving picture palaces.
Dallas County Heritage Society

Margo Jones pioneered "theater-in-the-round" in Dallas following World War II.
Dallas Public Library

Margo Jones presented her plays in a building at Fair Park constructed as the Magnolia Lounge for the 1936 Texas Centennial Exposition.
Dallas County Heritage Society

By 1935 the Dallas skyline glittered at night. *Dallas County Heritage Society*

(Far right) This song, composed about 1912, reflects the importance of Dallas, and specifically Deep Ellum, to the development of blues music. *Dallas Historical Society*

Alexandre Hogue was one of the Dallas regionalist artists who later achieved national renown. *Jerry Bywaters Collection on Art of the Southwest*

What went unappreciated by all but a few during the several decades following the turn of the century was the remarkable blues, jazz and early country music being played on the streets and recorded in Deep Ellum. Musicians such as Huddy "Leadbelly" Ledbetter and Blind Lemon Jefferson spent time at Deep Ellum, sometimes playing together on the streets. By the late 1920s Ledbetter had become one of the most recognized blues singers in the nation. His music influenced such well-known performers as Aaron "T-Bone" Walker, B.B. King and Henry "Buster" Smith. "Deep Ellum Blues," recorded in 1925 by Bob and Joe Shelton and the Lone Star Cowboys, broadly hinted at the temptations offered by the area:

> Once I had a sweetheart
> Who meant the world to me.
> But she hung around Deep Ellum
> Now she's not the girl for me.

Painter Jerry Bywaters supported the cause of regionalist artists through his writings and as director of the Dallas Museum of Fine Arts.
Jerry Bywaters Collection on Art of the Southwest

Music, gambling and nightlife flourished in the "Deep Ellum" neighborhood just east of downtown Dallas.
Dallas Public Library

CHAPTER SEVEN

7 PROGRESS ON MANY FRONTS

The idea to celebrate the centennial anniversary of Texas independence from Mexico had been floating around ever since Gov. James S. Hogg first mentioned it in 1903. Twenty years later in Corsicana, at a joint meeting of the Texas Press Association and Associated Advertising Clubs of America, a visiting speaker from New York pushed the idea more seriously. He advocated creation of a huge, new exposition

Robert L. Thornton, president of the Mercantile Bank, was the driving force behind winning the Texas Centennial Exposition for Dallas.
Dallas Public Library

Sketches by architect George Dahl helped persuade the State Board of Control that Dallas could stage a first-class exposition.
Dallas Historical Society

"city" and suggested the state's romantic history as a theme that could focus the nation's attention on Texas. From that moment on, energy mounted to put on a celebration.

Such an event would be the largest and most significant in Texas history. San Antonio, where patriots had given up their lives at the Alamo, was a likely site. Houston, just a few miles away from the battlefield of San Jacinto where the decisive victory over Santa Anna was won, was another. These two cities definitely wanted and believed they deserved the honor of hosting the Texas Centennial. But so did Dallas.

One of Dallas' most energetic business leaders, Robert L. Thornton, founder and president of Mercantile National Bank and head of the Chamber of Commerce's Industrial Dallas, Inc., program, was the inspired mastermind behind the move to bring the Centennial to Dallas. Sure, the one-time cotton-picking champion said in language he described as his "cotton-pickin' talk," those other cities had history, and sure it was true that Dallas did not even exist at the time of the Texas Revolution, but it was just as sure that Dallas was a city where things were happening, where the future of Texas was going and where such an event could best be produced. "From a cold-blooded dollars and cents view," Thornton said, "this exposition will mean more to Dallas than anything else."

Thornton, gutsy and aggressive, persuaded the city's other two leading bankers, Nathan Adams of First National and Fred Florence of Republic, to join him in the campaign to win the Centennial for Dallas. The trio enlisted the aid of other business and civic leaders, and they prepared a bid that San Antonio and Houston could not match. Dallas offered more money — $7.9 million to Houston's $6.5 and San Antonio's $4.8 — and it already had Fair Park, a fine facility accustomed every year to hosting hundreds of thousands of visitors. When the state's Centennial Commission measured the three cities' bids, it concluded that the upstart city from North Central Texas, Dallas, had submitted the best proposal and would play host to the Texas Centennial and Exposition.

Time was short. In the following 10 months, a $500,000 advertising and publicity campaign alerted the nation to the upcoming Centennial. An unbelievable transformation of Fair Park occurred under the direction of architect George L. Dahl, with 77 structures constructed or remodeled at a cost of some $25 million. Unlike so many other expositions with temporary buildings dismantled after the festivities, the central new buildings at Fair Park were permanent, architecturally significant additions that would forever give a new image to the fair grounds. They included notably the Hall of State, but also the Museum of Fine Arts, the Museum of Natural History, an aquarium and a series of matching art deco exhibition buildings on either side of an esplanade.

On June 6, 1936, some 250,000 spectators witnessed the inaugural parade for the Texas Centennial and

Exposition. A few days later President Franklin D. Roosevelt visited the grounds and proclaimed the Centennial to be not just for Texans but for people of all the other 47 states.

By the time the Centennial closed on November 29, 1936, it had attracted 6.3 million visitors, a tremendous boost to the city's economy in these Depression years. Businessmen interviewed by *The Dallas Morning News* agreed that the city had made more progress during the six months of the Centennial than it had in all its previous years of existence. The city could never be the same. "The 1936 Texas Centennial and its broad spectrum of experiences — social, cultural, and economic — had helped change the face and mood of Dallas forever," the historian of the Centennial, Kenneth Ragsdale, later summarized.

Dallas' image was transformed. Glowing descriptions of its accomplishments began appearing in the nation's press. The city began seeing itself as a place of sophistication and culture, an image enhanced considerably by an influential 1937 article in *Fortune* that described Neiman-Marcus, the Marcus family and the store's well-dressed customers in glowing terms. *Atlantic Monthly* in 1940 called Dallas a "new town in a new world," a place where one saw a marriage between the top hat of the East and the 10-gallon hat of the West. Families in the city had more purchasing power than those anywhere in the nation except New York City and Washington, D.C., according to the magazine, with an average family income of $3,600.

These and other articles created a new feeling of self-confidence for the city. The Chamber of Commerce's promotional material assumed a confidence never before seen. Dallas was "friendly, cosmopolitan, big," and "one of the best known cities in America." The chamber's 1938 annual report stated forcefully that "to MOST of the Southwest DALLAS is simply BIG D." The future had arrived.

The 1936 Texas Centennial Exposition played up the state's popular western image. *Dallas Historical Society*

Chapter 7

The Centennial Midway offered a colorful variety of attractions. *Dallas County Heritage Society*

One of the difficulties R.L. Thornton had encountered in organizing the campaign to win the Centennial was in pulling the leaders together for their meetings. The pay-off clearly had been more than worth it. There must be a simpler way, though, Thornton began to think, and after the Centennial he approached fellow banker Nathan Adams and broached an idea with him. "What we need is the boss men organized so we can act quick," he told Adams. Membership would be by invitation only, limited to an elite group of chief executive officers, presidents, or top executives of firms doing business in Dallas who possessed the power to make decisions without having to confer with someone else. Thus was born the influential Citizens Council, a body of businessmen who would yield enormous influence over Dallas into the 21st century. With regular meetings held out of the public's eye, the Citizens Council established community priorities and used the members' muscle and money to see that the goals were achieved.

The Centennial and founding of the Citizens Council were just two of the significant events that impacted Dallas during this Depression decade. The opening of the mammoth East Texas oil field, the taming of the Trinity through the levee system, the building of viaducts across the river, instituting a new form of municipal government and establishing the Citizens Charter Association were others that would impact the city for many years to come. All these developments had the happy effect of lessening the severity of the Depression.

Yet Dallas could not fully escape the economic ills that befell the American

The effects of the Great Depression were particularly evident in unincorporated West Dallas, where the enterprising owner of this dilapidated structure on Singleton Blvd. advertised an amazing variety of services. *Dallas Public Library*

Dynamic Dallas: An Illustrated History

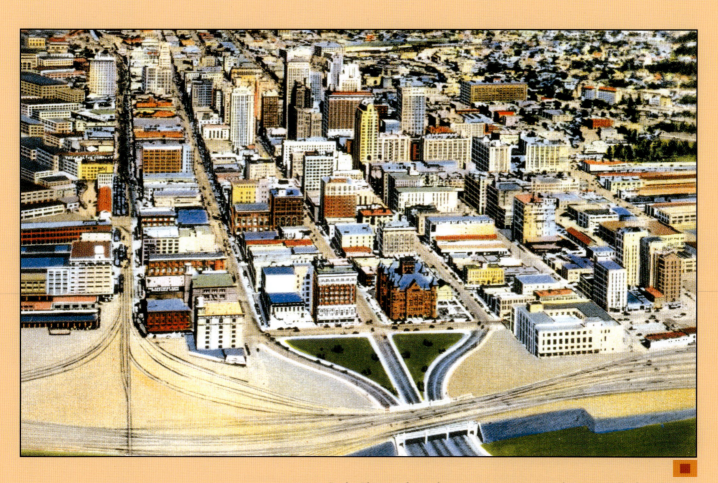

Dealey Plaza was designed as an attractive entrance to downtown Dallas from the west.
Dallas County Heritage Society

society during this unfortunate era. By the end of 1931 the number of jobless in the city was 18,500, and the Chamber of Commerce asked for $100,000 for relief projects. Federal funds generated by President Roosevelt's New Deal programs provided welcome assistance in the city. The Civilian Conservation Corps employed some 250 young men who helped improve White Rock Lake. The National Youth Administration, headed by Lyndon B. Johnson, had another 150 young men working on such projects as Dealey Plaza and the Triple Underpass. Works Project Administrations activities brought about a large number of improvements to city parks, destined to be useful and highly visible into the 21st century. There were adult education programs, nursery schools, recreational activities, sewing rooms, music projects, a toy-making and shoe-repair project, and many others.

Southwestern Medical School opened in prefabricated barracks in 1943.
UT Southwestern Medical School Archives

Despite such efforts at curtailing the Depression, not until the advent of a wartime economy did large-scale joblessness end, and even then life was far different than before. Long recruitment lines formed almost immediately after Pearl Harbor at five enlistment centers set up in Dallas. Only five days after U.S. entry into the war, more than 200 Dallas men departed from Union Station for training. They were followed by many, many others. By 1945 some 52,000 Dallas men and women had served in the armed forces; another 55,000 had worked in war-related industry; and 10,000 had helped coordinate defense-related activities. In the several war-loan drives, Dallas residents responded enthusiastically, raising millions of dollars more than their quota. North American Aviation workers, numbering as many as 30,000 and working several shifts, would build more than 20,000 aircraft for war use, including especially P-51 Mustangs and AT-6 Texan trainers.

Members of the Starlight Ballet practiced on the lawn outside the Casino (the bandshell) at Fair Park.
Dallas Public Library

More unexpected on the Dallas domestic scene was the presence of two prisoner-of-war camps established by the government. In 1944 German prisoners of war were placed in the old CCC camp on the east side of White Rock Lake. In nearby Seagoville, several hundred Japanese internees and some Germans and Italians were housed in the converted Federal Women's Reformatory.

The war effort overshadowed some promising developments in Dallas. One was the establishment in 1943 of a new medical school, Southwestern Medical

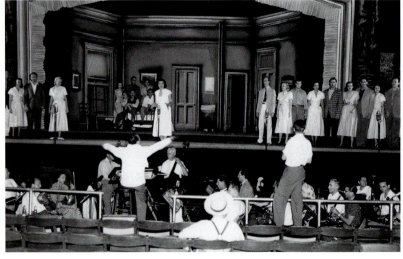

Kay Ballard, center stage, headed the cast of *Look Ma, I'm Dancin'*, shown here in rehearsals at the Fair Park Casino during the summer of 1949.
Dallas Public Library

Dynamic Dallas: An Illustrated History

College, begun modestly but destined to achieve status as one of the nation's most distinguished facilities as the University of Texas Southwestern Medical Center. Another was the beginning of a summer musical series called the "Starlight Operetta," held at the bandshell at Fair Park, a series that eventually moved inside Fair Park Auditorium as the Dallas Summer Musicals.

Yet another event with long-term consequences grew out of a dispute over the creation of a mid-city airport that could end the duplication of facilities at Fort Worth's Meacham Field and Dallas' Love Field. After an arrangement had been mutually agreed upon by the two cities in 1943 to create such a field, Dallas withdrew in anger after it blamed Fort Worth's Amon Carter for causing a change in the airport plans that favored Fort Worth. Love Field already was indisputably the leading airport in Texas in terms of passenger activity, and no Dallas civic leader wanted to jeopardize that asset. The result was a renewed dedication to Love Field. A new terminal was built and land was purchased for runway extensions that would continue into the 1960s.

Fort Worth, meanwhile, decided to build a new midway airport without Dallas. When Greater Fort Worth International Airport opened in 1953, it was only 12 miles away from Love Field. Its finer terminal and long runways caused a number of airlines to transfer flights from Love Field, causing anger and consternation in Dallas. But with the preponderance of travelers — approximately 75 percent — originating from Dallas, Love Field could not long be thwarted. It soon reclaimed the lost flights, opened a new runway in 1955 and a new terminal in 1957, and watched with a certain degree of smugness as Fort Worth's mid-cities airport entered a slow, downward spiral that ultimately saw its virtual abandonment as a passenger terminal.

The competition and acrimony between the two cities over aviation, understandably recognized by both as an important priority, flashed sharply over the next several decades. Arguments often were heard in courtrooms and before federal aviation agencies. Little could these two feuding cities imagine that not far ahead lay a happy resolution. They would come together and build a new mid-cities facility that when it opened in 1974 would be the world's largest airport.

Besides aviation, another major concern for Dallas that had lasted over several decades was the unrealized dream projected in 1911 by George Kessler — a central boulevard to tie together north and south parts of the city. The projected route was the old Houston & Texas Central Railroad, now owned by Southern Pacific. Voters approved bonds for this project in the amount of $450,000 in 1927, but not until Woodall Rodgers' four terms as mayor, 1939 to 1947, could the project begin in earnest with the first land purchases made from the railroad. Actual work began in 1947 when Mayor Rodgers broke ground one block north of Haskell Avenue, and when the first two-mile segment — now called Central "Expressway" instead of Boulevard — opened amidst festivities in June 1949, the state-of-the-art thoroughfare was said to be the finest such expressway in the world. Along that stretch it could move three times as much traffic, five times as safely, as an ordinary highway.

By 1950 Love Field was the busiest airport in Texas. *Dallas County Heritage Society*

From the day it opened in 1949, Central Expressway was considerably busier than this postcard indicates.
Dallas County Heritage Society

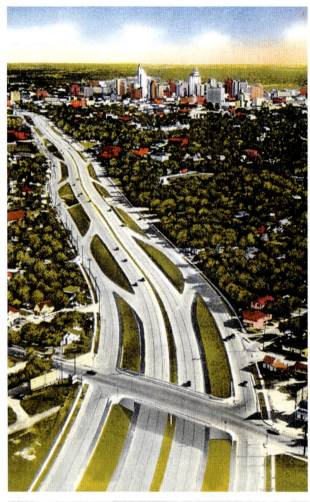

Mayor R. L. Thornton, center, and former Dallas mayors celebrated the "completion" of Central Expressway in 1956.
Dallas Historical Society

In 1956 five former mayors joined Mayor Robert L. Thornton in a ribbon-cutting ceremony to celebrate the "completion" of the project, but of course it was not finished, for extensions and improvements were to continue for decades ahead. Ultimately, it crossed the entire north-south length of the city and beyond. A complete refurbishing and widening was completed in 1999 at a cost of $441 million, vastly exceeding the original cost of $31 million, a figure which itself had dwarfed the amount of $450,000 provided in the 1927 bond issue.

The impact of Central Expressway was enormous, especially for the route developed first north of downtown. It promoted office development, erased slums along Central Avenue, prompted a suburban explosion for areas north of town as well as Richardson and Plano and gave a lasting bias toward development in that direction. In the years ahead many other expressways or freeways would be built, inevitably being named for civic leaders, mayors or ex-presidents — Stemmons, Woodall Rodgers, R.L. Thornton, Robert B. Cullum, Marvin B. Love, John Carpenter, S.M. Wright and Lyndon B. Johnson among them. None, though, would have the emotional or actual economic impact that had accompanied the long-delayed dream of Central Expressway.

By the end of the 20th century, Dallas and the Dallas area would be recognized as a major location for headquarters of major corporations listed in the Fortune 500. The roots of this new aspect of the city's history could be traced to the World War II period and immediately afterwards. What was described as "the greatest industrial development in the history of Texas" occurred in 1940 when North American Aviation of Inglewood, California, announced plans to build in Grand Prairie a $7 million plant that would employ more than 12,000 workers. It would be the largest single industry in the state. One of the reasons for choosing the area would turn out to be an important one for other corporations moving to the area: its convenient location on the continent midway between the East and West coasts.

In 1948 another major aircraft manufacturer, Chance-Vought in Connecticut, decided to transfer operations to the area. Chance-Vought's relocation was billed as the largest industrial move in the nation's history. In 1950 a major company in the oil and gas industry, Dresser Industries, came to Dallas from Cleveland, and in 1953 General Motors began building a $35 million assembly plant in Arlington. Ford Motor Co. had done so much earlier, in 1914. The postwar period also saw the emergence of another local company destined to have a worldwide impact — Texas Instruments, founded as a New Jersey company to provide seismic services to the oil industry but transformed under Erik Jonsson, Cecil Green and Eugene McDermott to emphasize its new product, the transistor, and thus to revolutionize the world of electronics.

Still another company whose outlets were destined to span the globe was born under more modest circumstances in Oak Cliff in the 1920s. John Jefferson "Uncle Johnny" Green, who sold blocks of ice at a small dock, began offering bread, milk, eggs and a few canned goods as well as a convenience to his customers. His success amounted to a new concept in marketing — the drive-in convenience store. The Southland Corporation implemented his idea throughout the state and soon the nation and before too long the entire world. The 7-Eleven Store had been born.

As the city prospered through the 1930s, 1940s and into the 1950s, one large segment of citizens continued to suffer from discrimination and failed to share in the improved economic conditions that so many residents enjoyed. This was the African-American population, 61,605 of the city's total of 294,734 in 1940. As was true for cities throughout the South, residential patterns and schools were strictly segregated by race; and productive jobs were almost entirely unavailable to African-Americans. For years the city's black population had accepted, largely without complaint, its disfavored status in society.

As early as the 1930s, however, a handful of African-American leaders determined to push harder for benefits and privileges previously denied them. The most ambitious of these leaders was A. Maceo Smith, who upon his arrival to the city in 1933 had energized the Negro Chamber of Commerce and the Dallas branch of the NAACP. A key partner was a minister, the Rev. Maynard Jackson, who had returned to his native city in the same year to take over as pastor of the New Hope Baptist Church. Besides their work with the Negro Chamber of Commerce and the NAACP, they formed a political organization that would endure into the 21st century, the Progressive Voters League.

One of their accomplishments, achieved only with difficulty, was the sponsorship of a building at the Texas Centennial called the Hall of Negro Life. Its exhibits demonstrated Negro advancements in all aspects of Texas life, and as African-Americans from throughout the state congregated in the building, the occasions were used to organize numerous chapters of the NAACP for communities throughout the state.

More direct was the voting strength achieved through a massive effort to encourage African-Americans to pay their poll taxes. With some 10,000 black voters registered, Smith and Jackson announced goals to secure

Texas Instruments revolutionized the electronics industry and anchored a "silicon corridor" along North Central Expressway.
Dallas County Heritage Society

The 7-Eleven convenience store chain got its start in 1927 at this market in Oak Cliff.
Dallas Historical Society Corporation

The Rev. Maynard Jackson (father of the future mayor of Atlanta) was the first president of the Progressive Voters League.
Dallas Historical Society

(Above) During the Texas Centennial Exposition, the Hall of Negro Life saluted the achievements of African Americans, but the building was torn down immediately afterward.
Dallas County Heritage Society

The Dallas Express, an African-American newspaper, encouraged its readers to pay their poll tax so they could vote.
Dallas Historical Society

a second Negro high school, the hiring of Negro policemen and letter carriers, street improvements for Negro neighborhoods, more and better parks to serve their community and opportunities for employment in all facets of municipal government. The concessions they won led to the building of a second high school for African-American students, Lincoln High, opening in 1940, and a new community house and recreation center at Wahoo Park. Not until 1947 were the first black police officers hired, and other employment opportunities at city hall were slow to come.

Other issues awaited remedy through the courts. One irritant was the fact that African-American schoolteachers in Dallas were paid less than their white counterparts. A black attorney, W.J. Durham, representing several Negro organizations, filed suit and in 1943 won a judgment granting pay raises that in two years made salaries of black teachers equal to that of white teachers. Another important lawsuit originating in Dallas was filed by Durham and C.B. Bunkley Jr. In this case, Smith v. Allwright, they challenged the constitutionality of all-white Democratic Party primary that effectively excluded African-Americans from participating in the important primary elections throughout the South. The U.S. Supreme Court in 1944 found the all-white primaries to be in violation of the Constitution. The case became an important first step in dismantling the segregated power structure throughout the South.

Efforts by African-Americans to win elected office in Dallas and Dallas County during the 1930s and 1940s failed, however. After Maynard Jackson's disappointing loss as a school board candidate in 1944, he accepted a pastorate in Atlanta, Georgia. There, his son, Maynard Jackson Jr., would become the first black mayor in Atlanta's history.

These efforts by African-Americans in the 1930s and 1940s laid the framework for the greater gains that would come later with the emergence of a new generation of activist-minded black citizens.

The first graduating class from Lincoln High School posed in front of the building in 1940.
Dallas Public Library

Attorneys C. B. Bunkley Jr., Cecil J. Partee and W. J. Durham challenged
laws that excluded African Americans from enjoying their full civil rights.
Dallas Public Library

CHAPTER EIGHT

Overcoming Trauma

8 DALLAS AND THE ASSASSINATION

One thing in Dallas had been consistent over the years — an unrelenting pattern of growth. This would continue unmitigated over the war years and the postwar period. The 432,927 residents who lived Dallas in 1950 reflected a 50 percent population jump over 1940. The 1950 city directory described the city as having "the charm of yesterday and the spirit of tomorrow," but it was the "tomorrow" that always had a priority.

Republican Congressman Bruce Alger articulated the conservative attitudes of many Dallas voters in the 1950s.
Dallas Public Library

Dallas was averaging a gain of five new businesses each day and 18 new manufacturing plants each month.

Its boundaries expanded at an even greater rate. The city limits grew by an amazing six-fold between 1945 and 1960. And census figures for 1960 showed that once more the population had soared more than 50 percent, now reaching 679,684.

If a characteristic could be ascribed to the population of any large city, one would have to say that throughout its history Dallas was marked by the presence of a large number of self-made individuals with a strong sense of independence. They, like the city they lived in, had prospered largely through their own initiative.

It was perhaps this characteristic that engendered a postwar political climate in the city noted for its ultra-conservatism. A series of events in Dallas brought national attention to the city in this regard. The first came in 1954 when the usual Democratic tradition was upset through the election to Congress of Bruce Alger — a Republican. He likely was the most conservative Congressman in the nation. He spoke ardently against creeping socialism, and he viewed the expanding role of the federal government as evidence of it. He vehemently favored local authority over federal, and he opposed federal expenditures that included even the popular school lunch programs. He sponsored bills for the United States to withdraw from the United Nations and to break relations with the Soviet Union. Dallas voters approved of his actions; they sent him back to Congress for four additional terms.

Alger's attitudes were reflected in several emotional controversies at the Dallas Museum of Fine Arts and the Dallas Public Library that brought unflattering national headlines to Dallas and further enlarged its growing reputation as a hotbed for political conservatism. Leaders of several local patriotic organizations questioned in 1955 the patriotism of art museum and library board trustees because they exhibited the works of artists who were either communists or had expressed sympathy for communism. (Pablo Picasso, Diego Rivera and Ben Shahn were among the artists whose works were attacked as improper for viewing in Dallas.)

Under pressure and concerned at being accused of a lack of patriotism, art museum trustees agreed not to display the work of any known communist or member of a communist-front organization. Local art patrons as well as art authorities and individuals across the nation expressed concern that political viewpoints could be used as a basis for censoring a work of art. Thus reinforced, trustees reversed their position and declared that they would exhibit and acquire works of art "only on the basis of their merit."

The library controversy, a similar one, surfaced the next year over an exhibition of paintings and rugs that included

Barely a year after its new central library building opened in 1955, the Dallas Public Library was caught in a controversy over the exhibition of two works by Pablo Picasso.
Dallas County Heritage Society

works by Picasso. To avoid a prolonged dispute, the library director simply withdrew Picasso's works. Protestors once more argued that the merits of a work of art had nothing to do with its creator's politics, but the library director and board — fearful of repercussions — preferred not to do battle.

In the fall of 1960 an episode occurred that brought even more unfortunate headlines to the city as a place where contrasting viewpoints were not tolerated. The incident involved one of the state's most noted Texans, Sen. Lyndon B. Johnson, the Democratic vice-presidential candidate and running mate to John F. Kennedy. Johnson and his wife, Lady Bird, in the city to attend a Democratic Party luncheon, were confronted by an angry, screaming crowd of demonstrators who pressed against them, taunted them, displayed insulting signs and almost held them prisoner. Congressman Alger, who bore a sign saying "LBJ Sold Out to Yankee Socialists," was the most prominent member of the demonstrators. His well-dressed Republican "Alger Girls," who had come downtown at his beckoning, were a part of the crowd. That such a raucous demonstration could be directed against a native Texan vice-presidential candidate in his own home state seemed remarkable to newspaper and television editors. The nation's press played up this surprising reception of this prominent Texas couple by their fellow Texans with all the details they could muster.

The episode rang an alarm bell in Dallas. Such scenes and headlines were not in keeping with the positive image the city's leaders had sought to foster for so many years. The event was, according to an editorial in the *Dallas Times Herald*, "completely foreign to usual Dallas manners and hospitality."

Unfortunately, the brand of ultra-conservatism that not only sought to censor the arts but viewed Johnson and Kennedy as traitors to the country was not uncommon. Former Army Gen. Edwin A. Walker, a pet of the John Birch Society and object of intense national interest, settled in the city to advance his controversial right-wing agenda. Famous oilman H.L. Hunt wrote and published ultra-conservative tracts and sponsored a radio and television commentary show replete with similar sentiments. An organization called the National Indignation Conference was founded in Dallas with the purpose of seeking the dismissal of all U.S. government officials responsible for granting military aid to

Billionaire oilman H.L. Hunt funded ultra-conservative causes in Dallas during the 1950s and 1960s. *Dallas Public Library*

Communist regimes anywhere. A chapter of the John Birch Society, probably the best-known of the nation's ultra-rightist organizations, flourished in the city and enjoyed periodic visitors from its founder, Robert Welch of Massachusetts. *The Dallas Morning News* nodded approvingly on its editorial pages at these activities.

Of course, there existed in Dallas many moderate and liberal individuals who held contrary viewpoints. Some of them belonged to the Dallas Council on World Affairs and the Dallas chapter of the United Nations Association. On October 26, 1963, these organizations sponsored a visit to Dallas by the U.S. ambassador to the United Nations, Adlai E. Stevenson, to speak on United Nations Day. A capacity crowd attended the evening event in Memorial Auditorium, but when Stanley Marcus introduced the ambassador it became clear that the evening would not be the pleasant and well-ordered affair anticipated. The audience was packed with a group of extremists who sought to disrupt Stevenson's speech with a bullhorn, noisemakers, heckling, constant coughing and movement. Outside, after his speech, a mob of demonstrators spotted Stevenson as he departed and rushed toward him. Shouts of "Communist" and "traitor" could be heard. One screaming woman hit him on the head with her picket sign. Another demonstrator spat on him.

Concerned about far-right elements, retail magnate Stanley Marcus urged President John F. Kennedy not to visit Dallas in 1963. *DeGolyer Library, Southern Methodist University*

The protestors began rocking his car until finally the driver was able to speed away. Television cameras caught the full anger of the scene. Viewers across the nation again were shocked at what they had seen in Dallas.

"What has happened to Dallas?" asked the *Dallas Times Herald* in disbelief. The display had brought the city to the realization that " 'harmless extremists' can not only cause physical harm but create destructive havoc." Mayor Earle Cabell, Citizens Council president Erik Jonsson, Chamber of Commerce president Robert B. Cullum and a hundred other leading citizens sent a telegram of apology to Ambassador Stevenson. Mayor Cabell urged Dallas citizens to reject the radical right now just as it had ultimately rejected the Klan in the 1920s.

Even more alarming was the foreboding realization that President Kennedy himself would be in Dallas in less than a month. What might the demonstrators do then? Concerned for the president's safety, Stanley Marcus urged him to stay away. But the president would not reconsider.

At this point, deeply concerned at the likelihood of further embarrassing demonstrations, the powerful Citizens Council announced that it would assume sponsorship of the presidential visit. Three years earlier, at another critical juncture, the Citizens Council had exercised its authority by conducting a powerful public relations campaign to permit the peaceful integration of Dallas' public schools. The success of this endeavor had been saluted by President Kennedy himself and also by his brother, Attorney General Robert Kennedy. Concerned once more about the city's increasingly fragile image, the Citizens Council initiated a broad campaign to promote a successful presidential visit. In speeches, sermons, newspaper articles, radio and television reports, and every means possible, speakers emphasized the need to treat the president with the respect he deserved.

On the day of President Kennedy's arrival, November 22, 1963, a full-page advertisement, "WANTED FOR TREASON," accompanied by simulated "mug shots" of President Kennedy and a list of "treasonous" charges, appeared in *The Dallas Morning News*. "We're really in 'nut country' now," Kennedy told his wife, Jackie, when he saw the advertisement that morning. On the streets some 5,000 leaflets repeating accusations of treason, printed by a close associate of Gen. Edwin A. Walker, had been scattered.

When the president and Mrs. Kennedy arrived at Love Field at 11:40 a.m. on November 22, a friendly, exuberant throng of spectators greeted them with spontaneous displays of genuine affection. Along the route of the presidential motorcade, an estimated 250,000 spectators further welcomed the president and Mrs. Kennedy, cheering, waving signs of greeting and showing clearly that they loved and supported their president and the First Lady.

Then, near the end of the motorcade route in downtown Dallas, came the worst moment in the city's history. At Dealey Plaza, a block from the Old Red Courthouse and at the very place where John Neely Bryan had founded

Dallas, three shots rang out from the Texas Schoolbook Depository. The president was fatally wounded; the governor of Texas, John Connally, riding in the same open limousine, was seriously wounded. The assassin, a recently hired employee in the building, was Lee Harvey Oswald, a 24-year-old ex-Marine, declared Marxist and one-time defector to the Soviet Union. Having fled the building for Oak Cliff, he stopped briefly at his rooming house to get a pistol, then shot and killed a Dallas police officer who sought to question him on the street. Minutes later, Oswald was captured in a movie theater a few blocks away.

Spectators on the "grassy knoll" in Dealey Plaza sought cover following the gunshots that killed President Kennedy.
John Fitzgerald Kennedy Library

On Sunday, two days after Oswald had been arrested, a nightclub owner named Jack Ruby slipped into the Dallas police station basement and shot and killed the suspect as he was being taken to a car for transfer to the county jail. An avalanche of hate mail and venomous long-distance telephone calls poured into the mayor's and police chief's offices. How, they asked, could Dallas have let the president be assassinated? And then, how could it have permitted the primary suspect to be killed while in police custody? The two events were simply incredulous. Worldwide opprobrium fell upon the city.

"We are a tormented town," said Joe Dealey of *The Dallas Morning News*. "All I could do was pray," said

Crowds at Love Field greeted President and Mrs. Kennedy warmly on November 22, 1963.
John Fitzgerald Kennedy Library

Chapter 8

Dallas Times Herald photographer Bob Jackson won a Pulitzer Prize by capturing the moment Jack Ruby shot Lee Harvey Oswald.
Belo Archives

(Far right) Mayor Earle Cabell resigned his office to run for Congress against Bruce Alger.
Dallas Public Library

The city council drafted J. Erik Jonsson, one of the men who had made Texas Instruments a technology giant, to serve as mayor in 1964.
Dallas Public Library

Robert L. Thornton. Dallas was "undergoing the dark night of the soul," editorialized the *Dallas Times Herald*. "In the name of God, what kind of city have we become?" asked the Rev. William A. Holmes.

The city was shaken to the roots of its soul. Although the assassin had been an avowed leftist, not a right-wing extremist, a realization dawned that extremism of any kind was harmful, that individuals with differing viewpoints should be treated with respect, and that accusations of treason were harmful and unfair.

A time for healing, a time for change, had come.

And change did come about. Extremist groups and individuals, seeming to realize that they had overstepped themselves, quietly faded away. Self-examination became the public norm. A determination to involve more of Dallas' citizens in decision-making arose. Out of tragedy, Dallas soon became a better place.

One of the first manifestations of the new mood came when Earle Cabell resigned as mayor to seek Bruce Alger's Congressional seat. With the support of much of Dallas' business-minded leadership, Cabell campaigned against Alger's extreme conservatism. His victory was surprisingly easy. Cabell billed it as "a return to sanity on the part of the people of Dallas County."

The new mayor, Erik Jonsson, announced a program designed for community self-examination. It was Goals for Dallas, a project which in its first five years involved more than 100,000 citizens who formed consensuses as to what kind of city they wanted, determined priorities and established deadlines for achieving the goals they set.

Goals achieved ranged from a new city hall and new central library to expanded cultural and ethnic-oriented programs. The success of the program was a key reason for *Look* magazine to designate Dallas an "All-America City" in 1970, the only city in its size category honored.

During this post-assassination period of positive thinking, a new challenge to Love Field arose. For years the city had wrangled with Fort Worth over aviation, especially a mid-cities airport, and it had fought tooth and nail against federal agencies that favored a mid-cities airport. In 1964 yet another serious challenge arose. The

Dynamic Dallas: An Illustrated History

Civil Aeronautics Board issued an ultimatum that the two cities must be served by a single regional airport. The cities had 180 days to agree upon a site or else it would be chosen for them.

It had been an accepted civic "truth" that all threats against Love Field must be resisted at all costs. The facility, after all, was one of the nation's busiest airports. By 1962 Love Field ranked seventh in the nation in the number of passenger departures. After overcoming many obstacles, an expensive new $4.5 million runway was being constructed. The new terminal was only seven years old. The city, justifiably, was very proud of this outstanding facility and its investment in it over the years.

But there were other considerations rarely mentioned. Continued growth in air transportation was absolutely certain, but further expansion of Love Field would be increasingly difficult if not impossible. Commercial and residential developments already surrounded Love Field. Longer runways to accommodate larger, supersonic aircraft just around the corner would be necessary, but getting them would be an arduous task, if possible.

Mayor Erik Jonsson, quietly contemplating the situation, concluded that the time had come for a major change in Dallas' thinking. He conferred with his friend, Robert B. Cullum, president of the Dallas Chamber of Commerce, who agreed with him. They initiated a series of quiet meetings with Fort Worth to see what might be arranged.

Jonsson, Cullum and Mayor Pro Tem Carie Welch represented Dallas in the negotiations. On May 28, 1965, the representatives from both cities signed a memorandum of understanding to be submitted to their city councils for approval. The negotiators had not only buried the hatchet, they created a bold, imaginative concept for what would be the largest airport in the world when it opened in 1974.

In its first year of operation, the new DFW Airport served more than 14 million passengers. Nine major airlines and eight commuter airlines offered more than 800 flights a day. The success of this new, spacious airfield with multiple "half-loop" terminals rather than an elongated single terminal was beyond all expectations.

Nearby cities such as Grapevine and Irving experienced substantial booms.

Love Field, rather than fading away from the public view in its new capacity of serving general aviation needs, had a surprising development. A new "commuter" airline, Southwest, insisted on remaining at Love Field to serve commercial passengers on short flights to such cities as Houston and San Antonio. Southwest developed into one of the nation's biggest and most profitable airlines, and Love Field continued to serve as one of Dallas' prized assets.

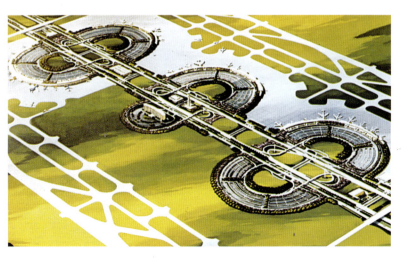

Mayor Jonsson launched Goals for Dallas, a massive city planning project, as one way to overcome the trauma of the Kennedy assassination. *Dallas County Heritage Society*

Located midway between Dallas and Fort Worth, DFW Airport opened in 1974 and served 14 million passengers during its first year of operation. *Dallas County Heritage Society*

Chapter 8

CHAPTER NINE

Suddenly Different

9 PREPARING FOR THE NEW CENTURY

Rapid change is an obvious hallmark of modern society, but as Dallas entered the 21st century its own transformation was unusually dramatic. Fundamental alterations had occurred in the makeup of its population, in the manner in which it was governed and in the people who governed it, in its relationship to large suburban cities surrounding it, in its growing partnership with Fort Worth and in a dynamic revival of the downtown area.

From its opening in 1978, Reunion Tower (part of the Hyatt Regency Dallas Hotel complex) became an instant landmark.
Carolyn Brown Photographer

The view of the downtown Dallas skyline from the revolving ball atop Reunion Tower is one of the most dramatic in the city.
Carolyn Brown Photographer

Its population seemed to have diversified overnight. Hispanics, rapidly growing in number, now constituted the largest single ethnic group, replacing African-Americans who throughout modern history had held that distinction. In the public schools Hispanic students also were a majority, followed by African-Americans, with white students now a distinct minority. There was a growing number of Asians, too, and a healthy sprinkling of immigrants from Africa, all of them attracted to the area's favorable economic climate.

Recognition of the city's diversity had changed the way Dallas was governed. Members of minority groups held a majority of the seats on the City Council, the makeup of which had been radically altered by a federal judge's ruling in 1991 mandating that districts be created to give minorities a better chance at being elected. Voters twice had chosen an African-American, Ron Kirk, as their mayor, the first person of his race to hold that office. His tenure was marked by a degree of harmony that had been missing at city hall for several years. Minorities either held or had held other top public offices in the city — city manager, police chief, fire chief, DISD school board president and DISD superintendent. At the county courthouse the same diversity was evident.

Dallas itself had grown by the year 2000 to a population of just over a million, about half of the 2.2 million people living in the entire county and only a third of those in the Dallas metropolitan area. The even larger Dallas/Fort Worth Consolidated Metropolitan Statistical Area (CMSA) held a population of 5 million.

On all sides, towns that for many years had been dwarfed by "Big D" were now major urban cities in their own right such as Richardson, Irving, Garland, Duncanville, Plano and Mesquite. In several instances their populations topped the 200,000 mark. Dallas' boundaries long since had ceased expanding because of these suburban towns, and the dramatic growth that had marked the city for so many decades now had shifted to these communities.

Communities within the CMSA had obtained a popular nickname — the "Metroplex" — a term invented as part of a marketing plan for DFW Airport that had somehow stuck. DFW International Airport, located almost precisely between Dallas and Fort Worth, was at the center of the Metroplex. Communities such as Irving, Grapevine, Coppell and Southlake were not the only ones that had thrived under the airport's immense shadow.

Dynamic Dallas: An Illustrated History

Fortune in 1999 proclaimed Dallas the "overall best city for business in North America," the second time the city had been so honored. Many of the nation's largest corporations — including Exxon, J.C. Penney and AMR — recognized the advantages of being near DFW Airport and transferred their headquarters to the area. They and others usually cited as their primary motivation the convenience of the airport, its capacity to handle a large volume of takeoffs and landings on seven runways, and its many national and international non-stop flights. Dallas' location in the center of the continent, once considered a remote setting, had become convenient in this age of jet travel.

The airport, with ownership shared by the cities of Dallas and Fort Worth, gave a tremendous impetus to the economy. As the third-busiest airport in the world, it was generating annual revenues of $11.2 billion, a figure that amounted to more than $1 million an hour, 24 hours a day, 365 days a year. Some 2,300 flights a day were being recorded at the end of the 20th century. Dallas and Fort Worth could be thankful that leaders of previous generations had had the wisdom to envision the future value of aviation to their communities.

Transportation within the growing Dallas metropolitan area also had undergone a transformation. Thirteen area cities were partners in Dallas Area Rapid Transit (DART), authorized by voters in 1983, a system that included buses and an expanding light-rail system. In the year 2000 some 96 million passengers took advantage of DART transportation. A notable expansion in 2001 was the inauguration of the Trinity Railway Express, a joint project with the Fort Worth Transportation Authority, providing rail service between Dallas and Fort Worth.

In downtown Dallas, long before the 21st century arrived, the skyline had become so congested with towering skyscrapers that the familiar flying red horse atop the Magnolia Building was all but lost to view. Several of the new downtown buildings were remarkable in ways other than soaring height,

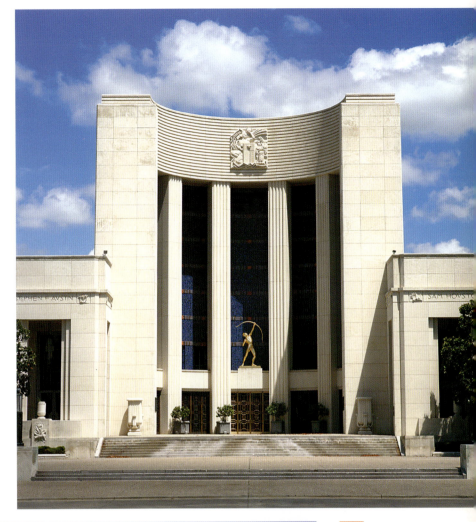

■ The gilt Tejas Warrior, sculpted by Allie Tennant in 1936, tops the entrance to the Hall of State at Fair Park, reminding visitors of the earliest inhabitants of Texas.
Carolyn Brown Photographer

■ DFW Airport prides itself on being the engine that drives the local economy.
Carolyn Brown Photographer

(Far right) The design of the Central Dallas Public Library, named in honor of J. Erik Jonsson, acknowledges I.M. Pei's City Hall across the street.
Carolyn Brown Photographer

Pegasus, the "flying red horse" atop the Magnolia Building, was once visible for miles in all directions. Today it is nearly lost among surrounding skyscrapers.
Carolyn Brown Photographer

(Bottom right) The "barrel vault" provides a dramatic centerpiece to the Dallas Museum of Art, designed by Edward Larrabee Barnes.
Carolyn Brown Photographer

Henry Moore's sculpture provides a dramatic counterpoint to I.M. Pei's angular Dallas City Hall.
Carolyn Brown Photographer

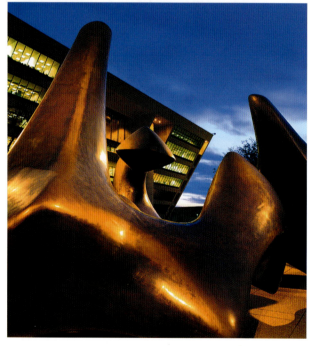

though. One was the dynamic city hall, designed by I.M. Pei. Each floor was larger than the one beneath it. Built as an outgrowth of the Goals for Dallas program, the modernistic, concrete structure, completed in 1978, instantly commanded the favorable attention of architectural critics. Across the street from city hall a new central library, complementary in architectural features and named for Erik Jonsson, opened in 1982 as a project also envisioned by Goals for Dallas.

I.M. Pei was also the architect of another spectacular ornament to the downtown area, a new concert hall, the Meyerson Symphony Center. Built at a cost of $81.5 million, it opened in 1989 and was acclaimed as one of the world's finest concert facilities. Located in the Arts District along Ross Avenue, it was not far from the new Dallas Museum of Art. The Arts District was destined soon to have another neighbor, the Nasher Sculpture Garden, where NorthPark developer Raymond Nasher's collection of outdoor sculpture, said to be the finest in the world, was under construction.

Yet another impressive addition to the downtown area was the American Airlines Center, home to both the Dallas Mavericks basketball team and the Dallas Stars ice hockey team. Built at an abandoned industrial site just north of the flourishing restaurants in the West End, the arena opened in 2001 as a joint project between the city of Dallas and the two sports teams' owners. The rest of the development, when completed, would include a much larger area containing entertainment, retail, residential and office projects.

The Morton Meyerson Symphony Center boasts some of the finest acoustics of any concert hall in the world.
Carolyn Brown Photographer

Before the American Airlines Center opened, a new owner had taken possession of the Dallas Mavericks and quickly become one of the most visible figures in town. He was Mark Cuban, the youthful Dallas billionaire who had made his fortune as founder of an Internet company, Broadcast.com, which he sold with his partner to Yahoo Inc. for approximately $6 billion. Cuban, a basketball "junkie," generally wore a T-shirt as he cheered on his team and made national sports headlines with his penchant for criticizing the officiating.

Sports were important in Dallas, and in fact the hugely successful and popular Dallas Cowboys football team had helped remove the stigma of assassination from the city's image in the dark days afterwards. The Cowboys' success in the 1960s and 1970s, and especially their regular appearances on television and two Super Bowl championships, led to a new nickname: "America's Team." Coach Tom Landry, owner Clint Murchison Jr., general manager Tex Schramm, quarterback Roger Staubach and other key players became some of the most admired citizens of Dallas. Then, under new owner Jerry Jones in the 1990s, the team and key players such as quarterback Troy Aikman once again climbed to the top of the professional football world, winning three Super Bowl championships. The fact that Texas Stadium, home of the Cowboys, was located in Irving, not Dallas, was testimony to the growing importance of the suburban cities around Dallas.

Collaboration between Dallas and Fort Worth, in addition to joint ownership of the airport and the Trinity Railway Express, extended these days to baseball. Neither city enjoyed specific identification in the team's title, the Texas Rangers, but from their uniquely named playing field — the Ball Park in Arlington — they represented both cities in the American League. In his efforts to bring a much-delayed championship to the area, owner Tom Hicks startled the baseball world in 2000 when he agreed to pay the highest sum of money ever to a baseball player — $252 million over a 10-year period to shortstop Alex Rodriguez.

Hicks' Southwest Sports Group also owned the Dallas Stars ice hockey team, which shared the American Airlines Center with the Dallas Mavericks. The Stars' success in 1999 brought to the city the coveted Stanley Cup, a trophy awarded the nation's championship ice hockey team. Southwest Sports Group also owned the Mesquite Championship Rodeo.

Hicks' announcement in summer 2001 of a new development gave clear indication of the continued northward thrust of Dallas that Central Expressway had started and Dallas North Tollway continued. Hicks said he planned to build in the rapidly growing town of Frisco a $300 million sports complex that would include a state-of-the-art ice hockey arena, a 9,000-seat stadium for a minor league baseball team, a hotel, 500 apartment units and retail establishments.

With such dramatic population explosions in areas so far north of the city limits, not to mention corporate relocations to those areas, downtown Dallas had taken on an entirely different character. In fact, its streets too frequently seemed deserted. Since the 1960s, familiar

For 50 years, "Big Tex" has greeted the thousands of visitors who flock to the State Fair of Texas each October.
Carolyn Brown Photographer

Dynamic Dallas: An Illustrated History

Still one of Dallas' architectural gems, the Wilson Building has gained new life as residential condominiums.
Carolyn Brown Photographer

department stores such as Sanger-Harris, Titche-Goettinger and Dreyfuss & Sons had disappeared through mergers or acquisitions and movements to shopping malls in outlying areas. Movie houses that for years had been located along Elm Street, too, had closed shop and moved to the suburbs as new multi-screen movie complexes. The skyscrapers in the downtown area, beautiful though they were, had taken up entire blocks with their massive structures, squeezing out pedestrian-enhancing sites such as small retail outlets, grocery stores, service stations and restaurants. Moreover, beginning in the 1990s office space vacancies were among the highest in the nation. Pedestrian traffic, once making downtown a beehive of activity, practically disappeared.

But just as wails of despair were sounding for the future of downtown, a new surge of life took hold. Abandoned buildings such as the Wilson Building, the Santa Fe Building, the Busch Building and the old Titche-Goettinger store, still handsome and solid, were reclaimed and converted into high-toned condominiums. Smaller buildings also underwent conversion into condominiums or lofts. New apartment complexes began to be built near the Farmers Market area, at the historic State-Thomas Historic District and elsewhere. The Deep Ellum district east of town and the former warehouse district now known as the West End, both revitalized, brought a cheerful nightlife to those separate ends of downtown. Suddenly, even with the explosion of the suburbs, downtown's future looked bright again.

Col. Belo's instincts certainly had been right when he sent George B. Dealey in 1882 to examine the promising North Central Texas area he was hearing so much about. But the prospects he saw as so evident then seemed barely to touch the surface of what lay ahead.

Chapter 9

Located on the southern edge of downtown Dallas, the Farmers' Market is a reminder that a rich agricultural region still surrounds the city.
Carolyn Brown Photographer

(Below) "Dallas Alley" is one of many entertainment venues that have developed in the historic West End district of downtown Dallas.
Carolyn Brown Photographer

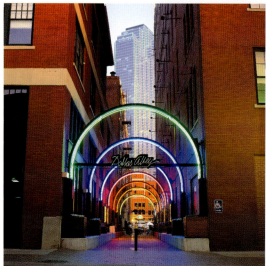

Growth through the years was spectacular. By the year 2000 the 16 counties in North Central Texas held a population of 5.3 million, an addition of more than a million since 1990. This accounted for nearly a third of the entire population growth in Texas during the decade. Within this region, Dallas County experienced the greatest increase, adding 366,000 to its population.

Since its founding in 1841 by a wandering frontiersman, Dallas has seen and overcome many obstacles. Those pioneers who founded and guided the city in the 19th century laid a sound foundation and kept the city ahead of its nearby rivals for area supremacy. The business/civic leaders who dominated affairs throughout most of the 20th century were wise and gave unselfishly of their time in pushing the city to new heights. The more diverse array of men and women who assumed positions of authority at the end of the 20th and beginning of the 21st century seemed to complete a natural evolution for Dallas. As they awaited the new and surely unpredictable challenges of the century ahead, they could look back with assurance on the successes of those who had preceded them.

The bronze cattle being herded down a slope in Pioneer Plaza are a reminder that Dallas was located on the early Shawnee Trail during its first two decades.

Carolyn Brown Photographer

PARTNERS IN DALLAS

122 *Building a Greater Dallas*

- *124* Briggs-Freeman Real Estate Brokerage
- *126* Dikita Enterprises
- *128* Frisco Square
- *130* Goodman Family of Builders
- *132* Harwood International
- *134* Mills Electrical Contractors
- *136* Ryland Homes
- *138* Sharif & Munir
- *140* Adleta & Poston, Realtors
- *141* Manhattan Construction Company
- *142* Pulte Homes

144 *Business & Finance*

- *146* Capital Alliance
- *148* KPMG LLP
- *150* Republic Group of Insurance Companies
- *152* State Farm Insurance®
- *154* Washington Mutual
- *156* JR Mortgage Corp.

158 *Manufacturing & Distribution*

- *160* Borden
- *162* Garrett Metal Detectors
- *164* Mary Kay Inc.
- *166* Occidental Chemical Corporation
- *168* Ceramic Tile International
- *169* Crown Computer Supplies, Inc.
- *170* The Stanley Works

172 *Marketplace*

- *174* Pilgrim's Pride
- *178* 7-Eleven, Inc.
- *180* Intervest
- *182* McShan Florist
- *184* Mrs Baird's
- *186* Carolyn Brown, Photographer
- *187* CourierGuy.com

188 *Networks*

- *190* American Airlines
- *192* Associated Air Center
- *194* WRR Classical 101.1 FM

196 Professional Services

- 198 AGUIRREcorporation
- 200 Baron & Budd, P.C.
- 202 Hughes & Luce, LLP
- 204 Huitt-Zollars, Inc.
- 206 RTKL
- 208 Snelling and Snelling Inc.
- 210 Strasburger & Price
- 212 Halff Associates, Inc.

214 Quality of Life

- 216 Baylor Health Care System
- 220 Dallas County Community College District
- 224 American Golf Corporation
- 226 ATI Career Training
- 228 Buckner Benevolences
- 230 Candlewood Suites
- 232 Dallas Can! Academy
- 234 Dallas VA Medical Center
- 236 Episcopal Diocese of Dallas
- 238 Kindred Hospital
- 240 Parkland Health & Hospital System
- 242 Presbyterian Hospital of Dallas
- 244 The Salvation Army
- 246 The University of Texas at Dallas
- 248 Ursuline Academy of Dallas
- 250 Catholic Diocese of Dallas
- 251 Catholic Education of Dallas
- 252 City of Plano
- 253 Dallas Christian School
- 254 Dallas Theological Seminary
- 255 Frisco, Texas
- 256 International Linguistics Center
- 257 Medical City Dallas Hospital
- 258 Old City Park: The Historical Village of Dallas
- 259 Preservation Dallas
- 260 Richardson Chamber of Commerce
- 261 The Bill Priest Institute
- 262 Dallas Historical Society
- 263 Dallas Public Library
- 264 The Shelton School And Evaluation Center

266 Technology

- 268 Abbott Laboratories
- 270 EDS

BUILDING A GREATER *Dallas*

123

*D*ALLAS REAL ESTATE AND CONSTRUCTION INDUSTRIES SHAPE TOMORROW'S SKYLINE, PROVIDING WORKING AND LIVING SPACE FOR AREA RESIDENTS.

BRIGGS-FREEMAN REAL ESTATE BROKERAGE

WHEN IT COMES TO RESIDENTIAL REAL ESTATE, Briggs-Freeman Real Estate Brokerage has generations of experience in Dallas' most prestigious neighborhoods. "Our company is relational, not transactional," says Robbie Briggs, a second-generation real estate leader. "We focus on our relationships with our clients, however large or small, because we know from experience that happy customers are loyal customers."

With over 70 years of tradition, Briggs-Freeman can be proud of its distinguished clientele, which ranges from former governors to chairmen of corporations, from Olympic celebrities to first-time homebuyers. Even entire corporations relocating into the Dallas area seek out Briggs-Freeman to handle their employees' real estate needs. Each of these clients comes to Briggs-Freeman Real Estate Brokerage because of its astute knowledge of the constantly changing residential real estate market and its reputation for strategic selling and buying of upscale properties in the Dallas area, as well as farms and ranches in Texas.

Briggs-Freeman is a full-service residential real estate firm. The company takes pride in handling whatever its clients need to make their real estate transactions smooth. Whether it is a new home sale, relocation service, marketing assistance, inspection coordination, market analysis, closing assistance, property management coordination, or in-house mortgage assistance, Briggs-Freeman does it all and with a smile.

Briggs-Freeman is one of the last remaining full-service independent residential real estate companies in Dallas. Being an independent company makes for greater flexibility in meeting the unique residential needs of its clientele, especially in the areas of real estate networking and marketing.

In fact, Briggs-Freeman Real Estate Brokerage is so dependable and consistent with sales performance and customer satisfaction that it has earned international accolades. Sotheby's International Realty, the property brokerage known worldwide for its celebrity clientele and high-end properties, selected Briggs-Freeman as its exclusive affiliate in Dallas. This prestigious affiliation allows buyers and sellers around the world to have access to Dallas properties and allows Dallas clients to have easy access to international properties.

Nationally, Briggs-Freeman is considered the cream of the crop for residential real estate brokerages. It is a member of Relo, the largest independent network of real estate brokerages. This membership is only conferred upon real estate companies that meet stringent criteria for network referrals, consistently high sales figures and thorough professionalism at every level of company operations.

One of the reasons Briggs-Freeman is so predictably successful in Dallas is its smooth internal operation

Previous listing by Briggs-Freeman

(Left to right) Charles Freeman and Robbie Briggs

as a company. Charles Freeman, a fourth-generation Dallasite and part owner of Briggs-Freeman Real Estate Brokerage, oversees all the crucial processes that make or break a deal. Freeman and his staff of trained professionals attend to the complex paperwork and procedures that make Briggs-Freeman well respected by customers, staff and industry leaders. Freeman's peers have recognized his expertise by electing him a director of the Greater Dallas Association of Realtors Board for three years.

Freeman and Briggs make an ideal team for tackling the evolving Dallas real estate market. Their combined experience, connections and real estate savvy enable them to market their properties with extraordinary success.

Briggs-Freeman takes a strategic service approach to marketing, leaving nothing to chance or luck. The company uses a wide range of marketing techniques including its state-of-the-art Web site, which provides easy access to property listings, services and an introduction to each of its experienced, energetic and resourceful broker agents. The Web site gives clients the information they need 24 hours a day.

In addition to a fast, resourceful Web site, accessible listings in international and national real estate databases, and referral services, Briggs-Freeman publishes a quality magazine four times a year. This full-color, well-written, well-designed magazine highlights special properties, recent awards the firm has earned, and provides useful and current information regarding sales figures in key neighborhoods.

With over 60 real estate brokers on staff, there is a team approach to all transactions. The philosophy of the company is to work together to make the customer happy. This approach is especially popular with corporate clients who need major relocation assistance for their employees. Briggs-Freeman has an extraordinary package that truly takes care of everything.

Offered at no cost to the corporation or its employees, Briggs-Freeman Relocation Services saves time, money, hassles and stress for workers who must move. Briggs-Freeman meets one-on-one with employees to give them guidance for house hunting, mortgage financing and Texas real estate legalities.

If the employee must move before the right house is found, Briggs-Freeman has the contacts to arrange interim housing all over the city. The company also provides assistance with the most annoying of tasks, including utility hookup, driver's license registrations and banking service. Moreover, the company can help a spouse with resources to find employment, help relocate an aging parent or relative who may need special accommodations, and help with school selection.

Briggs-Freeman offers such a full range of services because of its commitment to serving the customer and the Dallas community — not just making a real estate transaction. This commitment is one of the reasons that the company and both owners are highly involved in charitable causes such as the Juvenile Diabetes Foundation, church activities and many other community organizations.

Both Briggs and Freeman are also members of all the important local and national real estate organizations: Employee Relocation Council, Dallas Relocation Professional, Metroplex Relocation Forum, Texas Relocation Network, Greater Dallas Association of Realtors, Texas Association of Realtors and the National Association of Realtors.

Clearly, real estate member affiliations, commitment to the community, marketing savvy, state-of-the-art technology and experienced, enthusiastic brokers all make Briggs-Freeman a consistent success. It is its philosophy and dedication to the customer, however, that makes Briggs-Freeman stand out from the residential real estate crowd. One customer, the owner of the largest Cadillac dealership in Dallas, said it best: "When it comes to residential real estate in Dallas," the customer said, "I am a lifelong customer of Briggs-Freeman."

Previous listing by Briggs-Freeman

DIKITA ENTERPRISES

WHETHER PEOPLE ARE RIDING AROUND TOWN on a DART bus or train, enjoying a concert at the Smirnoff Center, or taking in the sights at Pegasus Park in downtown Dallas, they are surrounded by the works of Dikita Enterprises. The name of the firm, Dikita, translates as bringing the community together for its greater good,

and this goal continues to be the driving philosophy of the company. In keeping with that spirit, the founder of Dikita, Lucious Williams, has played a key role in the establishment of a number of local chambers, organizations and foundations geared at fostering industry partnerships and communication such as the Coalition of Minority Chambers and the North Texas Regional Certification Agency.

Williams founded the company in 1979 with two other principals after putting his car up as collateral to the Capital Marine Bank in Milwaukee, Wisconsin, for a $6,000 line of credit. He had been involved in a number of facets of engineering, from marketing development to administration, and he had a vision of building his own firm. Since its inception, Dikita has grown into a successful engineering and consulting firm providing services to public and private sector clients. The company is a Certified Disadvantaged and Minority Business Enterprise. Williams, with Chief Financial Officer Evalynn Warren, opened Dikita's Dallas office in 1993 after a number of successful years in Milwaukee. The company now has offices in Dallas; Milwaukee; Beaumont-Port Arthur, Texas; and Shreveport, Louisiana. Dikita Enterprises includes two elements: Dikita Engineering and Dikita Management Services.

DIKITA ENGINEERING

Dikita is one of the largest minority-owned engineering firms in Dallas, providing quality full-service planning, engineering and management services to three core service areas: transportation; water and wastewater; and institutional and residential development. Historically, Dikita's services have benefited municipal, state and federal governments as a prime contractor or indirectly through partnering relationships with other firms. The company strives to go beyond the problem at hand and look to the client's larger vision. Keeping true to the definition of its name, Dikita has made a significant contribution to the city of Dallas and is constantly striving to be involved in endeavors that improve the environment and infrastructure.

A notable residential development project is the Villages of Runyon Springs, one of the first in this area in many years. The program is structured to increase regional property values, improve local educational facilities, provide for natural resource conservation and promote strong community involvement to reduce crime. Another is Unity Estates, a development initiated by the African-American Pastors' Coalition, an organization of around 70 ministers from area churches representing over 50,000 congregational members. To bring affordable housing to south Dallas, this project overcame obstacles such as a battle to have the proposed location rezoned and a struggle to win community support. The result of both of these residential development undertakings will be the transformation of unused acres into moderately priced single-family homes.

Dikita also played a major role in the Dallas "Sprayparks" project, a Parks & Recreation Department initiative to replace closed city pools with water spraying towers to cool visitors off on hot summer days. The "Sprayparks" have been praised for their safety and economic benefits. The water from the towers is drained to an on-site treatment facility and is recycled back to the spray mechanisms.

The company provided services in support of an $8 million reconstruction project covering six blocks of downtown for the Dallas City Center, including the creation of a park facility from native stones, sculptures and streams with outdoor seating areas for concerts.

Throughout Dallas' transition into the city it is today, Dikita has participated in groundbreaking projects, including providing construction management for the Starplex Amphitheater, now the Smirnoff Center, and the Frank Crawley Courts Building. For DART, Dikita provided initial planning and studies that led to the current light rail system; provided engineering services for the South Oak Cliff line, the first section to be designed; and provided inspection services for the first 70 light rail vehicles purchased in Osaka, Japan. In addition, Dikita has provided the DFW Airport with various services over the years, including several runway and taxiway designs.

DIKITA MANAGEMENT SERVICES

Evelynn Warren, Dikita's CFO, organized Dikita Management Services in response to industry demands to complement the engineering division by augmenting transportation planning, particularly as it relates to data collection, analysis, reporting and management. Its mission is to address the specific and unique management needs of transportation agencies. Its services include data collection for bus and rail planning, survey services for marketing, and the public involvement and communication efforts of the agencies. Warren saw the industry's need for higher-quality data collection services and has incorporated a number of time- and cost-saving technologies into DMS' offerings.

A key client of DMS is Dallas Area Rapid Transit. The relationship between DMS and DART developed in the early 1990s when DART decided to outsource its data collection services, and the partnership has grown through several renewals of the initial contract. DMS pioneered the automation of the data collection process of boarding and alighting at each DART bus stop for all local and suburban routes. DMS also maximized the use of DART's handheld computers by digitally collecting 100 percent of all ridership data, which eliminated the need for data entry of manual ridercheck forms.

Dikita Engineering and Dikita Management Services, under the Dikita Enterprises umbrella, live up to the name by involvement in projects that bring the community together for the greater good.

FRISCO SQUARE

FRISCO SQUARE, THE INNOVATIVE PROJECT developed by Five Star Development Co., Inc., is one of the largest urban master-planned, mixed-use developments ever constructed in Texas and one of the largest in the Unites States. The 147-acre project is a classic example of "new urbanism" with a neo-traditional concept focused on a pedestrian-friendly environment.

Library Street town home building designed by Centerbrook Architects & Planners

Retail and Office Tower on Frisco Square

Apartment building on Frisco Street

Located 20 miles north of downtown Dallas, Frisco is one of the fastest-growing suburban cities in the United States with an estimated 300-percent growth between 2002 and 2005 and approximately 800 new residents each month during that period. Frisco Square will be the thriving center of Frisco, Texas, complete with luxury town homes, apartments, flexible office space and the most distinctive retail environment in north Texas. The city of Frisco is also relocating its entire municipal district, including Frisco City Hall, Library and a Senior Center.

Frisco Square is a multigenerational development specifically designed by a team of world-renowned architects to encourage residents and tenants to live, work and play in an intimate environment. The master plan design for the project is the work of nationally recognized Washington, D.C., architect David M. Schwarz, whose other notable Dallas/Fort Worth projects include The Ballpark at Arlington, Sundance Square, Bass Performance Hall, Parker Square and the American Airlines Center in downtown Dallas. Internationally renowned architects, including Robert A.M. Stern, Centerbrook Architects & Planners, and Albert, Richter & Tittmann, will design Frisco Square's residential community.

The residential element of Frisco Square will include 1,600 multifamily units and more than 300 luxury town homes with prices ranging from $250,000 to $700,000. Residents of Frisco Square will enjoy town home living with the latest upscale amenities and an unrivaled concierge service. In addition, all homes will be built under the city of Frisco's Green Building Program, which makes the homes more energy efficient, healthier and sustainable.

The first phase of town home construction neared completion in the last quarter of 2002, and the commercial phase commenced in August of that year. Once complete, the project will offer more than 4 million square feet of planned retail, office, restaurant, entertainment and residential space. The entire project is estimated to be complete in 12 to 15 years, with total revenue from property and sales taxes between $4 million to $6 million a year. The creation of more than 8,000 new jobs is anticipated.

BUILDING A QUALITY COMMUNITY

On the surface, the project may seem like a typical mixed-use development, but Frisco Square is anything but typical. This is perhaps best evidenced with an anecdote about Five Square Development President and CEO Cole McDowell. When McDowell and lead project architect David Schwarz were choosing the Texas limestone for the buildings, Schwarz chose limestone with a life expectancy of 150 years. McDowell, however, wasn't satisfied with 150 years. Always committed to quality and long-term development, McDowell wanted a 300-year limestone and, through the efforts of the limestone company, was able to get the 300-year variety in the exact color he needed.

This is the philosophy that sets Five Star Development and Frisco Square apart. Not a fan of disposable architecture such as strip centers with a 30-year life span, McDowell set out to make his developments, particularly Frisco Square, last for not only his lifetime, but for the lifetimes of his children, grandchildren and great-grandchildren. This commitment to quality will benefit every resident of Frisco.

THE LIFESTYLE CONCEPT

Five Star Development has created an entire community, a complete lifestyle, dedicated to convenience — the art of convenience. The unique concierge lifestyle isn't about escape, it's about streamlining life — the "to do" list happens effortlessly. Children can walk to a private school nestled within Frisco Square and adult residents can walk from their offices to their favorite restaurant for lunch, taking care of errands on the way.

Frisco Square provides residents and businesses alike with an unrivaled concierge service. Each residential unit has a combination closet where the concierge service can drop off dry cleaning, takeout food or other deliveries or the resident can leave items for pick up. The concierge meets repairmen for residents while they are at work.

Sidewalk Café in the Arcade on the Square

View of commercial building down Frisco Street from the Square

The corporate concierge provides business services and amenities such as arranging catering or dinner reservations, handling meeting and event planning, booking travel accommodations and acquiring suites at sporting events.

An amenities center is planned for the third phase of town home development. The center will provide a gym, pool, tennis courts and other leisure activities, all within walking distance from home.

Frisco Square's combination of residential, retail and office space, all within a community setting replete with civic buildings, churches, parks and town squares, is unique within Texas. Perhaps McDowell's own words sum it up best: "I'm inspired by the opportunity to create an entire community, a complete lifestyle, that's dedicated to convenience as an art form. Frisco Square is the culmination of my passion for blending an enduring design aesthetic with forward-thinking lifestyle elements."

GOODMAN FAMILY OF BUILDERS

WHEN THE TIME COMES TO SELECTING OR building a home, Goodman Family of Builders makes it easy. Goodman has been creating dream homes for more than 24 years in the Dallas-Ft. Worth area. Goodman understands that a home is not just built, it is created.

A home begins with a lifestyle vision. This is why Goodman Family of Builders offers three distinct brands of homes catering to an individual's budget, space needs, desired amenities and community location. All of these brands — Goodman, Diamond and Westminster — maintain Goodman's sterling reputation for quality and excellent customer service.

Goodman Family of Builders is divided by three distinctive brands.

Westminster Homes are priced from the $110s. These homes range from 1,400 to 3,000 square feet. They offer floor plans that have several pre-planned options for the buyer to choose from. Options include bonus rooms, fireplaces, bay windows and more.

Diamond Homes are priced from the $150s to the $250s. These homes range from 2,000 to 3,500 square feet. Diamond offers design flexibility at an affordable price. Diamond Homes are so popular that their sales have grown almost 200 percent since 1996. It comes as no surprise then that Diamond Homes was recognized as Dallas Builder of the Year in 1996 and 1997.

Goodman Custom Homes are priced from the $250s to the $600s. They are the ultimate, "anything goes." A customer's dream home is built exactly the way the owner envisions it. Whether the customer's statement is traditional or contemporary, elegant or casual, Goodman will create an environment rich in style and sophistication.

Moreover, Goodman Family of Builders understands the bottom line: customer service. Unlike other builders, each home is assigned a Community Builder who is responsible from start to finish on each home. In this way, there is a point-person to contact for any issues that a buyer would like to communicate along the design, construction and follow-up phases for their dream home.

One of the most important considerations for anyone buying a home is the neighborhood. Goodman Family of Builders has more than 45 residential communities across the Metroplex. Each is carefully chosen for its schools, easy access to shopping, business centers, medical facilities, parks and recreational facilities.

Master Planned Communities are also available for those buyers who wish more natural surroundings and social amenities. Some of these Master Planned Communities offer lakes, golf, biking and hiking trails, swimming pools and a clubhouse.

All of the Goodman Family of Builders are owned by K. Hovnanian Enterprises, one of the top 10 builders in the United States. This allows for national purchasing of the highest-quality materials at a lower cost than a local independent builder. Moreover, the stability and financial backing of a national builder can be comforting for the long-term investment aspects of buying of home.

The Goodman and Diamond Homes brands share the same enjoyable decorating starting point. The Homes Design Gallery has all the options that a custom homebuyer could ever want and more. Owners will never feel rushed at The Home Design Gallery, which is full of samples to consider. The hardest part is making a decision, but even that is easier with The Home Designers, experienced professionals who understand how to translate vision into materials and how to stick within a budget.

Another benefit to working with Goodman Family of Builders is that it has its own mortgage company, which simplifies the financing process. Moreover, all the cumbersome title and closing materials are handled for the buyer internally. This eliminates all the hassle of the paperwork.

As a one-stop source, Goodman Family of Builders is committed to customer satisfaction. It conducts followup surveys after the sale of the house at closing and two months after move-in. The goal is to make sure that the customer is satisfied all along the way. If a problem arises, Goodman Family of Builders simply follows the philosophy of taking care of the customer and doing what is right.

Realtors, who often guide homebuyers who seek to customize and build, are especially fond of Goodman Family of Builders. Realtors know that Goodman is one of the top 10 largest builders in the Metroplex, with a reputation for design and building excellence. They know that Goodman Family of Builders consistently makes donations to many worthwhile organizations. They also know that the employees of Goodman are loyal professionals who enjoy their jobs. Goodman has very little turnover because employees are proud to work for such reputable, stable, growing company.

Goodman Family of Builders believes that a home is more than an investment. It is a place where memories are made. For over two decades, its philosophy has been centered around personal attention and unparalleled service. Goodman employees take the time to listen to their customers all the way through the sales, design, building and move-in stages. They take the time to resolve any problems. They take the time to understand the individual nuances and little touches that make all the difference.

Goodman Family of Builders knows that customers do not want to just buy or build a house. They want to create a home.

HARWOOD INTERNATIONAL

HARWOOD INTERNATIONAL HAS REDEFINED the standard for real estate excellence and consistency in Dallas and in select markets throughout the world. Clients worldwide appreciate Harwood International's comprehensive approach to real estate services and its commitment to providing quality office environments that enhance their businesses, exceed their expectations and improve their neighborhoods.

Founded in 1988 by Swiss-born Gabriel Barbier-Mueller, a Dallas resident since 1979, Harwood International is best known for leading the effort to transform Uptown Dallas from a declining area just north of the Central Business District into one of the most sought-after neighborhoods in Dallas. Located in the heart of Uptown between American Airlines Center and the Crescent, Harwood International Center provides an Uptown address within blocks of the city's finest sports, entertainment, dining and cultural institutions, as well as a plethora of upscale residential venues.

Harwood International Center is a master-planned campus that offers a Class A office environment, a host of client services and amenities, and extraordinary green space. The focal point of the center is a 1.5-acre European-inspired collection of gardens. Featuring reflecting pools, seating areas nestled under mature trees, private enclaves, and oversized chess and checker boards, the gardens offer visitors an oasis throughout the seasons. This extraordinary green space was created for the benefit of Harwood clients as well as the community

Tranquil pools reflect the natural beauty of the gardens and the timeless lines of the modern architecture.

and exemplifies Harwood International's commitment to responsible development and excellence.

A unique skybridge system allows clients access to the gardens, fitness centers, restaurants and various tenant support services as well as the other buildings within the complex. The bridges not only provide a function, they also create a sculptural link between architectural forms that anchor the campus. For example, the Centex Bridge is visible from the busy adjacent street, sidewalk and nearby buildings. This skybridge adds a warm and elegant accent to the dramatic buildings from which it begins and ends. Formed from Pau Lope — an ironwood — and paved with granite, the bridge brings a new combination of elements to use in

As dusk falls on the campus, everything from the gardens to the buildings take on an entirely new ambiance, affording clients and visitors a renewed sense of discovery.

A growing collection of museum-quality objects and antiquities rewards and informs while providing a symbolic extension to the nearby Arts District.

the campus. International Center's skybridge system not only provides a means of connecting buildings, it connects people. As the campus continues to grow, the importance of connecting "people places" will grow as well.

The first phase of the campus, the Rolex Building, was constructed in 1982 and has been a Dallas landmark for decades. In 2001 the building was renovated and expanded to include a seventh-floor tower.

The Centex Building, International Center's second phase, received notoriety as the first new office development in Dallas in 10 years. Since it opened in 1996, the Centex Building has received numerous community and industry awards. In 1999 it was named by the EPA as the most energy efficient building in the nation and continues to set the benchmark within the industry.

The Jones Day Building, Phase III, was completed in 1999. It serves as a backdrop for the campus's 1.5-acre gardens. As a bonus, clients enjoy a view of the arena as well as the Downtown skyline. In January 2000 Phase IV opened in record time: groundbreaking to grand opening transitioned within only 14 months. To date, three additional buildings are being designed for International Center. Ultimately, the campus will include 4 million square feet. With each subsequent phase that is created, the campus gets even better and additional amenities are added.

Each building at International Center is distinctive while maintaining a continuity of quality design and construction. Patterns of granite, metals and glass create a striking yet elegant presentation. Varying shapes of the building tops, window-wall spacing and materials coloration give each building its own identity. Lobbies feature a unique selection of stone, glass, metal and wood. They are finished with fine art pieces and modern classic furniture.

Meticulous planning and attention to detail have been key in the success of Harwood International. The long-range effects of the company's projects are of great consideration throughout the design, development and management processes.

Rather than reacting to client needs and market demands, the company strives to anticipate them. This philosophy allows Harwood International to better serve its clients and community. As a long-term owner, Harwood International is committed to Dallas' continued growth and prosperity.

HIC is shaping a new Dallas skyline creating a distinctive presence for the city's thriving Uptown district.

Building a Greater Dallas

MILLS ELECTRICAL CONTRACTORS

MILLS ELECTRICAL IS A FULL-SERVICE ELECTRICAL contractor that has served the Dallas area since its inception in September 1972. The business quickly grew and prospered during the real estate boom of the 1970s and 1980s, thanks in part to strong relationships with Dallas developers and a focus on their needs to quickly build cost-efficient buildings. Mills Electrical was privately held until 1998, when the president, Tim Cummings, was instrumental in the merging of Mills Electrical and 16 other electrical contractors to form Integrated Electrical Services (IES). Today, IES is a $1.7 billion enterprise with 82 member companies, is traded on the New York Stock Exchange and provides a strong platform for Mills Electrical to service customers on a nationwide basis.

Mills Electrical began adding to the Dallas skyline in 1972. In 1974 one of its first major projects involved providing electrical work for the Promenade Towers, a 16-story office building. Other recognizable projects carried out over the next quarter century were Hughes Tool Manufacturing Plant, Frito Lay Headquarters, Dallas Market Center, Wyndham Anatole Hotel, The Holtze Magnolia Hotel, Nortel Regional Headquarters, Childrens' Hospital, Presbyterian Hospital, World Trade Center-Dallas, The Wyndham Hotel (now The Renaissance Hotel), American Airlines Headquarters, DART Light Rail Service Facility, Texas Instruments' Kilby Center, Federal Express Sorting Facility at Alliance Airport, Lone Star Park at Grand Prairie, Willow Bend Mall, DFW Airport Terminal "D" and Grapevine Opryland Hotel & Convention Center. If one looks in virtually any direction in Dallas, one can see a building that has been powered up by Mills Electrical.

Over the years Mills Electrical has grown into a full-service electrical contractor — one of the nation's premier electrical companies. Its capabilities extend far beyond those of the traditional electrical contractor. Mills Electrical "New Construction" credentials include providing pre-construction services, prefabricated electrical components, design-build expertise, value-engineering assistance, exceptional project management, highly skilled electrical installation and technically advanced data cabling services. Mills Electrical's Service Group provides fully-trained technicians for design, installation, maintenance, testing and upgrades of all complex systems including high-voltage systems, back-up power systems, voice and data solutions, and fire alarms systems, along with a variety of preventive and maintenance programs.

From the onset of a building project, Mills Electrical starts with a focus on what a customer needs from its electrical systems. Every aspect of the project is examined. Building system functionality, installation cost, system reliability, constructability, maintenance factors, energy efficiency, scheduling requirements and customer preferences are all reviewed in great detail to ensure that all needs are fully met. Once the plan is in place, Mills' project management team uses world-class management processes to ensure that safety, quality and schedule are maintained. Mills Electrical has worked hard to build a

The Wyndham Anatole Hotel is an important repeat customer of Mills Electrical.

reputation of integrity by showing how it responds to and performs in meeting its customers' needs.

Because of its reputation and variety of services, Mills Electrical is now one of the largest electrical contractors in the Dallas-Fort Worth Metroplex. The company has also expanded into other areas and has offices in Fort Worth, Austin, Denver and Colorado Springs. Today, Mills Electrical is capable of providing services for large projects involving facilities in multiple states. One example is the $250 million project for WorldCom that involved 13 complex Network Information Centers in separate locations across the nation.

Thirty years of continuous business have given Mills Electrical a wide range of project experience including airport terminals and hangars; business complexes; call centers; religious facilities; theaters; data centers; Web-hosting facilities; distribution centers; health care facilities; hotels and resorts; industrial and manufacturing plants; military facilities; multi-family and assisted living centers; office buildings; power generation; prisons and detention centers; retail properties; and stadium facilities. If a type of project has been built in the Dallas area, odds are Mills Electrical has done it.

Mills Electrical is rightly proud of the many times it has been selected by industry peers for notable projects. Mills Electrical has received Associated Builders & Contractors (ABC) National Excellence in Construction awards for Texas Instruments 15 K.V. upgrade in 1994; The Rachofsky House in 1996; Wyndham Anatole Trinity Hall expansion in 1998; The Potter's House in 2000; and The Mount Vernon renovation in 2001. No other electrical contractor has been the recipient of this high number of National Excellence Awards.

With the ever-growing shortage of skilled service sector workers, Mills Electrical recognizes the industrywide need to develop employees. All employees are given training opportunities annually and are rewarded for their participation in training. Mills Electrical has a state-of-the-art training facility and staff in Dallas that trains thousands of class hours per year. "Only through development of our people are we able to meet our clients' needs in a manner they can find nowhere else," states Tim Cummings, president of Mills Electrical. "Our commitment to training far exceeds the industry norm and the results show in the quality of work performed by this company."

Two of the many service technicians that have helped Mills Electrical become one of the nation's premier electrical companies.

In addition to providing exceptional electrical and telecommunications services to the public and private sectors, Mills Electrical employees donate time, energy and materials to charitable concerns, including Scottish Rite Childrens' Hospital, The Family Place, Habitat for Humanity, The Vogel Alcove, Hearts & Hammers and Fogelsom Forum. Assisting the Dallas community's needs is important to the employees at Mills Electrical, and they put great effort into giving back to those who are less fortunate.

Mills Electrical's plans include continuing to grow its market in Dallas, and both broadening and increasing the services it provides. Mills Electrical wants to be the provider of choice for every customer with wire or fiber needs. As the requirements of buildings and their owners grow more complex, the services at Mills Electrical will expand to meet these new needs. This has always been the approach taken at Mills Electrical, and its consistently satisfied customers show that this approach has worked to date.

Mills' senior management: (seated) Bill Memory, Tim Cummings and Marty Gatenby; (standing) Dale Payne, Russ Crawford, John Zelman and Earl Ward

Building a Greater Dallas

RYLAND HOMES

RYLAND HOMES HAS ALWAYS TRIED TO MAKE it easy for home buyers in Dallas and the surrounding areas. Unlike custom home builders that require buyers to know exactly what they want in a home, Ryland Homes offers choices of homes that can become a dream home.

A good home begins with a good neighborhood. Location is everything for a homeowner, and Ryland Homes has always carefully developed on solid property, near good schools and parks and convenient shopping. It is close enough to businesses that workers have a short commute but far enough away to leave the stress at the office. The neighborhoods are purposefully designed to bring calmness with their beautiful landscaping and attractive homes.

Ryland Homes understands home ownership. Each family has its own rhythms and lifestyles, so Ryland Homes has the largest, most diverse product portfolio for home builders in the area, including its Crescent series ranging from $80,000 to $140,000 and move-ups to Ryland Homes ranging from $140,000 to $300,000. It builds low-maintenance patio homes on small lots and neo-traditional homes on big lots all over the Metroplex.

Ryland Homes is known throughout the country for building a quality home using only the best materials. As part of a national company, Ryland Homes has the purchasing power to buy the best lumber, pipes and faucets, roofing and windows. Moreover, Ryland Homes tries to exceed safety and environmental codes. Each of its homes is geared for environmentally cleaner air-conditioning and heating.

Ryland Homes is also known for having experienced construction crews who get the job done right and on time. It was the first home building company in the nation to develop a formalized training program specifically aimed at recruiting and training a diverse base of future managers. This includes a unique program honoring veterans by recruiting ex-military personnel.

It is the floor plan that truly determines the beginning of a home's character. Ryland Homes offers between 10 to 15 floor plans for any given neighborhood. Within these floor plans, there are many pre-designed options so home buyers can make the home more suitable to their needs. Whether it is an extra game room, a home office or a sunroom, Ryland Homes has plenty of choices to work with.

Another way Ryland Homes simplifies home buying is through its interior design support. Ryland Homes creates selection centers that are comfortable spaces where customers can relax and view options, upgrades and color selections. All the options are in one convenient location so there is no hassle in comparison-shopping. With the assistance of a professional design consultant, most Ryland home buyers select from a variety of choices for cabinetry, plumbing fixtures, lighting, flooring, appliances, fireplaces and other options based on their individual budgets and tastes.

The Springhill — Mansfield National Golf Community, Mansfield, Texas

Even the legal and financial aspects of buying a home are made easier at Ryland Homes. Ryland Mortgage Company handles it all, from initial application to close of escrow. Ryland Mortgage Company reviews hundreds of loan alternatives and presents the smartest and most competitively priced options. There are FHA, VA and conventional financing and interest-rate lock-in options. There are also a variety of unique programs to accommodate home buyers with income or credit concerns, such as extending qualifying features and lender-paid closing cost assistance. Ryland Homes also has its own title company.

It is the personal service that makes the process of purchasing a Ryland Home so appealing to so many customers and repeat customers over the years. The staff is knowledgeable, enthusiastic and loyal. Each home buyer works directly with the superintendents along the construction process starting at the beginning through the framing stage until the final, satisfying walk-through.

Ryland Homes stands behind its product. It is one of the top three highest-rated, financially stable homebuilding companies listed on the New York Stock Exchange. The company only works with reputable vendors and offers a 10-year standard warranty that covers a wide range of items.

Ryland Homes adds a unique value for the first-time home buyer by providing every new homeowner with a comprehensive homeowner's guide. This homeowner's guide offers helpful home maintenance tips and puts service policies, warranty programs and performance standards in writing.

If it is ever necessary to utilize the warranty, Ryland Homes is quick to respond in an efficient and timely manner. When a request is received, it is logged in and referred to employees who are assigned to specific neighborhoods. Typically this is an employee who can handle a variety of construction issues.

Because of this reputation for reliability in the most important purchase of a lifetime, a home, Ryland Homes has exploded with business. Over 1,200 homes were built in 2001, and the numbers keep increasing because Ryland Homes keeps living up to its promises. It builds a good home in a good neighborhood for a fair price that will have long-lasting market value.

Ryland Homes is also committed to the Dallas community. In addition to sponsoring many local charitable

The Clayborn — The Homestead, Sunnyvale, Texas

and educational programs to help the citizens in a myriad of ways, it has entered into a unique alliance with a coalition of African-American pastors to develop communities in South Dallas where many residents don't know how to buy homes and are intimidated by consumer credit issues. This outreach program is part of Ryland Homes' overall dedication to making Dallas one of the best places to live in the United States.

Ryland Homes has created many beautiful neighborhoods with lovely homes and yards in Dallas and the surrounding areas. It has created the serenity of suburbs amidst the business of city life. It has made home ownership more accessible to thousands of people who enjoy well-built homes and the financial satisfaction of making a sound housing investment that will maintain and appreciate in value. Ryland Homes has made the dream home real.

The Marquette — Mansfield National Golf Community, Mansfield, Texas

SHARIF & MUNIR

MANY FACTORS DISTINGUISH SHARIF & MUNIR as a singular enterprise. Beyond being unique in its field, the firm's originality marks it as a different type of business altogether.

The company's slogan, Uncustomary Custom Homes, calls attention to its special approach and to the distinctive, awe-inspiring homes it creates. Yet it is the joy and pride shared with its clients in the accomplishment of a dream that forms the curious blend of business and artistic endeavors which marks Sharif & Munir as one-of-a-kind.

More than an architect or designer, more than a contractor or a project manager, Sharif & Munir is participating in the revival of a practice that combined art and craft and gave birth to the term artisan. It all began in ancient Rome, when the word architect was synonymous with builder, and the person who divined the design was also the one who conveyed that image into the imaginations of the craftsmen and organized and coordinated the creation.

Today, that practice is called design/build, and one of its leading practitioners in Dallas is Mickey Munir, A.I.A., a licensed architect, interior designer and Graduate Master Builder. Since 1978 Sharif & Munir has built stunningly unique homes for hundreds of satisfied clients and has earned a spot at the pinnacle of the luxury home market.

A luxury home is now more than ever the product of many professional disciplines. Each tradesman or professional is necessarily focused on its area of specialty. Most contractors are capable of coordinating the various construction trades through the completion of a home. However, without an understanding of the underlying design elements and a personal understanding of the client's vision, there always remains a risk of a less-than-perfect result.

At Sharif & Munir, a staff of professionals all work together from start to finish to coordinate the entire process of building a client's dream home. A cohesive team of architects, builders, subcontractors, engineers, landscape designers and interior decorators, many of whom have worked with the company for decades, join Sharif & Munir to leave no detail unattended. The team's guiding force is the client's vision, as communicated by Mickey Munir and company Vice President Michael Munir, A.S.I.D. The result is consistency, exceptional communication, excellent documentation and accountability.

An important element distinguishing Sharif & Munir is its complete attention to its clients' individuality. The first thing Sharif & Munir does is listen. The company's professionals guide prospective homeowners in developing their vision and transform it into a reality. The result is a floor plan that flows from and fits the client's way of life. The relationship of

Dynamic Dallas: An Illustrated History

setting, lifestyle, finishes and details, including gardens and pathways, are all carefully considered, integrated and infused with the client's personality. Whether it's a floor inlaid with granite and marble, an intricately beveled mirror, rough-hewn slate surfaces or distinctive Florentine wrought iron selections, the details delight the eye and inspire the heart.

This is not cookie cutter or repetitive homebuilding. The company's clients are not one-dimensional people, and Sharif & Munir creates an environment that caters to all of their moods and needs. It can encompass a world of differences that all flow into a harmonious whole — a home that is at once opulent and exotic, dignified and discreet; a lavish setting for spectacular entertaining and a cozy, comfortable, personal space; a statement of status and achievement; and a private harbor of peace and serenity.

The firm's architects and designers have experience with a wide variety of styles, including Mediterranean, Neo-Classic, French and contemporary. But Sharif & Munir's expertise can manifest virtually any design possibility. The company offers attractive, nominal-risk programs to assist prospective clients with site selection or with the evaluation of an already owned site's suitability. Particularly popular is Sharif & Munir's "Look Before You Leap" program, which provides clients with a high level of comfort prior to beginning the building process.

Client satisfaction is assured because Sharif & Munir takes care of everything from start to finish, from mastering the architectural, engineering and construction challenges to fulfilling the client's dreams through exquisite decorating and design.

Sharif & Munir's reputation has been earned by taking on a monumental task — fulfilling people's dreams — and then exceeding their expectations.

Building a Greater Dallas

ADLETA & POSTON, REALTORS

THE YEAR WAS 1979, AND THE METROPLEX area of North Texas was becoming one of the country's more prestigious addresses. The economy was thriving thanks to the opening of the Dallas/Fort Worth International Airport. Companies came calling, eager to set up shop. For Lynda Adleta, a Dallas native, it was time to get moving.

"Dallas was fast becoming a rather sophisticated, world-class city," she says. "The city was going to be a relocation hub for people in the near future, and we realized that there wasn't anybody targeting the relocating executive."

Adleta's business sense kicked into high gear and she, along with two partners, decided to set up their own shop, a real estate agency that would cater to this demographic. Some 22 years later, Adleta is still at it, keeping her clients' needs as the top priority at the single-office boutique real estate office in North Dallas. "The company is probably much the same as it was 20 years ago — only it's bigger."

In fact, Adleta & Poston is one of the largest single-office independent real estate brokerage firms in the city, sporting 84 agents and a support staff of nine. Adleta says that despite the relative size of the company, it's amazing that they've been able to run the business on their own terms. "Many single offices have not survived," she says. "They have been absorbed by the larger companies."

Perhaps Adleta & Poston has persevered because the company owns a clear business plan. Many of the properties that the agency lists are in the same area as its office. This includes homes in Dallas' most exclusive neighborhoods, including the Park Cities, Preston Hollow, Turtle Creek and Lakewood areas of Dallas. By specifically dealing with homes in these areas, the firm has been able to successfully carve out a niche for itself. Kimberly Poston, who has been a co-owner since 1979, explains that their focused business plan is what sets the company apart from other real estate brokerage firms. More importantly, she says the firm is entirely dedicated to its clients' needs. "We all can show and sell the same houses," she says of their competition. "But I think our level of commitment to our clients is unsurpassed."

The company has also made a priority of being an integral part of the Dallas business community. Adleta, who talks of her associates as if they were family, says their interest in Dallas doesn't stop at merely selling homes. The company is involved in many area community endeavors and makes a point of supporting charities with which its associates are involved. Organizations that the company works with include the Dallas and Highland Park independent school districts, the Junior League of Dallas, the Salvation Army, and the Leukemia and Lymphoma Society, to name a few.

Clearly, Adleta & Poston is a company that volunteers its talents in an array of areas. The company's roots are firmly planted in the Dallas community, and as for the future, Adleta has no problem selling the city. "Our vision for the future is one of great optimism," she says. "Dallas is a wonderful place to live and to enjoy the privilege of home ownership. We may not have mountains and lakes to look at, but we have a diversified economic base and a wonderful city filled with people who possess a 'can-do' attitude toward life and who epitomize success."

(Far right) Lynda Adleta and Kimberly Poston

A traditional home in Highland Park
Photo by Matrix Tours

MANHATTAN CONSTRUCTION COMPANY

FOR OVER 100 YEARS, MANHATTAN Construction Company has been the "Builder of Choice" for some of the most impressive buildings in the nation. In Dallas, Manhattan Construction Company's work has been an integral part of the city's history and growth.

The company handles a diverse project mix that includes corporate headquarters, office buildings, health care facilities, high-tech research and educational complexes, museums, libraries, industrial installations, hotels and high-rise condominiums, churches and sports stadiums.

In the heart of downtown Dallas, for example, is Thanksgiving Square, a landmark for tourists and locals. Thanksgiving Square is a simple, well-designed, beautifully built structural oasis designed to bring calm and comfort amidst the hustle and bustle of the city.

From the serenity and simplicity of Thanksgiving Square to the massive Dallas Convention Center and elegant Vendôme Condominium Tower on Turtle Creek, Manhattan Construction Company has extensive experience with projects of all shapes and sizes.

Whether it is building the award-winning The Ballpark in Arlington, the Bush Presidential Library Center, facilities within the Texas Medical Center in Houston, or the five-star Four Seasons Resort and Club Villas in Las Colinas, Manhattan Construction Company has a reputation for getting the project built on time and within budget.

Customer satisfaction is the reason that Manhattan Construction Company is a leading contractor in the Dallas metroplex, ranking 4th in total revenue for Texas contractors.

Repeat projects make up a large part of the company's annual business. The company has a long list of repeat clients who have turned to Manhattan to build their facilities repeatedly over the years, including American Airlines, Southwest Airlines, Lincoln Property Company, Koll Development, Worldcom, Archon and Delta. In addition, a vital strength to Manhattan Construction Company is its important corporate headquarters experience including Nokia House, Omnicom and NEC America to name a few.

Manhattan's integrity has been an important factor in attracting such clients as the Prestonwood Baptist Church. The church, among the largest in the area, chose Manhattan Construction Company to build its new 7,000-seat sanctuary, educational and administrative complex in the suburb of Plano, and when expansion plans ensued, the church turned to Manhattan to build the Prestonwood Sports Fitness Center and the Prestonwood Christian Academy.

While Manhattan is a company that makes its mark with steel, concrete, glass and stone, the company's success has been built with the minds and hearts of its staff. It was founded in 1896 by L.H. Rooney and continues to be operated by his heirs and loyal employees. The company is known for being an excellent employer with good benefits, safe work sites, career opportunity, educational training and the latest technology to maximize productivity. The emphasis on teamwork and respect for the individual carries over to client relations, making Manhattan Construction Company an ideal builder for projects small and large.

Headquartered in Dallas, Manhattan Construction Company prides itself on its core values of excellence in all actions and integrity in all transactions. These values translate into happy employees, satisfied customers, and buildings and landmarks that will last generations.

The Ballpark in Arlington

Building a Greater Dallas

PULTE HOMES

PULTE HOMES HAS DELIGHTED HOMEOWNERS for over half a century. In 2000 the company celebrated the 50th anniversary of Bill Pulte building his first home in Detroit. Over 407,000 homes later, Pulte Homes now operates in 44 markets, including 25 U.S. states, Puerto Rico, Argentina and Mexico, where it is the fifth-largest builder. The company became publicly owned in 1969 and in 1995 became the largest homebuilder in the United States. Pulte entered the Dallas market in 1978 and closed 1,385 D/FW homes in 2001.

Pulte Homes has grown by following a simple formula for success — build the best-quality home for the money in the right location and delight the customer throughout the entire home buying experience. Bill Pulte understood the winning strategy was to provide the homebuyer with added value and exceed the customer's expectations. To set himself apart from competitors, Pulte began building model homes in his communities in 1960.

Product lines were expanded in the 1980s and the Pulte Quality Leadership (PQL) initiative was created to guarantee customers the highest level of craftsmanship and service. A PQL component, the Customer Care Program, educates buyers about properly maintaining their homes, thus creating another layer of customer service. The 1990s ushered in a focus on Pulte's core competencies of homebuilding and related operations. The Pulte Preferred Partnerships (P3) program is an example of the new focus, setting industry standards for home quality by closely working with preferred contractors. Another program, the Pulte Production Plan, offers a 10-year insured warranty package to all Pulte homebuyers.

Pulte's Customer Satisfaction Measurement System (CSMS) was set up to track a homeowner's experience at each stage of the homebuilding process. This system allows for increased communication between each element of the buying experience: sales, construction, mortgage and the homebuyer. This constant communication allows Pulte to measure the customer's experience with a CSMS score and supports the ultimate goal of Pulte Homes: creating a homeowner for life.

Environments For LIVING, a heating, cooling and comfort program, incorporates stringent design guidelines into Pulte homes resulting in improved indoor air quality and more-energy-efficient homes. Pulte is the first builder in the D/FW Metroplex to offer such an extensive program, which guarantees a reduction in homeowners' energy bills.

Pulte Homes has won a number of awards and honors during its 50-plus years. These include being recognized as "America's Best Builder" by the National Association of Homebuilders and *Builder* magazine and "2002 Builder of the Year" by *Professional Builder* magazine. In 2001 Pulte ranked as the "Best Performing Company in Housing and Real Estate" by *Business Week* magazine and was the recipient of the 2001 Summit Award for exceptional quality in construction and outstanding customer service to its new homebuyers. By delighting homeowners for over 50 years, Pulte Homes has established itself as one of the nation's industry leaders and created homeowners for life. Pulte Homes — The Way It Should Be.

Dallas Historical Society

BUSINESS & *Finance*

Banks, securities brokerages, insurance companies and diversified holding firms provide a financial foundation for a host of Dallas companies.

CAPITAL ALLIANCE

INVESTMENT BANKING FIRMS THAT DEAL WITH privately held companies in the middle market — companies with annual sales between $10 million and $500 million — generally have a lower public name recognition than their Wall Street peers but are equally important to economies around the world.

Dallas-based Capital Alliance is one such firm. Incorporated in 1976, this firm is a specialist in brokering deals for privately held middle market companies. Edward J. Dawson, the company's chairman and president, sees his firm as a boutique with a very focused approach, finely tuned and highly skilled in its area of expertise.

That area of expertise is mergers and acquisitions in the aforementioned middle market. Within this area, Capital Alliance is very successful. In the last six years the company closed 74 transactions representing over $1 billion in transaction value.

The firm's success comes from engaging serious, interested principals and then finding well-matched acquirers, sellers or financing sources. "The company," Dawson says, "is very good at negotiating the highest values for its clients, bringing liquidity to shareholders and growth to companies."

Capital Alliance has extensive experience closing a wide variety of transactions throughout the United States and in several foreign countries. Seated in the lobby in front of some of the firm's closing announcements is Edward J. Dawson, president of Capital Alliance.

M&A INTERNATIONAL

Some of the companies that have benefited from relationships with Capital Alliance are Dallas-based companies such as Processors Unlimited, The National Motor Club and Heritage Press. However, the majority of the firm's business comes from national and international clients.

In fact, the international aspect of the firm's business is so important that it has representative offices in Mexico and has been a member of the prestigious M&A International since 1986. M&A International is an alliance of 40 of the top middle market investment banking firms located in the major economic countries throughout the world.

Dawson has served two terms as president of M&A International and currently serves as chairman of the Technology Network, an industry specialty group within M&A International. Capital Alliance has also won M&A International's coveted "Dealmaker of the Year" award on the only three occasions it entered the contest.

Capital Alliance received its first award in 1995 for outstanding negotiating during the largest acquisition ever completed by the Avis Rent-A-Car Company. In 1997 the company was again honored for the sale of numerous USConnect computer systems integration companies to IKON Office Solutions and Inacom Corporation. The following year Capital Alliance won again, this time due to the acquisition of PCM, Inc. by Aztec Technology Partners.

The "Dealmaker of the Year" is a competitive award given annually to the M&A International firm that generates truly outstanding results for its clients.

THE BUSINESS

Capital Alliance works with both buyers and sellers. On the selling side, the firm has a comprehensive program to assist in the sale of a corporation that involves, among other things, continual consultation, an in-depth guidebook on the merger and acquisition process, establishing goals and strategies to meet those goals, negotiating, and, of course, closing the transactions.

One of the company's fundamental strengths is the enormous database of over 8,000 contacts it has built up in over a quarter century of business dealings. The data can be analyzed to quickly develop hundreds and sometimes even thousands of prospects that are then further reviewed. This facilitates the selling process by ensuring that each company is presented to a number of financially sound potential suitors who are a good match for the selling firm's business.

On the acquiring side, Capital Alliance often functions as a corporate development department by, among other things, helping to formulate acquisition plans, contacting prospects and assisting in negotiations that create closings. The firm also offers financing services for major purchases or recapitalizations.

To facilitate these operations with the highest level of efficiency, Capital Alliance hires only the best and brightest minds in industry, with an emphasis on CEO and/or entrepreneurial experience. In fact, executives and principals at the company have more than 100 years of combined CEO experience.

Dawson is quick to point out that the 20-plus professionals of Capital Alliance are the company's greatest asset. Even though his firm is on the cutting edge of technology and has one of the most comprehensive databases in the industry, it is the people that drive the business. Computers are great for many things, such as tracking thousands of contacts made over a quarter century of business, but there are many things the computer can't do — like effectively negotiating the transaction, as well as properly handling many people with diverse interests in a transaction, Dawson says.

PREPARING TOMORROW'S M&A LEADERS

As the leader of a world-class investment banking firm that specializes in mergers and acquisitions, Edward Dawson has acquired a wealth of knowledge in the field. He is using that knowledge to prepare the next generation of business professionals in two courses he teaches at the Business Leadership Center of Southern Methodist University's Cox Graduate School of Business — "Effectively Negotiating Merger and Acquisition Transactions" and "Trust in Business Transactions: Who and When."

Through the negotiating course, Dawson presents his students with an opportunity to understand the forces impacting the M&A negotiating environment. By practicing different negotiating techniques, students come to understand the importance of people in the process, Dawson says. The other course focuses on the important subjects of personal trust and personal integrity in business transactions.

Capital Alliance is a name synonymous with excellence in middle market investment banking. Its reputation has been earned by consistently delivering its clients the things that they most desire — liquidity to shareholders and growth capital to companies — through an elegant blend of technology, experience, contacts and highly skilled people.

KPMG LLP

KPMG WAS BORN IN 1897 AS THE BRAINCHILD of two Scotsmen, James Marwick and Roger Mitchell. Today, the figures are impressive. Worldwide, KPMG employs more than 100,000 partners and professionals providing assurance, tax, and financial advisory services from more than 750 offices in 152 countries with revenues of $11.7 billion. More than 20,000 people are based in the United States.

KPMG LLP is the U.S. member firm of KPMG International. Founded as Marwick, Mitchell & Co., the firm sought an international practice and merged in 1925 to become Peat, Marwick, Mitchell & Co. In 1987 the firm gained a worldwide presence when it merged to become KPMG Peat Marwick in the United States and KPMG around the world. In January 1999 the firm changed its legal name to KPMG LLP. The strength and equity in the KPMG name is the result of more than a century of unwavering commitment to serving clients by analyzing their businesses with true clarity, raising their level of performance, achieving growth, and enhancing shareholder value.

CLIENT-CENTRIC FOCUS

The Dallas office of KPMG was founded in 1915. At that time, Dallas was on the cusp of its transformation from a rural cow town to the booming marketplace of free enterprise that it represents in today's economy. Today, the Dallas office is the regional headquarters of KPMG's Southwest area and is one of the oldest and largest accounting firms in the city. The firm's Assurance and Tax practices have grown dramatically, offering deep industry experience and market-focused professional services. Tax offers State and Local Tax, International Tax and Federal Tax, including Compensation and Benefits and the firm's Engagement Services Practice, while Assurance offers its Business Measurement Process, Financial Advisory Services, and Risk Advisory Services, including Internal Audit, to name a few.

Dallas KPMG professionals understand the issues driving today's business climate. As a result, KPMG helps its clients recognize risk, plan strategically, and continually improve the way they operate not simply to stay in business today but to thrive as the industry leaders of tomorrow. With client satisfaction as an ongoing commitment to ensure overall client business needs are being met, KPMG's Dallas client base includes companies that have been with the firm for more than half a century.

As the types of businesses and industries in Dallas have diversified, so has KPMG's impressive client base. The firm serves clients across industries including consumer markets; financial services and real estate; information, communication and entertainment; industrial markets; and health care and the public sector.

Inspired by the increasing demands of corporate responsibility and a changing regulatory environment, KPMG formed the Audit Committee Institute (ACI) in 1999 to support the evolving needs of corporate audit committee and board members. The ACI publishes materials on issues of importance and teams with leading universities and law firms to sponsor roundtables and industry-based conferences.

KPMG CENTRE

Since its inception, the Dallas office of KPMG has steadily grown to meet the needs of many of the prominent Dallas entrepreneurs, visionaries, and community leaders

Together, P. Scott Ozanus (right), Dallas Office managing partner and Southwest Area Managing Partner of Tax, and Donald C. Spitzer (left), Southwest Area Managing Partner of Assurance, provide integrated, synergistic leadership that reflects the culture of the Dallas office.

who have woven the fabric of the city's rich history. KPMG continues to grow in Dallas, having added nearly 30 partners and nearly 300 professionals in the year 2002, increasing the firm's bench strength to more than 1,100. This expansion extends to the firm's location. After 10 years at the Crescent Court building in Uptown Dallas, in addition to its Fort Worth office, KPMG now occupies 200,000 square feet of office space at KPMG Centre, one of downtown Dallas' renowned skyscrapers. The move to KPMG Centre, formerly the Maxus Energy Tower, adds new life to the city's core and embodies KPMG's commitment to the Dallas Central Business District.

LEADERS WHO SERVE

At the helm of this large and talented practice are two Texans with more than half a century of combined experience in Dallas/Fort Worth. P. Scott Ozanus, Dallas Office Managing Partner and Southwest Area Managing Partner of Tax, and Donald C. Spitzer, Southwest Area Managing Partner of Assurance, are forward-thinking leaders who believe in building quality, long-term relationships with their clients.

Ozanus brings more than two decades of technical capability and knowledge of financial advisory services, transaction advisory services, and mergers and acquisitions to his role leading the Dallas office and KPMG's Tax practice in the Southwest area, which includes the firm's major business units in Dallas, Houston, and Denver that serve Texas, Louisiana, Oklahoma, Arkansas, New Mexico, and Colorado.

"Our vision is to be the professional services firm and employer of choice in Dallas/Fort Worth," says Ozanus. "With outstanding people, you'll have outstanding clients. KPMG provides an atmosphere centered around teamwork where our people contribute the best of their knowledge and talents, knowing we value their integrity and loyalty. We are a team of diverse individuals who share a passion for what we do — helping our clients achieve their aspirations."

Spitzer leads the firm's Assurance practice in the Southwest. With more than 30 years serving KPMG, Spitzer also serves on KPMG's U.S. Assurance Leadership Team and the U.S. firm's board of directors.

Together, Ozanus and Spitzer provide integrated, synergistic leadership that reflects the culture of the Dallas office and the firm's overall core values including leaders who serve; teamwork and collaboration; open and honest communication; continuous learning and active sharing; recognition and respect; commitment and accountability; and ethics and integrity.

"We are positioned to thrive during the changes and challenges ahead, with our clients at the nucleus of our efforts," says Spitzer. "Our dominance in the Dallas marketplace is the direct result of the dedication of our partners and our employees and their commitment to the opportunities in our future."

COMMITMENT TO COMMUNITY

KPMG wholeheartedly believes in civic and community involvement. The firm supports not-for-profit organizations including the United Way of Metropolitan Dallas, the American Heart Association, the Dallas Women's Foundation, Junior Achievement and the American Red Cross through volunteerism, fund raising, and participation in citywide events, enhancing the lives of those in need.

KPMG has formalized its volunteerism through the firm's Involve program, a national initiative that has been embraced by the managers and employees of the Dallas office and the Dallas community at-large. Through this unique program, employees are encouraged to volunteer regularly in communitywide and individual volunteer activities.

KPMG partners serve on community boards including the Greater Dallas Chamber of Commerce, the United Way of Metropolitan Dallas, the Southern Methodist Cox School of Business, and the March of Dimes.

KPMG occupies 200,000 square feet of office space at KPMG Centre, one of downtown Dallas' renowned skyscrapers. Formerly the Maxus Energy Tower, KPMG Centre embodies KPMG's commitment to the Dallas Central Business District.

REPUBLIC GROUP OF INSURANCE COMPANIES

THE HISTORY OF THE REPUBLIC GROUP OF Insurance Companies began in Dallas, Texas, in 1903 with the formation of The Commonwealth Fire Insurance Company of Texas. Through mergers, acquisitions and formation of new companies, Commonwealth evolved into Republic. From its beginning a century ago to its current position as the "Regional Company of Choice," Republic has sought to provide exceptional service to its customers — policyholders who rely upon Republic to provide insurance protection for homes, automobiles, and businesses and independent agents who represent Republic.

Republic, with primary operations in Texas, Louisiana, New Mexico and Oklahoma, is dedicated to remaining a regional multiline property and casualty insurer. As Bruce R. Milligan, president of Republic states, "Republic's desired corporate look as the 'Regional Company of Choice' is achieved by the efforts of our employees in delivering desired products and services to our agents and policyholders at an appropriate price with the least inconvenience. Republic's regional focus allows it to remain close to its policyholders and agents, both physically and philosophically. This focus, coupled with Republic's careful attention to underwriting and claims handling in both personal and commercial lines insurance, has resulted in its consistently better than industry performance." Republic is rated A (Excellent) by A.M. Best, the recognized source of insurance company ratings.

Republic's statement of purpose is simple: to assume financial risks from individuals and businesses and to manage these risks in a responsible and conservative manner for the benefit of its stakeholders — policyholders, agents, employees, shareholders and the community. Dedication to these stakeholders is the unifying force behind Republic's success. Republic recognizes that the interests of its stakeholders are mutually dependent. Each stakeholder must benefit in order for the relationship to grow and prosper.

POLICYHOLDERS

Because of its regional operations, Republic is close to its policyholders. Decisions can be made locally and quickly. Republic's hands-on approach enables it to better identify its policyholders' needs and provide a wide variety of services. Policyholders can report claims directly to local representatives any hour of the day, any day of the year. Safety professionals are available to assist commercial policyholders in identifying potential risks and developing training and safety programs to reduce claims. Republic's workers' compensation policyholders have access to return-to-work programs, medical management plans and other cost-containment programs. Additionally, a wide range of billing options is offered to meet policyholders' needs.

While personal lines insurance (homeowners and automobile) has been Republic's mainstay since its beginning, Republic also offers a full line of commercial insurance products. Republic works closely with its agents to develop and offer new products to meet the needs of policyholders. Republic strives to make available a wide array of business insurance, from products providing specific and limited protection to package products providing complete business protection. Republic also helps policyholders reduce operating costs by identifying insurance needs and recognizing better-than-average risks with fair pricing.

In addition to traditional personal and commercial insurance, Republic offers a variety of specialty insurance products, including non-standard automobile liability, collateral protection insurance, prize indemnification, surplus lines and other niche products.

Bruce R. Milligan, president and CEO of Republic

AGENTS

Republic recognizes the contributions its agents make to its success. Its agents know the people of Republic and have immediate contact with its employees, including underwriters, claims adjusters or the president of the company.

As part of Republic's long-term commitment to its agents, Republic developed RepubLink, an extensive proprietary agency automation system. Using the convenience of the Internet, RepubLink provides a comprehensive set of services to facilitate insurance transactions, expediting all steps of the insurance process, saving both time and money. RepubLink is a secure system that provides a link between Republic and its agents, making it convenient to do business with Republic. Agents can use the system to obtain insurance quotes and forms and to submit applications online. Daily business processing from application to underwriting can be conducted quickly and easily.

But even with extensive use of technology, Republic has not forgotten that its agents, like its policyholders, still need and deserve personal attention. With its regional focus, Republic provides the personal touch that distinguishes it from other insurers. Its regional strategy gives Republic the advantage of the flexibility and responsiveness of local operations, allowing it to compete effectively with national insurance companies.

EMPLOYEES

Republic incorporates the "team" concept into its operations. Personnel from all disciplines participate as members of teams that facilitate the design and implementation of products, procedures, systems and strategies. The immediate input of critical personnel in team settings results in expedited decision making, critical in Republic's desire to be responsive to the needs of agents and policyholders. Its employees are involved in and critical to the success of Republic.

SHAREHOLDERS

Republic recognizes its responsibility to create value for its shareholders and, to that end, seeks always to return an underwriting profit while judiciously increasing its volume of business.

Corporate headquarters in Dallas

COMMUNITY

Republic gives back to the community in various ways, from providing employment to members of the community to participating in charitable activities and organizations. For many years, Republic and its employees have been active participants in events that make for a better community, including the United Way and other charitable organizations. Each Christmas holiday season, employees sponsor gifts for the underprivileged in the Republic community. The depth of this generosity is demonstrated by the fact that in addition to the necessities identified on each person's gift list, employees attempt to ensure that each child sponsored by Republic receives every toy on his or her wish list.

Republic has changed in many ways since its beginning in Dallas almost 100 years ago. One way it has not changed is in its dedication to its stakeholders.

Insurance policy issuing companies of Republic include: Republic Underwriters Insurance Company, Republic Lloyds, Republic-Vanguard Insurance Company, Southern Insurance Company, Southern County Mutual Insurance Company, Republic Fire and Casualty Insurance Company, Southern Vanguard Insurance Company and Southern Underwriters Insurance Company.

STATE FARM INSURANCE®

THE HISTORY OF STATE FARM® IN DALLAS reflects its strong commitment to providing its policyholders unsurpassed customer service, while also being uniquely involved at the community level as a "good neighbor." The successes of State Farm and Dallas have been, in many ways, parallel ones.

DALLAS BEGINNINGS

The historic rise of State Farm as an insurance leader in Dallas began back in 1928, when it first started selling auto insurance in Texas. By 1929, Dallas was a city of 250,000 people and State Farm life insurance was being sold in Texas — but the Depression loomed.

Dallas had a ready answer for the Depression: the discovery of oil 100 miles east of Dallas in 1930. As the local economy improved due to the wealth produced by oil, State Farm boomed as well. In 1936 State Farm began offering fire insurance in Texas, and its presence in Dallas continued to grow.

In 1940, Dallas was selected as the site of the first Service Office in Texas on South Ervay Street. Six years later, in 1946, State Farm was insuring more automobiles than the next two largest companies combined, and the decision was made to decentralize operations from the corporate office into several branch offices throughout the country. One of those branch offices for auto and fire operations came to Dallas.

GROWING IN STATURE AND SERVICE

Continued growth in Texas resulted in Dallas being named as the site for a Texas Branch Office. An office on Luther Lane in Dallas was leased, and it became the sixth branch office of State Farm. The new office opened in Dallas on November 1, 1951, with the Dallas mayor in attendance to welcome State Farm to Dallas. It is interesting to note that on the day it opened, the branch office had no heat, unfinished floors and only two working phones for 109 employees.

Growth quickly overcame those initial obstacles. In February 1952, the first activities board was elected, the Credit Union was formed and the employee publication, the "Howdy Podner," was born. The "Howdy Podner" would continue to be the employee publication for 48 years. Continued growth would eventually cause a space problem that could only be solved one way — construction of a new office.

In April 1956, a site on Preston Road in Dallas was purchased for the purpose of building a new office facility. At the time of the land purchase, there were 250 employees in the Regional Office in Dallas servicing 208,000 auto policies in the region.

In August 1957, State Farm announced the "Y" Plan, continuing the management decentralization, giving leadership to a structure of regional offices headed by a regional vice president. On October 14, 1957, the new Texas Branch Office opened on Preston Road in Dallas.

Today's Dallas Operations Center facility on Preston Road — inset: (top) Preston/Forest Lane office (1957-81); (bottom) Luther Lane office (1951-57)

In 1960 the office was renamed the Southwestern Regional Office, serving Texas, New Mexico and Oklahoma.

CHANGES AND CHALLENGES

Tremendous growth and change continued to be a hallmark for State Farm in Dallas. By 1970, the Southwestern Region had 1,500 employees. In 1971, reorganization within the company created the new Southwestern Regional Office in Dallas, now handling only North Texas and Oklahoma business.

A quick look at the Southwestern Regional Office in Dallas in 1972 reveals a region with 837 employees servicing nearly 695,000 policies in force. By 1980 total policies in force jumped to over 1.4 million.

The tremendous growth State Farm experienced was evident in more than just policies and claims numbers. The company's associates in Dallas have historically been committed and involved in their local communities, and State Farm as a corporate entity in Dallas has displayed a strong commitment to bettering their communities with both funds and volunteerism. Although State Farm has supported many organizations and worthwhile community events, since 1965 its primary charitable focus has been the United Way. The company's associates have over the years proved time and time again their belief in the important work the United Way does in Dallas. Over the last decade, its United Way focus has been on education and safety. The commitment from both leadership and associates to the United Way is a proud part of the history of State Farm in Dallas.

By 1980 the growth fueled by the commitment of State Farm associates and agents required a larger facility to house the regional operations in Dallas. By 1989 over 2.4 million policies were in force, reflecting Dallas and the surrounding area's continued confidence in State Farm. On August 1, 1989, the Southwestern Region was replaced by the North Texas Regional Office with 2,104 associates.

NEW OPPORTUNITIES, NEW HORIZONS

State Farm entered a decade of new challenges as the new North Texas Region settled into its new facility in North Dallas. By the year 2000, the North Texas region headquartered in Dallas boasted 3,198 employees, and 2.7 million policies in force. In spite of all this success and growth, a major change was in store for State Farm.

On August 17, 2001, State Farm announced a reorganization plan to better serve its customers. On January 1, 2002, the North Texas Region based in Dallas and the South Texas Region based in Austin became one Texas Zone.

Dallas' growth from a town of 250,000 people in 1928 to today's cosmopolitan city of 1 million people is a modern success story. The growth of State Farm from its Texas arrival in 1928 to being the leading insurer in Dallas, with over 2.7 million policies in force, mirrors Dallas' success. But that success isn't based on the number of policies that have grown through the years — it's based on the trust and confidence policyholders have in the values State Farm practices every day.

State Farm fosters the belief that making a difference professionally and in its communities is a fundamental value of the company. From the first arrival in Texas in 1928 to today, State Farm associates in Dallas have been committed to helping policyholders manage the risks of everyday life, recover from the unexpected and realize their dreams. State Farm is truly part of the story of Dallas.

State Farm employees enjoying a break at the Luther Lane office, early 1950s

The "Howdy Podner" debuted on March 21, 1952, and would be the employee publication for 48 years, chronicling the community involvement and growth of State Farm in Dallas.

WASHINGTON MUTUAL

WASHINGTON MUTUAL ENTERED THE DALLAS area like a lamb, quietly moving into the competitive Texas banking arena in the late 1990s with just 48 offices around the state. But by 2001 the lamb transformed into a lion as the largest thrift in the nation staked its claim on Texas. The acquisition of nearly 150 Bank United branches around the state put 100 Washington Mutual offices in the Dallas-Fort Worth region alone.

While Washington Mutual is just developing its history in Dallas-Fort Worth, the bank has a rich past. A long dry spell and a burning glue pot sparked "The Great Fire" that swept through downtown Seattle, Washington, in 1889. The blaze cut a destructive path through 120 acres, blackening the business district and engulfing 25 city blocks. Residents, many of whom lost everything, took shelter in a tent city. Six Seattle businessmen looking for a solution created the Washington National Building Loan and Investment Association to help people build homes. The bank helped to finance the resurgence of the city.

During The Depression, banks all over the country began to fail as people emptied out accounts. Washington Mutual worked to reassure its customers: officers set up in front of the bank, ready to dole out interest payments to customers who kept their money at the bank. Still, panic over the safety of their accounts caused depositor "runs" on the bank. Washington Mutual met every withdrawal request even as other banks closed. By the 1940s Washington Mutual was on the road to expansion when World War II put a snag in those plans. But the company actually emerged from the war years with a solid reputation as the strongest savings institution in Washington state. Assets and depositors both increased dramatically by the late 1950s, and computerization in the 1960s and 1970s made the bank more efficient.

Washington Mutual didn't blink as losses added up in the 1980s and other thrifts folded. Instead, the bank acquired a full-service brokerage firm. The acquisition was the first of its kind by any bank in the nation. Soon after, Washington Mutual converted from a mutual form of ownership to become a savings bank owned by holders of capital stock. On March 11, 1983, the bank's common stock debuted and raised $72 million. Within six years of going public, the bank's assets more than doubled. Originally traded under the name WaMu, Washington Mutual stock trades under the symbol WM on the New York Stock Exchange.

Acquisitions and rapid growth marked the 1990s and the early part of the new millennium. Washington Mutual doubled its size in 1993, branching into Oregon with the acquisition of Pacific First Bank. Western Bank, with 42 locations in Oregon, became a part of the Washington Mutual family in 1996. That same year, Washington Mutual rode into California, doubling its size, buying up American Savings Bank. Not limiting itself to the West Coast, the bank moved into Florida, adding Great Western Financial Corporation, a Fortune 500 financial services company. Beginning in 2000, Washington Mutual expanded by entering Arizona, Colorado, Georgia, Nevada and New York. At the same time, Texas became Washington Mutual's second-largest market.

Consumers in Dallas and elsewhere enjoy Washington Mutual's new retail banking concept called "Occasio," Latin for "favorable opportunity," which mimics contemporary retail stores. It features casually dressed employees, eliminates teller windows, incorporates a children's play area and a retail store selling money

In 2002 the Points of Light Foundation, the nation's leading volunteer organization, awarded Washington Mutual its annual Points of Light Award for Excellence in Corporate Community Service. In 2001 approximately 17,500 employees donated nearly 200,000 hours to volunteer service across the nation. Pictured at the award ceremony receiving the honor from former President George H.W. Bush is Kerry Killinger, chairman, president and CEO of Washington Mutual.

Dynamic Dallas: An Illustrated History

management software and books, piggybanks and even the bank's own action figure, the "Action Teller" doll.

Washington Mutual's diversified umbrella of products and services caters to consumers and small- to mid-sized businesses. Operations now serve customers in all 50 states. The Consumer Banking Group assists 5.5 million households through multiple delivery channels that include financial centers, online banking and automated teller machines. The Home Loan and Insurance Services Group serves individuals nationwide through 277 branches and generates mortgages on a wholesale basis through 32 offices. The nation's No. 1 originator of multi-family loans in 2000, Washington Mutual provides property owners and developers commercial and multi-family real estate loans through 19 regional offices. The Financial Services Group comprises three lines: a licensed broker-dealer, a mutual fund complex and a full-service insurance agency. The Consumer Finance Group, operating 450 offices under Washington Mutual Finance and Long Beach Mortgage, makes direct consumer installment loans and real estate secured loans, and purchases secured retail installment contracts. Long Beach Mortgage originates, purchases and sells specialty finance mortgage loans.

Currently operating more than 2,400 consumer banking, mortgage lending, business and SBA lending, commercial banking, consumer finance and financial services offices throughout the country, Washington Mutual and its subsidiaries showed consolidated assets of $275.22 billion as of March 31, 2002. But the bank that rose out of the soot and smoke of a catastrophic fire, created to comfort a displaced lot of people, always returns to its roots, sending profits back into the communities in which it conducts business. Washington Mutual returns 2 percent of pre-tax earnings to the communities through grants, sponsorships, loans at below-market rates, in-kind donations and paid volunteer time for employees. Its volunteer efforts earned Washington Mutual the coveted Points of Light Award for Excellence in Corporate Community Service, one of the most heralded community service awards in the country. In 2002 Washington Mutual announced the largest-ever community lending commitment of $375 billion over 10 years to aid low- to moderate-income areas throughout the United States. Also in 2002, Fortune magazine ranked Washington Mutual one of the top U.S. companies for minorities.

The seventh-largest financial institution and the largest mortgage originator and servicer in the country, Washington Mutual wants to remain at the top of its game and keep growing while still "doing right by people," a philosophy invoked at inception. From the headquarters, a post-modernist skyscraper in Seattle, to the bank branches across Dallas and Fort Worth, current and past CEOs stress a code of ethics emphasizing respect for employees and customers, asking each officer to use good judgment rather than just follow rules and regulations. Washington Mutual welcomes the diversity and dynamics of North Texas into its family, accepting change, welcoming it, and promising to constantly evolve in its role as a banker and a good neighbor.

In the late 1910s Washington Mutual Savings Bank moved to new offices to accommodate the larger staff, photographed here in front of the new location on Second Avenue in Seattle. By the end of 2001 Washington Mutual had approximately 45,000 employees nationwide.

On March 13, 1923, Washington Mutual launched its School Savings program, teaching children the value of saving their money. In 2001 over 115,000 children at 900 schools across the country were participating in the program. Pictured here are some of the students who participated in Washington Mutual's first School Savings program.

J.R. MORTGAGE CORPORATION

J.R. MORTGAGE CORPORATION, A DALLAS-based mortgage broker, opened its doors in January 1995. The firm was founded by Angela Ragnauth and James Ragnauth, respectively the president and operations manager of the company. The firm opened with the objective of providing faster and better services to first-time homebuyers in assessing their mortgage needs.

J.R. Mortgage acts as an intermediary between its clients and bankers or wholesale lenders. The firm has successfully serviced all sections of the communities in which it operates. While the firm concentrates on first-time homebuyers, it also services investors and commercial clients. A recent expansion of its service area has allowed the company to garner business from military members in the Fort Hood area.

The firm has earned a reputation within its service area as a company that goes the extra mile to assist previously under-served minorities, particularly African Americans, Asian Americans and Hispanics, to obtain mortgages. The firm's administrative personnel bring together decades of mortgage experience to provide the best possible service to all its clients.

J.R. Mortgage is a member of many local and national business organizations. Locally, the firm belongs to the Oak Cliff Chamber of Commerce and the Texas Association of Mortgage Brokers. On the national level, J.R. Mortgage is a member of the National Registry of Who-Is-Who and the Better Business Bureau.

A small organization, J.R. Mortgage employs a receptionist, a courier and a handful of processors, loan officers and administrators. The firm has achieved steady growth and expansion in a challenging and competitive market by leveraging the talents of its small group of employees to its utmost potential.

J.R. provides numerous services to its clients. The company's home buying seminars are both popular and successful. The seminars teach potential buyers how to get the home they want, explain various loan options — including FHA, VA and conventional, all of which the firm offers, and discuss current interest rates that are available to different buyers. J.R. Mortgage also aids its clients by assisting them in gathering the requisite documents, providing information for self-employed clients, educating them on mortgage terminology and, finally, by processing their mortgage pre-approvals.

The firm also helps to educate its clients in credit. Good credit scores are vital to obtaining an affordable mortgage, so the firm counsels clients on how to track their credit and advises on necessary steps to improve the credit score if it is low. The firm offers information on defaulted student loans and helps make arrangements for paying off debt and problematic accounts.

With a strong sense of community and the ability and desire to help first-time buyers purchase their dream homes, J.R. Mortgage is well situated for the future. The firm's dedication to customer service will continue to enhance its already golden reputation and will allow the company to be a leading mortgage broker in the Dallas area for years to come.

Dallas Public Library

MANUFACTURING & *Distribution*

𝒥N ADDITION TO PRODUCING EXCEPTIONAL GOODS FOR INDIVIDUALS AND INDUSTRY, DALLAS MANUFACTURING AND DISTRIBUTION COMPANIES PROVIDE EMPLOYMENT FOR RESIDENTS.

BORDEN

BORDEN IS A COMPANY NAME KNOWN nationwide. It was first known as the Borden Company and came into existence in 1857 as the result of a zany idea by Gail Borden Jr., who envisioned food concentrates as a means of safeguarding humans' food supply. Borden, an inventor, newspaper publisher, surveyor and (ultimately) philanthropist, is said to have experimented with large-scale refrigeration in the mid-1840s as a means of preventing yellow fever. In 1849 he perfected a meat biscuit, made of dehydrated meat compounded with flour, which he spent the next seven years trying to market. The project left him deeply in debt — but not defeated.

In 1853 Borden turned his attention to finding a way to condense milk in a vacuum — prior to that time dairy products were shipped in unsanitary oak barrels, which caused the milk to spoil — and by 1856 had received both American and British patents. After a couple of setbacks, through the help of New York financier Jeremiah Milbank, Borden opened another factory in Connecticut. His timing was perfect: when the Civil War brought intensified demand for condensed milk, sales grew so much that Borden's success was assured. He opened additional factories in Connecticut, New York and Illinois, licensed other concerns in Pennsylvania and Maine, and went on to invent processes for condensing various fruit juices, for extract of beef and for coffee. The company Borden founded was renamed Borden, Inc. in 1968.

In the early 1940s the Borden Company acquired Mistletoe Creamery, a butter plant, and Dallas Milk Company, the latter located on Leonard Street at Flora Street, for its milk operation. By the mid-1950s Borden had 90 home delivery routes in Dallas, delivering milk, cream and cottage cheese in returnable glass containers. Borden also sold its products through many mom-and-pop grocery stories, but as operations gave way to the new, giant supermarkets that were being built, the home milk delivery business began to diminish. By the early 1960s home delivery had largely ended.

As the city of Dallas grew in the 1960s through the 80s, so did Borden Dairy and its distribution. Recognizing that Dallas would be expanding its arts district, Dallas mayor Jack Evans contacted Borden chairman Eugene Sullivan in 1984 to see if Borden would sell its property for the arts district's use. Borden responded by donating a parking lot and agreed to sell the remainder of its land on Leonard Street to the city of Dallas once Borden had found another site for its dairy. The Morton H. Meyerson Symphony Center today stands on the former Borden plant site.

Borden purchased property in the Red Bird addition to build its dairy but found an alternative site by acquiring the Metzger Dairy in southern Dallas. Borden temporarily shut down the dairy in order to totally refurbish and

The Borden plant on Leonard Street — The Morton H. Meyerson Symphony Center stands on the site today.

The beautiful, newly renovated mural at the Borden Milk Products facility in South Dallas

renovate the structure. In February 1985 Borden reopened in its new location. Today, this plant supplies Borden products north to the Red River, south to Waco, west to Abilene and east to Texarkana and Shreveport, Louisiana. The company currently has distribution through all major supermarkets and all independent grocers in Dallas. Borden is the No. 1 brand supplier of dairy foods in Dallas. General managers of Borden have been Ted Robinson, Jim Wilson, L.B. Parker, Lewis Torrance, W.G. McMillan, Elmer Pillars, Carl Todd, Don Yeatman, Glen Harrington, Brian Haugh and James McBride.

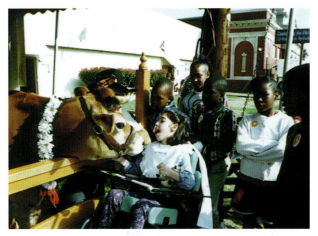

Elsie the Cow, an American icon, brightens the lives of youngsters during visits to Children's Hospital.

Raw milk supply for Borden's Dallas operation comes from Dairy Farmers of America, primarily from Dallas' neighboring counties. Borden receives and processes milk seven days a week. Borden offers a wide variety of dairy products — from whole vitamin D milk, 2-percent hi-protein milk, 1-percent hi-calcium milk, Lite Line fat-free milk, cottage cheese, sour cream, dips and yogurt to frozen pops, ice cream sandwiches and old-fashioned ice cream. Borden brand juice products include orange, apple, grape and fruit juices and a variety of Borden brand specialty drinks include orange, lemon lime, blue raspberry and strawberry drinks, citrus punch and pink lemonade.

Sponsor of the Special Olympics-Texas; Elsie is pictured here with Borden volunteers.

It is impossible to think of the Borden Company without conjuring up an image of Elsie the Cow. Elsie was born in Brookfield, Massachusetts, in 1932 and has been a "spokes-cow" for Borden brand dairy products since 1939, when she first appeared in national magazines and attended the New York's World Fair. During World War II, Elsie sold $10 million in U.S. war bonds while on tour. She was present to celebrate Borden's 100th year in business in 1957; appeared in television commercials in 1971 and at the opening of Walt Disney World in Orlando, Florida; and led the Rose Bowl parade in Pasadena, California, on January 1, 1974.

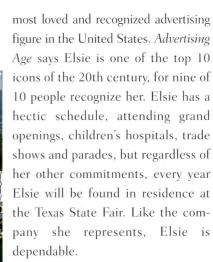

Elsie has come to stand for excellence in the dairy business and a time-honored symbol of trust. In 1966 a national survey showed Elsie to be the most loved and recognized advertising figure in the United States. *Advertising Age* says Elsie is one of the top 10 icons of the 20th century, for nine of 10 people recognize her. Elsie has a hectic schedule, attending grand openings, children's hospitals, trade shows and parades, but regardless of her other commitments, every year Elsie will be found in residence at the Texas State Fair. Like the company she represents, Elsie is dependable.

Elsie with her lifelong friend, Jim Cavanaugh

The Borden brand is distinguished as America's premier dairy brand. The Borden brand difference — making Borden brand products better than competitors' — is based on exceeding high-quality standards and establishing a taste, trust and tradition that consumers have learned to depend upon.

Manufacturing & Distribution

GARRETT METAL DETECTORS

MANY PEOPLE CONSIDER CHARLES GARRETT, co-founder of Garrett Metal Detectors in Garland, Texas, one of the luckiest men in the world — one of those rare persons who successfully transforms a beloved hobby into a global industry. Rarer still, Garrett has retained the thrill of the avocation while realizing financial profit from the vocation.

The story of Garrett Electronics, more familiarly known as Garrett Metal Detectors, began when Charles Garrett saw the movie *Treasure Island* in 1939 and became enthralled with stories of hidden wealth. He later began treasure hunting in earnest with a surplus World War II mine detector. Electronic training that Garrett received while serving in the U.S. Navy stimulated new ideas about treasure hunting.

Charles Garrett personally tests every new Garrett detector line before it is offered to customers.

After the Korean Conflict ended, Garrett returned stateside to marry Eleanor Smith of Pennington, Texas; earn a bachelor's degree in electrical engineering from Lamar State College of Technology (now Lamar University); and become deeply engrossed in development of systems and equipment required by America's space effort. During stints at Texas Instruments and Teledyne Geotech, Garrett participated in a number of important developments in military aircraft, space and earth-science electronics. These included developing a seismograph amplifier that Apollo 11 astronaut Neil Armstrong "planted" on the moon and an automatic flight control for the U.S. Air Force F-111 fighter plane.

During these years Garrett remained devoted to his lifelong love of treasure hunting and in his spare time built metal detectors whose features and capabilities outshone other commercially available detectors. In 1964 Charles and Eleanor Garrett founded Garrett Electronics in order to produce Garrett's inventions. Although the Garretts operated on a shoestring budget, their most important assets were a deep belief in the viability of their products and a genuine desire to serve customers. At times the fledgling company sold only a single detector per month, but the Garretts soon flourished. By 1982 Garrett Metal Detectors was leveraging its hobby industry success into the security business, which gave the company a worldwide exposure it had not previously enjoyed.

Garrett's first patented detectors set an engineering standard that other manufacturers soon began to emulate. Today, after three decades of success, Garrett is the acknowledged worldwide leader in the design and manufacture of metal detection equipment. From the outset of his business, Charles Garrett vowed to practice what he preached: Before any new Garrett equipment is offered to customers, he tests it personally to ensure its workability regardless of terrain or environmental conditions. Garrett continually creates innovative, simple-to-operate detectors such as the popular GTI 2500. Garrett's development in detector technology has helped to open new markets in such areas as beach and surf hunting and gold prospecting. Today, the name Garrett is recognized worldwide by anyone who uses an electronic metal detector, ranging from a hand-held security detector to the famed Garrett Magnascanner™ walk-through unit to treasure-hunting detectors.

Garrett products have become the world's most respected metal detectors for security and law enforcement. The company manufactures numerous types and styles of walk-through, hand-held and ground search equipment, varying in sensitivity, to satisfy the specific security or law enforcement need. Garrett products are used in courtrooms, by corporate security and for one-night events such as concerts and sporting events.

Garrett provided security equipment for the 1984 Los Angeles Olympic Games, and Garrett detectors have successfully guarded athletes and spectators at every Olympics since and earned the company the sobriquet, "a national treasure," from Olympic officials in Australia in 2000. Because the Olympic Games present a natural opportunity for massive terrorist threats, absolute security is essential. Garrett's elaborate security systems provided the biggest Olympic security effort in Winter Games history for the 2002 Salt Lake City Winter Olympics.

The unfortunate spate of school shootings in recent years and the terrorist attacks of September 11, 2001, have directly impacted Garrett Metal Detectors' business. Garrett now develops most of the security detection systems for U.S. public schools, and in response to Americans' desire for travel safety, Garrett is creating more sophisticated walk-through security systems for airports. Garrett has long been the foremost supplier of hand-held wands that easily pinpoint metal on a person's body.

Garrett also provides hands-on training in the proper uses of metal detectors in a security environment. Garrett, the only provider of academic training for metal detector users, has trained thousands of U.S. Secret Service, Federal Bureau of Investigation and other law-enforcement agency workers, school security officers and governmental bodies of all sizes.

Charles Garrett pioneered electronic prospecting, using electronic metal detectors of his own design to search for and find gold, silver and other treasure on

Garrett, an official supplier to the U.S. Olympic Team at the Salt Lake City Olympics, provided the world's most elaborate security systems at the 2002 Olympics.

every continent except Antarctica. He has even scanned under lakes, seas and oceans. Garrett detectors have discovered millions of dollars of gold nuggets in the United States, Canada, Mexico and Australia. The greatest finds in treasure-hunting history, using Garrett equipment, include the 61-pound Hand of Faith gold nugget found in Australia in 1980 and now on view at The Golden Nugget hotel-casino in Las Vegas, and the 15th-century Middleham Jewel, a splendid golden pendant found in 1985 near Richard III's Middleham Castle and acquired by the Yorkshire Museum for £4.5 million. Garrett's famed Sea Hunter detector was used to discover the Spanish treasure galleon, *La Senora de Atocha*, wrecked on the Florida Keys in 1622.

Garrett's unbounded enthusiasm for his lifelong hobby has caused him to share his knowledge through hundreds of free instructional seminars, lectures and discussions and in articles, books and films. Ram Publishing Co., founded by Charles and Eleanor Garrett to give Charles' writings the widest possible circulation, has sold more than a half-million Garrett titles, including *Treasure Hunting for Fun and Profit*, and hundreds of thousands of imprints by other treasure-hunting authors. Charles Garrett has also produced and starred in treasure hunting and adventure videos.

Garrett Metal Detectors today has the largest engineering staff for metal detection in the world. In 1964 the name Garrett stood for a commitment to develop the most advanced, highest-quality metal detection equipment and an unwavering dedication to customer satisfaction. Nearly four decades later, it still does.

MARY KAY INC.

IN 1963 MARY KAY ASH HAD BIG DREAMS FOR her small cosmetics company. She hoped that she could help women overcome obstacles she had faced in the workplace. The Dallas legend not only did that, she founded a principles-based organization that — four decades later — continues to enrich the lives of millions of women and their families throughout the world.

Direct sales was the industry she knew and cosmetics was the product category Mary Kay chose. With the help of her then-20-year-old son, Richard Rogers, Mary Kay forged a path of economic liberation for women that is heralded worldwide. Perhaps more than any other business figure of the 20th century, Mary Kay Ash is credited with providing women unlimited opportunity for both personal and financial success.

Mary Kay Inc. has grown from a small direct sales company to one of the largest direct sellers of facial skin care and color cosmetics in the world. Mary Kay has been recognized as one of The 100 Best Companies to Work For in America three times and one of the 10 best companies for women. With 2001 sales that surpassed $2.8 billion at the retail level, Mary Kay's independent sales force is approaching 1 million independent beauty consultants worldwide.

Using the Golden Rule and priorities of God first, family second and career third as their guiding philosophy, these women entrepreneurs determine their own level of success. They have within a Mary Kay career not only unlimited earnings potential, but the flexible schedules and career portability that have proven extremely beneficial as women work to achieve a balance between career and family life.

Mary Kay's simple and profound genius is a proven business plan, studied and taught by many universities, including the Harvard School of Business. In the book, *Forbes Greatest Business Stories of All Time*, published in 1996, Mary Kay is the only woman profiled among the greatest names in commerce. She is credited by the authors with "shattering the glass ceiling for women 20 years before the term even existed."

Her many honors include the Horatio Alger Distinguished American Citizen Award and the National Business Hall of Fame Award. In 1999 viewers of Lifetime Television voted Mary Kay Ash the most outstanding woman in business in the 20th century. In her native Texas, Mary Kay was named as the state's Woman of the Century.

Today, Mary Kay's son and company co-founder Richard Rogers serves as chairman and CEO. Rogers has emphasized his singular focus is to see that Mary Kay's dream continues to enrich the lives of women around the world.

Even though women's role in the workplace is now a given, the Mary Kay opportunity continues to open new doors for women. Although its principles continue to resonate with what women want, the company constantly blazes new trails for women's achievement.

Mary Kay Inc. employs nearly 2,000 people at its world headquarters in Addison, its manufacturing plant in Dallas and two other facilities.

Dynamic Dallas: An Illustrated History

(Far left) Some 15 million pounds of raw materials are processed annually at the state-of-the-art Dallas manufacturing facility

(Center) The famous Mary Kay Career Car Program includes pearlized pink Cadillacs.

Mary Kay Ash provided women with an opportunity to make beautiful lives for themselves.

Upon her death on Thanksgiving Day, Nov. 22, 2001, Mary Kay Ash was mourned worldwide in headlines that recognized her contributions to American business as well as to women. Even posthumously, Mary Kay continues to be honored. In early 2002 she received recognition from the Junior Achievement Business Hall of Fame, the Sales and Marketing Executives International Academy of Achievement and the National Conference on Medical Care in Domestic Violence.

The Mary Kay Ash Charitable Foundation, established in 1996, is dedicated to funding research on cancers affecting women and supporting efforts to prevent violence against women. In 2001 the company underwrote a documentary on domestic violence that is being aired through 2004 on the Public Broadcasting System (PBS). That documentary, "Breaking the Silence: Journeys of Hope," has been nominated for a prestigious Emmy Award.

With its traditional values, the corporation also prides itself on remaining innovative. In 2000 the magazine *Interactive Week* named Mary Kay among the top five companies in the world for online sales in the retail sector. In 2001 the company received the Direct Selling Association's Industry Innovation Award for the Mary Kay Personal Web site program, which provides each Independent Beauty Consultant the opportunity to have a high-impact personal Web site of her own.

Product innovation is another area where the company excels. Since the start of the new millennium, Mary Kay has launched TimeWise™ skin care products — which became its most successful launch in company history — as well as the Velocity™ brand of products for teens and the MK Signature™ color products line. These highly successful categories are part of a product line that includes more than 200 premium products in eight categories: facial skin care, color cosmetics, nail care, body care, sun protection, fragrance, men's products, and dietary supplements for men and women.

Dallas has been corporate headquarters to the company since its founding in 1963. The firm employs nearly 2,000 in the Dallas area at its world headquarters in Addison, its manufacturing plant in Dallas and two other facilities. Both the Mary Kay Museum at corporate headquarters on the Dallas North Tollway and the manufacturing plant off of Regal Row and I-35 offer public tours at no charge. Some 20,000 visitors are drawn to these sites annually for tours.

At the state-of-the-art manufacturing facility, some 15 million pounds of raw materials are processed annually. The Dallas site is an Occupational Health and Safety Association (OSHA) Star worksite. In addition to the Dallas plant, Mary Kay also manufactures products in China.

Mary Kay's dream continues today to enrich the lives of millions of women. The company's excellent products enjoy great loyalty. The Mary Kay philosophies and her business acumen have brought unparalleled recognition to both her native state and to her hometown of Dallas. The pride of association is evident in the independent sales force and employees who carry forth Mary Kay's vision today.

It is still true after four decades, as Mary Kay always said: "If one more woman today finds out how great she really is, then it has been a good day."

Manufacturing & Distribution

OCCIDENTAL CHEMICAL CORPORATION

DALLAS HAS BEEN HEADQUARTERS TO Occidental Chemical Corporation (OxyChem) since its relocation from Connecticut in 1987. While Houston and the Texas Gulf Coast are home to most of the state's massive chemical industry investment, OxyChem chose Dallas for its excellent business and residential climate as well as its superior domestic and international air travel capabilities. In the ensuing years, the company has consolidated nearly all of its general sales and administrative functions here, relocating them from various parts of the country.

OxyChem, a wholly owned subsidiary of Los Angeles-based Occidental Petroleum Corporation, is a leader in the chemical industry, with 2000 annual sales of approximately $4 billion. Through its participation in two alliances (Oxy Vinyls, LP and Equistar Chemicals, LP), OxyChem is a highly integrated producer of polyvinyl chloride (PVC) with its own network of raw materials supply. This manufacturing capability includes chlorine, ethylene, ethylene dichloride and vinyl chloride monomer (VCM), and together forms North America's largest vinyl producer. OxyChem is the largest merchant marketer of chlorine and caustic soda and the largest producer of chrome chemicals (Chromic Acid & Sodium Bichromate) in North America. Worldwide, the company is the largest producer of potassium hydroxide and chlorinated isocyanurate products.

President and CEO
J. Roger Hirl

Separately and in combination with other materials, these products find their ways into our cars, households and other aspects of our daily lives. Water treatment and purification; vinyl siding and window frames; irrigation pipe; automobile dashboards; television and computer screens; pharmaceuticals and medical devices; swimming pool sanitizers; detergents; brake fluids; industrial and household bleach; wood preservation; leather tanning; and crop protection all depend on products manufactured by OxyChem.

There is, however, much more to the company than just its output. Led by President and CEO J. Roger Hirl, OxyChem is recognized nationally and locally for its contributions to the industry and its communities. Performance in the areas of health, environmental protection and safety receive the highest level of attention and are an integral part of all employees' daily functions.

OxyChem's safety philosophy is perhaps best contained in an excerpt from a 1996 address by Hirl to a national industrial safety conference: "... [safety] should be paramount throughout the company — for every employee, contractor and visitor — whether in our plants or in our offices."

This mandate has resulted in OxyChem having qualified 18 separate sites for OSHA Star certification, including its 24-story headquarters building at the intersection of the Dallas North Tollway and the LBJ Freeway in north Dallas — the first office structure to be so honored. The OSHA Star is the highest award for safety excellence given by the U.S. Occupational Safety and Health Administration. And within the chemical industry, OxyChem is the only company to have earned the American Chemistry Council's Responsible Care® Sustained Excellence Award for three years in a row.

But the company's safety efforts don't stop just with its employees. Along the way OxyChem has helped other businesses and organizations with their own safety missions. Among these are NASA's Johnson Space Center in Houston, Searle Pharmaceutical and ExxonMobil. OxyChem representatives are also frequent speakers at regional and national safety conferences, both in the chemical industry and before other major industries, including pulp and paper and textiles.

Not long after relocating to Dallas, OxyChem was instrumental in helping form the chemical industry's Responsible Care® initiative, which revolutionized the way industry reaches out to and reacts with its various constituents. Simply put, this voluntary effort is built around a code of management practices to assure continued improved performance relative to health, the environment and safety. OxyChem and the chemical industry know that no matter how much improvement is made in these areas, it will only be meaningful if surrounding communities and the general public have a voice in the process, are aware of the changes and understand the objectives. So the company takes every possible opportunity to meet with neighbors and citizens, demonstrate concern and engage in a two-way dialogue about its effect on its communities.

"The chemical industry can only operate when it has the trust and support of the people — particularly with regard to safety and environmental issues," says Hirl. "I think of this as nothing less than a public franchise, and it is my goal to see that we renew it each and every day."

Keeping with its program of responsibility and working to improve on its already strong safety standards would leave an average company with perhaps too much to juggle. Not so for OxyChem.

Since arriving in Dallas nearly 15 years ago, OxyChem quickly set about establishing itself as a leader in corporate community involvement. Public schools and related facilities such as The Science Place received

OSHA Star — In July 1998 OxyChem's headquarters in Dallas became the first office building in the country to be awarded the OSHA Star Award.

prompt attention, in terms of financial support as well as the involvement and volunteerism of employees at all levels. From the start, OxyChem has taken part in Dallas Public Schools' Partners in Education Program, through which it has adopted several nearby schools. On average approximately 20 percent of the company's more than 500 Dallas-based employees volunteer each week, working with students in need of academic help and attention. OxyChem is also committed to the Junior Achievement program, once again with volunteers and financial resources.

The company has become one of the best-known supporters of the area's United Way campaign, with one of the highest annual levels of per capita giving. Nearly 100 percent of OxyChem employees regularly contribute to these efforts — one of the highest rates of participation by any similar-size company in the Metroplex.

"We recognized early on that Dallas is a city that truly appreciates the involvement of people and the financial resources of its business community," says Hirl. "We looked for opportunities that best matched our capabilities, found the ones where we felt we could make a meaningful difference, and we've been involved ever since. There's no better way for our company and our employees to truly become part of the community."

Whether it's helping a student with his math problems or helping a large company solve its safety issues, OxyChem has proven that it is at once a diverse and unique company. OxyChem is proud to be an integral part of the Dallas community.

Occidental Chemical Corporation's headquarters in North Dallas

CERAMIC TILE INTERNATIONAL

PEOPLE LOOKING FOR TILE PRODUCTS across the south and southwest United States need to look no further than Ceramic Tile International (CTI). CTI is a wholly owned subsidiary of Interceramic, Inc., one of the largest ceramic floor and wall tile manufacturing and distribution companies in the world. It markets the products of its parent company along with international imports. The company targets all floor and wall tile market segments — floor covering dealers, builders, residential and commercial flooring contractors, and home improvement centers. CTI rounds out its product mix with setting materials, tools, and cleaning supplies to provide a full range of tile products for its customers.

Ceramic Tile International opened in 1988 in El Paso, Texas, the home of Interceramic's U. S. distribution headquarters. Both companies moved to Carrollton, Texas, later that year and the original location remained open as CTI El Paso. Expansion began in 1991 when CTI acquired an existing independently owned distributor of Interceramic tile in San Antonio, Texas.

The 1990s were a decade of consistent growth at CTI. In 1992 the company moved its Carrollton distribution center to a large and visible Dallas location facing LBJ Freeway, and later the same year it opened a new location in Fort Worth. Through the middle of the 1990s CTI bought existing tile distributors in Houston and the Atlanta, Georgia, area and built new locations in Plano, Austin and San Antonio. A relocation and expansion of the main distribution center in Houston added an import depot to receive, stock and distribute import products to other CTI sites. A new San Antonio location opened, specializing in discontinued material and second-quality tile products. During this time CTI also opened a new DFW Distribution/Service Center warehouse close to the old Interceramic headquarters in Carrollton, serving as a distribution point for the Dallas, Plano and Fort Worth CTIs.

1997 took CTI west with centers in Phoenix, Arizona, and Las Vegas, Nevada. The end of the 1990s found CTI in Albuquerque, New Mexico; Scottsdale, Arizona; Tulsa, and Oklahoma City, Oklahoma. This expansion took CTI into new markets with fast-growing urban areas. The 21st century opened with CTI distribution centers in 18 locations across six states — Texas, Georgia, Arizona, Nevada, New Mexico and Oklahoma — distributing both international imports and Interceramic products.

Looking to the future, Ceramic Tile International intends to continue its regional growth across the south and southwest United States. Remaining regional allows CTI to keep transportation cost low and delivery time fast because of the close proximity to its factories. The company also expects to exploit growth in the southwest region and its expanding residential market. CTI has enjoyed a rapid expansion in the world of ceramic tile and with a plan for growth, it has the future covered.

Ceramic Tile International, Dallas, Texas

CROWN COMPUTER SUPPLIES, INC.

ON THE SURFACE, RICHARDSON-BASED CROWN Computer Supplies sells computer and printer products and provides a wide range of printer service solutions — but that description does not *define* the company. To understand Crown Computer, one should learn of its beginnings and its founder.

When Crown Computer was started by Lorraine Ballard in 1982, she wasn't a computer expert or a printer specialist. She didn't even have a degree — but she *knew* people. "Her employees didn't just *work* for her, they *adored* her," says Karen Quay, Crown's Vice President and Lorraine's daughter. "She had the unique ability to inspire people to action."

Lorraine was powerful and eccentric. When she arrived at the office each day, she darted through the building, greeting everyone in her wake with her creative jibes. She blasted music through the PA system and danced in the halls. She attended meetings with her cockatoo on her shoulder. Her dogs frequented the halls. On an impulse, she would *command* everyone to drop what they were doing and meet up at the local bowling alley (or whatever struck her fancy at the time).

Through her actions, Lorraine expressed her love for her employees. She loaned money, cars, clothes and even jewelry. She helped employees buy homes and cars, adopt children and enter drug rehab. Lorraine encouraged her people to go to college and expect more from themselves, both personally and professionally.

Her earnestness reached beyond Crown's four walls. Lorraine was an early participant and active promoter of hiring the disabled. For her efforts, Crown was honored as "Employer of the Year" by the Mayor's Committee for the Employment of People with Disabilities. Since Lorraine's death in 1996, Crown has continued to work with the Garland Rehab Center, Bethphage and was honored as "Employer of the Year" by the Association for Retarded Citizens in 2001. "It is important to us that we keep Lorraine's goals alive. Crown was built on her standards, and it continues to thrive there," says Lisa Hanes, Crown's President and Lorraine's daughter.

Hanes affectionately remembers the excitement at Crown when they first opened their doors, with inventory consisting of only a single case of greenbar computer paper and two boxes of floppy disks. "It is amazing to think how far we've come, especially since we had such a limited concept of what technology held for us back then." Now, with a fleet of vehicles, printer service certifications from Hewlett-Packard, Lexmark, Tektronix, Brother and Xerox, as well as its own InfiniMAX™ laser toner and inkjet cartridges, selling *supplies* is only a small part of what Crown does.

Today, Crown continues to foster the development of innovative products and the family environment that Lorraine inspired. From its enthusiastic and tenured staff to its perennial inclusion in lists of top Texas women-owned businesses, Crown's success is a tribute to the firm's founder and the values she instilled in both her daughters and her employees.

This rendering of Lorraine Ballard (September 3, 1943 – September 19, 1996), "Eyes, Mind & Heart," was painted by her friend Jerry Lee. It now hangs in Crown's lobby as a memorial to her spirit.

(Left to right) Sheri Philips; Lisa Hanes, President; Audrey Bowen, VP Manufacturing; and Karen Quay, VP Operations
Photo by Evie Rossi

Manufacturing & Distribution

THE STANLEY WORKS

One of Dallas' high-end Proto Industrial Tools — the Big Dawg™ Pearhead Ratchet

Quality, durability and dependability are built into all Stanley Mechanics Tools' products such as the new toolbox shown here.

THE STANLEY WORKS IS A GLOBAL MANU-facturer and marketer of tools, hardware, doors and home decor products for home improvement, consumer, industrial and professional use. Its origins are traced back to 1843 when Frederick T. Stanley founded the company that manufactured hinges, bolts and other door hardware in a one-story wooden building in New Britain, Connecticut. Stanley's vision was to create a hardware company with unsurpassed customer service and innovative products that would become the first choice among professionals worldwide. His principles for doing business — value, respect, integrity and quality — are the foundation for what makes the company successful today.

Stanley's vision has become a reality as The Stanley Works continues to grow with expansion and diversification — more than 54,000 different products are currently offered to professionals and consumers. The company is committed to innovation and will continue to create a steady stream of new products and business opportunities worldwide.

Innovation has led Stanley to become one of the largest hand tool suppliers in the world with more than $2.7 billion in sales. The Stanley Works has paid cash dividends in each of 125 consecutive years — a record unmatched by any industrial company listed on the New York Stock Exchange — and has regularly increased dividends for the past 34 years.

Contributing to the success of The Stanley Works are 10 business units, one of which, Stanley Mechanics Tools, is headquartered in Dallas, Texas. Stanley Mechanics Tools serves the industrial, automotive, professional and consumer markets by manufacturing and marketing the Stanley® Proto, Blackhawk and Stanley Mechanics Tools brands, along with several private brand products. Professionals worldwide prefer these products for their outstanding quality, durability and dependability — qualities that are built into the tools starting with their design and continuing through their production.

Stanley Mechanics Tools operates four plants in the United States. Mechanics tools are produced in Dallas, Texas; tool boxes are made in Georgetown, Ohio; the Sabina, Ohio plant produces forgings; and industrial custom storage cabinets are made in Allentown, Pennsylvania, under the Vidmar® brand. Stanley Mechanics Tools also has five factories outside the United States — in Smith Falls, Canada; Chiro, Taiwan; Tona, Czech Republic; and two in Israel.

As a result of this diverse manufacturing base, Stanley employees represent a broad range of cultures, religions, ethnic backgrounds and abilities. This diversity gives Stanley Mechanics Tools a competitive edge by allowing the company to be more responsive to the needs of its ever-changing markets. In order to increase the effectiveness and energy of its work force, Stanley Mechanics Tools offers classes in English as a Second Language and has created teams that serve as interpreting groups.

Stanley Mechanics Tools, like The Stanley Works, is committed to excellence through innovation. Its experienced management team and diverse employee base are constantly searching for better ways to get the job done. This desire affects the way they design and produce their tools, their sales strategies and their programs. As a result, Stanley continues to earn its reputation as one of the world's most recognized and trusted brand names for tools.

Dallas Public Library

MARKETPLACE

173

*D*ALLAS RETAIL ESTABLISHMENTS, SERVICE INDUSTRIES AND LEISURE/CONVENTION FACILITIES OFFER AN IMPRESSIVE VARIETY OF CHOICES FOR DALLAS RESIDENTS AND VISITORS ALIKE.

PILGRIM'S PRIDE

WHAT STARTED AS AN EAST TEXAS FEED STORE has grown to become a North American power in the poultry industry. Pilgrim's Pride, headquartered in Pittsburg, Texas, with strategic offices — including sales and marketing — in Dallas, was founded by Aubrey Pilgrim and Pat Johns as Farmer's Feed and Seed Company in 1946. Pilgrim and Johns purchased the business from its owner for $3,500. By the 50th anniversary of the purchase, Pilgrim's Pride was a billion-dollar business (annual sales).

Change and growth marked the early years of the company. In 1947 Aubrey bought out Pat Johns' interest in the company and asked his brother Bo to become his partner at the Feed and Seed. Lonnie "Bo" Pilgrim eagerly joined his brother's company and the two set out to build an empire.

Bo Pilgrim as he appeared in many Pilgrim's Pride television commercials

Business in those days consisted of selling baby chicks, feed, seed and fertilizer. The brothers also sold fruit they purchased wholesale from area farmers. By 1950 growth had prompted the company to add a feed mill, which they did by purchasing the Hudson Cotton Gin and converting it to mill use. The firm began crimping oats, cracking milo and making corn chops. This allowed the company to begin selling semi-raw materials to other feed mixers in East Texas.

The following year, 1951, Bo Pilgrim was drafted for the Korean War. This would prove beneficial to Farmer's Feed and Seed, albeit in a roundabout way. Bo didn't see action in Korea. Instead, he was chosen for officer training. He did well and was selected to stay at the school to train new recruits. The school was in California. While there, Bo had a chance to study the bulk feed trucks and large mills then in use on the West Coast. When he returned from the Army in 1953, Bo convinced Aubrey of the benefits of the production methods used in California and the company installed its first large grain tanks.

The large tanks proved successful, and by 1955 the Pilgrims had added a railroad siding to the mill. Shortly thereafter the firm added six new 64-foot grain tanks to its operation. The remainder of the decade was marked by increasing technological innovation at the mills, such as the installation of automated bagging and sewing machines, and gradual expansion of its marketing area. Until 1958 the Pilgrim brothers dealt in chickens only to the extent that it supplemented their feed business. However, all of that changed when the firm purchased a bankrupt hatchery, moved it from its original location in Mount Pleasant to the Market Street location that today houses Pilgrim's Pride Farm Supply store, and integrated its operation with their feed and seed business. This would mark the beginning of the company's growth into an international poultry powerhouse.

The next decade would begin with the firm winning several awards from some of its largest business partners, including Purina and the Quaker Oats Company, both of which still do business with Pilgrim's Pride. The Purina award recognized Pilgrim Feed Mills, as the firm was then known, for reaching the 50,000-tons-sold plateau of Purina chows. Quaker awarded the firm for selling 4,500 tons of Ful-O-Pep Feeds during a year. Their success in this area of their business encouraged the brothers to actively pursue their vision of building a fully integrated poultry operation. In 1960 the Pilgrims purchased a Mount Pleasant chicken processing plant that had been mostly unsuccessful in its three years of operation under various owners. The processing plant was quickly turned around and the now-profitable business was named Pilgrim Poultry Company.

In the mid-60s the firm was producing 150,000 turkeys a year, but by the end of the decade turkey was a money-losing business and Pilgrim Poultry decided to cease turkey operations and concentrate on chicken and eggs. Chicken production during this period was approximately 15 million broilers a year, 100,000 breeder hens and 100,000 layers.

Nineteen sixty-six would be a year of sorrow for the company as founding partner Aubrey Pilgrim passed away. However, Bo would step in and take complete control of the company that he had helped build with his brother. The firm opened a new hatchery in 1966 that added a capacity of 300,000 chicks a week to the firm's rapidly growing business. The feed mill's capacity would also be increased during this period to 2,400 tons a week.

The 1970s would be a decade of growth by acquisition. Market Produce Company of Fort Worth was the first company acquired. It had operations in Arlington and El Paso, amongst other locations, which helped expand Pilgrim's area of operations. Pilgrim's then added 300,000 bushels of storage capacity with the purchase of the Graham Feed Elevator in Rosser.

The company would also continue its aggressive move into the processing plant business. In 1973 it purchased a 50-percent stake in Golden Feast Poultry. A year later, Pilgrim's leased the Abalon Poultry Processing Plant in Dallas — a plant it would eventually buy. These additions would strengthen the firm's presence as a poultry processor and would also increase its byproducts business, which sold to large pet food companies such as Ralston Purina, Iams and Carnation.

A variety of Pilgrim's Pride products: healthy, delicious and mouth-watering

In 1975 Pilgrim's opened its second hatchery and set a goal of producing a million chickens a week by 1979, which it accomplished. By the 1980s Pilgrim's was ready to move onto the national scene, which it did by acquiring

the Mountaire Poultry Company. This acquisition moved Pilgrim's into the top 10 of broiler producers in the country. By this time the company was extremely diversified in agribusiness. It owned two hatcheries, three processing plants, two feed mills, 28 farms, a farm supply division, an egg marketing and distribution division, and 2,700 acres of owned and leased land on which it raised cattle. The purchase of Mountaire allowed Pilgrim's to enter the pre-packaged chicken business after years of selling strictly in bulk to its customers.

In 1984 Bo Pilgrim perfected the whole boneless chicken. The product was unique in the industry and received major recognition from around the world. In 1986 the firm went public and began trading on the New York Stock Exchange under the symbol "CHX." That same year the firm began producing further-processed chicken and deli products in its new state-of-the-art production facility in Mount Pleasant. Today, further-processed foods are a core business at Pilgrim's.

At the end of the 80s, the firm made a stronger push into the Mexican market, purchasing the Purina Feed Mill in Queretaro, Mexico, giving the company three wholly owned mills in that country. The increase in business from Mexican operations helped push the company onto the list of Fortune 500 companies in the United States. The firm would eventually add 400-plus chicken houses and a new hatchery in Mexico by the end of 1991.

Pilgrims Pride employees attend to the chicken nugget conveyor at the firm's further-processing plant.

Through the remainder of that decade and into the early years of the new millennium, Pilgrim's Pride would continue to grow through acquisitions and new operations. The firm expanded operations in the further-processed and Individually Quick Frozen Markets, giving it a broader base of customers on the national scene.

Pilgrim's Pride is a major supplier to a vast array of major restaurants, grocery stores and other food vendors. Technological innovation plays a key role in Pilgrim's dealings with many of these firms. One large retail outlet, for instance, uses a just-in-time computerized inventory system that automatically tracks the amount of chicken sold at its retail units and automatically places an order with Pilgrim's to replenish the in-store supply. Typically, this firm places an order Sunday, for example, and Pilgrim's will have that order filled and on the road by Sunday night for a delivery by Monday. This system allows the retail outlet to stock the freshest available chicken at all times.

Ability to meet the needs of clients has always been a key factor in the success of Pilgrim's Pride. The just-in-time inventory replacement technology is one example of this. Another example comes from the company's dealings with a major fast food restaurant. When one of the restaurant's major suppliers faced some extensive problems that threatened its chicken inventory, the restaurant called on Pilgrim's to help remedy the situation. Pilgrim's put 6 million pounds of product on the road within days, saving the restaurant from running out of chicken. The firm's ability to deliver at a critical time earned Pilgrim's a larger percentage of that company's business, a substantial increase from its previous level.

In 2001 Pilgrim's Pride acquired WLR Food in Broadway Virginia, which included chicken and turkey operations. They put the Pilgrim's name on turkey.

When Bo and Aubrey Pilgrim began building their business in 1946, the brothers envisioned having a business that would one day be an industry leader and would have a reputation for providing customers with the highest-quality product available in the most efficient manner possible. Today, Pilgrim's Pride is the No. 2 value-added poultry producer in the United States and Mexico and has a stellar reputation amongst its clients. Indeed, Pilgrim's Pride has achieved the original vision of the Pilgrim brothers.

Today Pilgrim's Pride Corp. is the No. 2 poultry processor in the United States and No. 2 in Mexico. What sets it apart from others in the industry is their business model. It is processing and further processing a large percentage of its product for distribution in restaurants and supermarkets nationwide in Mexico and for export to many countries.

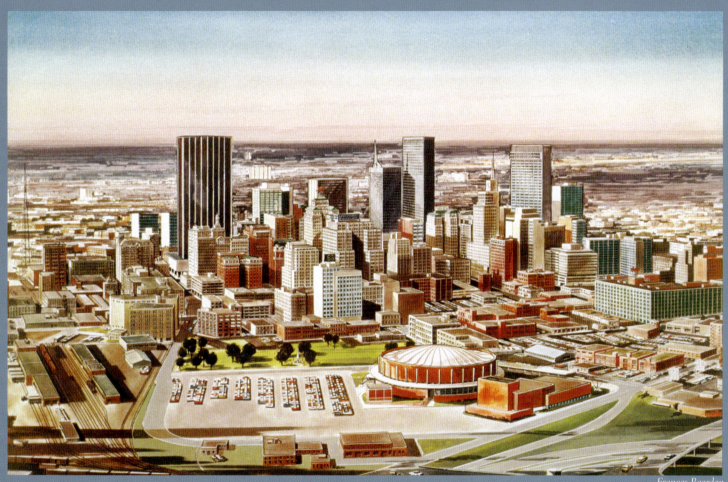
Frances Bearden

7-ELEVEN, INC.

THE STORY OF 7-ELEVEN HAS NEVER BEEN conventional! From a meager beginning in 1920s Oak Cliff, 7-Eleven has provided convenience to consumers for 75 years, growing exponentially to become a multibillion-dollar international operation with more than 22,000 convenience stores in 20 countries and U.S. territories.

Convenience retailing was born in Dallas during the summer of 1927 when "Uncle Johnny" Green ran one of 16 ice docks for The Southland Ice Company. His customers began asking him to stock staples such as eggs, bread and milk. Not only did the enterprising Uncle Johnny see the value of the idea, he extended his hours of business to evenings and weekends, when other retailers were closed. The staples sold so well he kept his ice dock open through the winter and added cigarettes and some canned goods. The experiment was successful, and in 1928 10 Southland stores — known as Tote'm stores — opened and soon added gasoline to their product mix.

By 1946 Southland was operating convenience stores under various names across Texas. Following a decision to keep all the stores open from 7 a.m. to 11 p.m., the single name "7-Eleven" became official. During the next 20 years the stores expanded across the country and in the 1960s and 1970s the company ventured outside U.S. borders, bringing its retail concept to Canada, the United Kingdom and Japan. It was in 1963 that 7-Eleven took its concept to the next level by offering convenience around the clock.

Through the years, 7-Eleven products have answered customer demand, inspired consumer trends, and even become cultural icons. Undoubtedly the most well-known 7-Eleven product, the Slurpee® beverage, was introduced in 1965 and named for the "slurping" sound it makes coming through the straw. The Slurpee phenomenon included specially named flavors like "Fulla Bulla" "Kiss Me, You Fool" and "Miami Ice." Today, 7-Eleven stores sell more than half a million Slurpee drinks a day.

Also in the 1960s, 7-Eleven began testing coffee-by-the-cup in its East Coast stores. Today, the company sells a whopping 365 million cups of coffee a year. In the 1970s, 7-Eleven became the first retailer to offer self-serve fountain drinks, introducing the now legendary Big Gulp® beverage, the patriarch of large-size drinks.

With the 1980s and 1990s came more new products and services, like the "Super Big Gulp®" drink and "Big Bite®" hot dog — a staple of American "dashboard dining" — as well as daily delivery of fresh food items and the widespread introduction of ATMs.

7-Eleven continues to be nimble in its response to and anticipation of consumer needs, always with a sharp eye on assortment, quality, value, cleanliness, and fast and friendly service. Today, there are department-store quality pantyhose in a lipstick-sized package, CDs for young consumers, and nutritional bars and drinks for the health-conscious.

Another aspect of 7-Eleven that sets its stores apart from most retailers is its

Southland Ice Company employee Johnny Green began stocking eggs, milk and bread in 1927 to sell to his ice customers in Oak Cliff. Thus, the convenience store industry began. Eventually named 7-Eleven to reflect the business hours at that time, the stores added more products as customers responded to the unique, quick-shopping concept. 7-Eleven spawned the industry that has grown to some 120,000 stores with approximately $270 billion in sales in the United States.

use of technology. In 2000, the company began testing its Vcom™ kiosks, Web-enabled integrated financial services machines. These kiosks combine the convenience of an ATM with the benefits of the Internet. 7-Eleven envisions that the Vcom kiosks will eventually provide customers with touch-screen access for bill payment, deposit capability, event ticketing and travel directions.

The company introduced its proprietary lines of fresh food and baked goods in 1994, offering a wide variety of items prepared and delivered to its stores daily by food preparation and distribution experts. 7-Eleven's proprietary technology ensures each store gets the items they order through the company's Retail Information System.

Just as 7-Eleven is "part of the neighborhood" as a convenient retail store, the company's community relations programs have been designed to strengthen the community and empower the people in neighborhoods where its stores operate. More than $95 million has been raised by 7-Eleven for worthy causes, such as education, disaster relief, health care and crime deterrence. The company has sponsored numerous local and national programs to benefit communities across the country and donated tons of product to local food banks through its Harvest Program to fight hunger.

The company also donated the land and building on the site of the world's first 7-Eleven store to the League of United Latin American Citizens (LULAC) for its local office and Youth Leadership Academy.

7-Eleven created the modern convenience store by listening to Uncle Johnny Green's customers, who wanted to be able to pick up bread, milk and eggs. The neighborhoods have changed; lifestyles have changed. And time and again 7-Eleven has responded, providing products and services to meet and exceed its customers' needs. The company has grown from those humble origins to become a 21st-century multinational corporation with annual revenues exceeding $9.45 billion. In recognizing its 75th anniversary, 7-Eleven celebrates the ideas, innovations and people that invented and continue to redefine the convenience-retailing industry.

7-ELEVEN® FUN FACTS

- July 11 (7/11), 1927, is the official birthday of the 7-Eleven® convenience store chain.
- Of all U.S. retailers, 7-Eleven sells the most: *USA Today* newspapers, *Sports Illustrated* magazines, cold beer, cold single-serve bottled water, cold Gatorade, fresh-grilled hot dogs and single-serve chips.
- In a four-week period, customers visit a 7-Eleven store an average of 17 times — 80 percent of their total trips to any convenience store.
- Who? What? Where? Who's buying the most 7-Eleven stuff where? The answer is: the most Slurpee® drinks in Detroit; hot dogs in Washington, D.C.; coffee on Long Island; nachos in Colorado; and Big Gulp® drinks in sunny Southern California.
- Of all its proprietary products, 7-Eleven sells more fresh-brewed coffee than anything else —1 million cups each day. That's more than 10,000 pots of coffee an hour every hour of every day of the year.
- 7-Eleven sells approximately 100 million fresh-grilled hot dogs every year, more than any other retailer in America, and could feed every person in hot dog-loving Chicago a Big Bite® hot dog each day for a month.
- 7-Eleven sells 41 million gallons of milk each year — enough to pour more than two glasses of milk for every man, woman and child in the United States.

One of the 7-Eleven stores' best-known products is the Slurpee® beverage, which is a semi-frozen, carbonated drink served at a frosty 28 degrees. 7-Eleven began selling the product in 1965 under the name of "Icee," which was changed to "Slurpee" in 1967 when the company's advertising agency recognized the "slurp" sound made when the beverage was sipped through a straw. More than 11 million Slurpee drinks are purchased at 7-Eleven stores each month.

Today, 7-Eleven, Inc. is the premier convenience retailer in the world, with more than 22,000 convenience stores operating in 20 countries and U.S. territories. The company continues to reinvent convenience retailing through innovative product developments, its use of technology and involving its merchandising processes to meet the ever-changing needs of the time-pressed consumer.

INTERVEST COMPANIES

INTERVEST COMPANIES HAS BEEN INVOLVED IN real estate development, investment and management since 1974 when Michael B. Schiff founded the company. This development includes one of Intervest's most recent projects, Bradford Homesuites, a high-end residential hotel concept with locations in Dallas, Houston, Austin, Colorado Springs and Denver and plans to expand. Bradford Homesuites grew from a mid-1990s initiative at Intervest to develop extended-stay hotel projects with large, well-designed suites, complete kitchens, separate sleeping areas and a high level of amenities. The product has been well received and generated excellent returns for Intervest's investors.

Schiff formed Intervest Companies in 1974 and immediately began buying, developing and operating multi-family units. Before founding the company Schiff spent a number of years working with a large Dallas-area apartment builder and operator and a national real estate development firm with projects in a number of states. Schiff has been active on the boards of many organizations including financial institutions, the Anti-Defamation League and the Apartment Association of Greater Dallas.

John A. Raphael and John J. Wilson are the other Intervest principals. John A. Raphael earned an M.B.A. from the University of Texas and then became a C.P.A. in 1966. Raphael joined the international accounting firm of Touche Ross & Co. and became a partner there in 1976. He joined Intervest Companies as a partner in 1979 and has been involved in many projects including the development and ownership of large multi-family properties, several large single-family home subdivisions developments and Class A office developments.

John J. Wilson first became associated with the company in 1974 while in college. Wilson went on to earn a business degree from the University of Texas at Arlington and became a Certified Public Accountant. He joined the international accounting firm of Arthur Young & Co. before returning to Intervest in 1982 as president of Intervest Property Company, Inc., the company's property management division. Wilson's experience includes property management, financial planning and analysis, property sales, acquisitions and financing. He has also been involved in all major property developments over the last eight years, including Bradford Homesuites.

Over its first 10 years Intervest focused on multi-family projects, but in the early 1980s the principals saw what they believed was an overpriced multi-family market and trouble on the horizon. Unlike many companies involved in Texas real estate during the 1980s, Intervest successfully weathered the downturn in the market. Intervest sold close to 3,000 apartment units between 1983 and 1986 anticipating poor market conditions, and held a core group of around 3,000 units, which allowed the company to remain fiscally viable until conditions improved.

During the weak real estate market of the mid- to late-80s, Schiff and Raphael helped form Americity Federal Savings Bank, a savings

Bradford Homesuites. Austin, Texas

and loan association in Dallas. Americity became a successful Dallas-area financial institution and in 1992 was sold for a substantial profit.

The 1990s brought a stronger real estate market to Texas and a new round of investment from Intervest Companies with a new focus on single-family subdivisions. A 1993 joint venture between Intervest and GE Capital Corporation purchased all the remaining lots in Caruth Court, a zero-lot-line luxury home development located next to the Park Cities and the final phase of the Caruth Homeplace subdivision. Intervest acquired 63 acres of land in West Plano in 1992 and developed Glenhollow Estates, a 216 single-family residential subdivision. All 216 lots were sold to large Dallas-area home builders and all phases came in under budget and ahead of schedule and were very profitable.

Other early 1990s development includes The Trails subdivision in Plano with 296 single-family lots located between Legacy Business Park and the Plano/Richardson High Tech Corridor, a development that became one of the most successful in Plano.

Intervest Companies continued its growth through the 1990s. In 1995 the company assembled 14 pieces of property and bought five contiguous acres of land adjacent to the Mansion on Turtle Creek Hotel, land that was quickly resold for a substantial profit. That same year Intervest bought three acres of land in North Dallas to develop Churchill Pointe, an upscale 26 lot zero-lot-line luxury home gated community. In 1996 the company developed Valley Oaks, a 104 lot single family subdivision in the suburb of Lewisville. Intervest completed luxury multi-family projects in the Dallas market totaling over 700 units in the late 90s. Both of these developments have already been sold for substantial profit.

In 1999 Intervest bought a high-rise condominium site in the Oak Lawn/ Preston Road area and plans to build an upscale 14-story condominium development. The company has also acquired a 5.85-acre tract of land in the

The Bradford at Lincoln Park, Dallas, Texas

Turtle Creek Green Belt across from the Mansion. Intervest is planning a luxury high-rise mixed-use development at this location.

The late-90s also led Intervest into extended-stay residential hotel concepts and its Bradford Homesuites hotel properties. Intervest has opened nine Bradford Homesuites: four in Dallas, two in Houston, one in Austin, one in Colorado Springs and one in Denver. Intervest is developing additional Bradford Homesuites in Austin and looking to break into various Northeast markets.

The company developed a 17-acre commercial tract on the North Dallas Tollway for a three-phased office park containing approximately 600,000 square feet. The first 200,000-square-foot, eight-story Class A office building is complete and over 98-percent occupied. In 1998 Intervest acquired several office buildings in Houston totaling approximately 500,000 square feet.

Bradford Homesuites, Colorado Springs, Colorado

McSHAN FLORIST

FIFTY-FOUR YEARS AGO, BRUCE MCSHAN WAS the youngest member of the McShan family, having arrived just three weeks after his parents opened their doors for business on December 1, 1948. As a toddler he swept floors and accompanied his father on local deliveries. Today, Bruce McShan and his wife, Sheri, are well known for developing McShan Florist into one of the industry's most technologically advanced florists in the country, clearing more FTD orders than any other single-location florist in the world.

Sheri and Bruce McShan celebrated 25 years of marriage as the company celebrated 50 years of operation in 1998.

The original McShan Florist and Nursery as it looked in 1948, with two first-class delivery trucks and the McShan family home at left. Freelance artist Celeste Askew charged $5 for drawing the caladium leaf logo.

The story began on a lonely country road in the cotton fields of East Dallas. It was a red-letter day in the lives of Lee A. McShan Jr. and his wife, Velma, who had purchased the Faltejsek Florist and Nursery — now renamed McShan Florist and Nursery — and moved into the tiny house behind it with their 2-year-old son, Mike. Four days before Christmas, newborn Bruce joined the family.

On opening day the McShans had three employees, two delivery vehicles and relatives with serious doubts about the business' chance to survive in its remote, rural location. At the end of the first day, with only $11 in the cash register, the McShans must have had a few doubts, too. But Lee McShan had an unwavering determination and a sound business philosophy based upon the Golden Rule, which he encouraged his employees to practice as the company's fundamental law.

The greenhouse, nursery and all its stock were part of the original purchase, but Lee McShan wanted to focus on developing the florist business. His opportunity to deplete the nursery merchandise came in the early 50s when the Federal Housing Authority paid McShan $12.50 per house to landscape the new Casa View subdivision. Thereafter, Lee McShan was able to concentrate on his floral business. By 1955 business was booming. The McShans began to give back to the community, whose support they deeply appreciated. They donated the use of their original home to the newly formed White Rock YMCA for offices and much of their precious free time to numerous civic, neighborhood and church activities.

McShan Florist's growing reputation as a full-service florist was confirmed when Stanley Marcus of Neiman-Marcus selected McShan to service his personal and corporate accounts. The long-term relationship allowed the McShans to show the nation the scope of their creative capabilities. In 1971 the McShans transformed the downtown Dallas store into a floral wonderland during the Fortnight celebration Fete des Fleurs (Festival of Flowers). In preparation for the two-week extravaganza, Bruce McShan, his parents and a plant broker traveled to

California on a special buying trip. They returned to Dallas leading two 18-wheelers loaded with plants and flowers. A crew of 60 employees worked from 5:30 p.m. on a Saturday until Sunday noon to create the memorable displays.

It was 1970 when both McShan sons — Mike, following his discharge from the U.S. Navy, and Bruce, upon graduation from Stephen F. Austin State University — joined the family business and became instrumental in the company's continued growth. By 1975 the delivery fleet had grown to eight vehicles, with an average load of 250 deliveries daily. The family discussed expansion, and on January 3, 1979, the original McShan Florist structure was demolished. The business operated out of temporary quarters until June, when a new two-level facility was completed, designed to serve employees' future needs as the business grew. To accommodate the volume of the store's operation, the brothers streamlined the business by implementing computers to print customer accounts and payments. Sadly, Mike McShan died suddenly at the age of 36 in 1982, but the McShan family moved bravely forward.

Since completion of the new facility, the company expanded twice with the purchase of two adjacent properties for storage and parking. Bruce McShan assumed the role of president following the death of his father on June 25, 1990. His mother, Velma, died suddenly on March 10, 1996. Bruce and Sheri, married in 1973, shared a heartfelt passion to continue the family business.

In the early 90s Bruce McShan unexpectedly became a leader in the green movement when he chose to convert the McShan fleet to compressed natural gas (CNG), a clean-burning alternative fuel. In 1992 McShan Florist was recognized as Texas' first small business to begin conversion to CNG, and in June 2002 Bruce McShan installed a CNG fueling station on site to benefit his growing fleet.

Always with an eye to the future, Bruce McShan and computer expert Abner Maldonado began creating a new state-of-the-art computer program in 1997 specifically designed to enhance operations in every department. McShan has since created an innovative software program that tracks an order from time of origin to time of delivery, providing customers with up-to-the-minute status on any order. Many U.S. florists now use this valuable time-saving software.

Throughout their careers the McShan family has received numerous important honors and awards, but none as meaningful as the faith the Dallas community has shown in their business for more than 50 years. Bruce McShan credits four key elements to the company's success: a well-trained, dedicated employee family; a proven creed of Quality, Style and Service; practicing the Golden Rule; and a thoughtful, genuine philosophy — that McShan Florist is in the business of sharing life's meaningful moments, which means every expression of love is special for the person ordering the gift, the person who receives the flowers and to McShan as the "messenger of love."

Today, McShan Florist continues to operate by the Golden Rule, always putting the customer first. From humble beginnings to 150 employees and 45 custom-painted delivery vans, the McShans are proud of their store's continued growth. Bruce and Sheri's college-age daughter, Jodi, assists part-time, and Sheri also volunteers as a chaplain at Baylor University Medical Center. The family's dedication to succeed has never been greater — Bruce and Sheri's commitment is truly a labor of love they have carried into the 21st century — guided steadfastly by the Golden Rule, just as when the family business was founded in 1948.

Elaborate holiday decorations are an annual event at McShan Florist, attracting the attention of even the most casual passerby. Santa Fe-style luminarias provide a dramatic evening accent to the store's exterior design.

Velma and Lee McShan, McShan Florist co-founders, are pictured here on their 50th wedding anniversary, April 21, 1990.

MRS BAIRD'S

A Texas Legend

THE STORY OF MRS BAIRD'S BREAD IS ONE that is steeped in the history of a family working together — a company started by an idea, inspired by circumstances and motivated by the determination to succeed and overcome adversity while building a Texas tradition. It all started from a humble beginning in a small rented house in Fort Worth in 1908 and has grown into Texas' leading bakery. Throughout the years, much has changed but the values of quality, freshness and service that made Mrs Baird's Bread a success remain unchanged.

Around the turn of the 20th Century, baking was a challenging task. Enduring the heat of her wood-burning stove in the sweltering Texas summer heat and maintaining a consistent oven temperature came naturally to Ninnie L. Baird. She loved to bake breads, cakes and pies for her family of four boys, four girls and her husband, William. She was a talented baker who often gave bread to her neighbors. Soon, everyone in the neighborhood began asking about Mrs. Baird's delicious bread. Ninnie recognized fairly quickly that she could make a living by selling her bread. Due to her husband's deteriorating health, Ninnie was faced with having to support her large family. So in 1908, Mrs Baird's Bread was born. Shortly after, in 1911, William died.

Ninnie began baking and selling bread from her home on Hemphill Street in Fort Worth. The family was no stranger to hard work. Baking in a tiny kitchen with a wood-burning stove capable of baking only four loaves at a time, Ninnie worked side by side with her four sons who helped bake, sell and deliver the bread. Her four daughters helped out at home.

At first, all deliveries were made on foot. The boys would carry baskets full of freshly baked cakes and bread to houses in the neighborhood. As sales grew, so did the delivery area. So the Baird boys soon traded in their walking shoes for bicycles. Soon after, the family converted its buggy into a sales wagon pulled by a horse named Ned.

It didn't take long for Ninnie's business to outgrow her tiny kitchen and the small wood-burning stove. Around 1915, Ninnie purchased her first commercial oven from a local hotel. She financed the $75 oven with $25 cash and payments of her famous bread and rolls. Ninnie's new oven was capable of baking 40 loaves of bread at a time and helped her meet the growing demand for her baked goods. Even though bread production increased, demand for Mrs Baird's Bread continued to grow. So, Ninnie moved her baking outside of the house and into a small wooden building in the backyard.

By 1917, the horse and wagon was replaced with Mrs Baird's first motorized delivery truck. A panel body was built for it, the passenger seats were removed and the truck was painted a cream color. The words "Eat More Mrs Baird's" were painted on the side.

In 1918 the company built its first bakery located

at 6th and Terrell in Fort Worth. The family installed a Peterson gas-fired peel oven with a capacity to bake 400 one-pound loaves at a time. They also purchased a hand-wrapping machine. The total initial investment for the new bakery — $8,800. But the new bakery and equipment was not enough.

Demand for fresh Mrs Baird's Bread continued to grow. Therefore, the bakery was expanded nine times during the next 10 years to keep up with production demand. In 1928 Mrs Baird's opened its first Dallas bakery and began a long affiliation with the North Dallas neighborhood. The Dallas bakery located at Mockingbird and Central Expressway will always be remembered for the aroma of fresh baking bread.

History offered challenges to Mrs Baird's Bakeries, which endured financial hardships and short supplies during the Great Depression and World War II. Through it all, growth continued. Although her children, grandchildren, and great-grandchildren ran the company's day-to-day operations, Ninnie Baird kept a careful eye on the business until her death in 1961 at the age of 92.

With a commitment to quality, freshness and service, the demand continued to grow for Mrs Baird's products. New bakeries were built in new neighborhoods across Texas producing the freshest varieties of bread, cakes, pies and other sweet goods.

Along with the expansion of new bakeries, Mrs Baird's delivery system also saw exponential growth. Delivery methods have grown from a horse named Ned, who pulled a delivery wagon and snacked on the customers' lawns, to a fleet of modern, computer-equipped delivery trucks making 20,000 stops a day. Today, Mrs Baird's operates six baking facilities strategically located throughout Texas in order to provide the freshest products for their customers.

Mrs Baird's modern bakeries include technology that helps meet the growing demand for the company's products. But technology hasn't changed the baking process that has made Mrs Baird's the leading brand of bread in Texas. The dough is still handtwisted and allowed to rise naturally twice. Quality ingredients, including real milk, are still part of the baking process to ensure an outstanding loaf of bread.

Mrs Baird's philosophy of regional bakeries is key to delivering the freshest bread, buns and sweet goods every day throughout Texas, Oklahoma and parts of Louisiana, Arkansas and New Mexico. As the company has always looked at it: "We're still baking bread for the neighbors. The neighborhood has just gotten a little bigger, that's all."

Another historic step in Mrs Baird's growth was marked in 1998 when the company became part of one of the world's leading baking companies, Grupo Bimbo. Mexico's market leader in bakery products, Grupo Bimbo, like Mrs Baird's, is a family tradition that holds the same commitment to quality, freshness and service. Even though Mrs Baird's is no longer a family business, it still has family heritage.

The bakery that started just a few miles from downtown Fort Worth with an old hotel oven and horse-drawn wagon is now headquarters for one of the nation's fastest growing baking companies — Bimbo Bakeries USA.

"We are continuing to build on Mrs Baird's success," says Juan Muldoon, president of Bimbo Bakeries USA. "We are committed to the legacy Ninnie Baird created through innovation, support, competitive position and the highest commitment to quality, freshness and service. We're proud of Mrs Baird's local heritage and look forward to a bright future."

CAROLYN BROWN, PHOTOGRAPHER

CAROLYN BROWN HAS BEEN PHOTOGRAPHING ancient architecture since 1980, when her talents were commissioned for the texts, *Upper Egypt*, and later for *Aswan and Abu Simbel*. Through the years, she has received travel grants to photograph in Iraq, Rwanda, Guatemala, Belize, Honduras, Mexico, Lebanon and Syria. With the assistance of the Mexican Government Tourist Bureau, she continues to work in Mexico to enhance a large archive of Mexican architecture.

Carolyn has traveled the world to photograph famous places, yet some of the best images are found in her own backyard. In June 1994, *Dallas: The Shining Star of Texas*, co-authored with Jim Donovan, was published, and in 1997, *Dallas, World Class Texas*, co-authored with Annette Strauss, was published. Her photographs were the subject of a large exhibit, "Sacred Spaces: Man and the Divine in Mexico, Central America and Southwestern United States." This exhibit of over 200 images is currently traveling in Mexico and the United States. Presently Carolyn is working on another large exhibit on the ancient Middle East.

(Above)
Exconvent of San Andrés Calpan and Iztaccíhuatl Calpan, Puebla, Mexico
©*Carolyn Brown*

(Top right)
Smoking Volcano Popocatepetl and Spanish Mission on Cholula Pyramid Puebla, Mexico
©*Carolyn Brown*

(Bottom right)
Al Khazneh at Petra, Jordan
©*Carolyn Brown*

Vegetable Market at Chicicastenango, Guatemala
©*Carolyn Brown*

COURIERGUY.COM

MICHAEL MINER SHARPENED HIS BASIC computer programming skills while trying to solve various service and data delivery problems for the courier services he managed in Dallas for more than 13 years. After much tinkering, Miner developed a program that would make his supervisor's company more efficient and potentially save the firm $60,000 a year. When his employer refused to consider the program, Miner decided to set out on his own.

In 2000 Miner started CourierGuy.com, a Dallas-based courier service built around Miner's software and the CourierGuy Web site. The firm is quickly gaining a reputation for its attention to detail, personalized service and willingness to do almost anything for a client.

WHEN CROCODILES ATTACK

When MGM Studio's *Crocodile Hunter* was about to open nationwide, the studio decided to pull a publicity stunt in several major cities. In Dallas, MGM's marketing reps hired CourierGuy.com to hand-deliver inflatable crocodiles throughout the city. To properly complete the assignment, CourierGuy employees spent most of the day inflating the rubber crocs and then worked the graveyard shift to deliver them as discreetly as possible. From 10 p.m. until 8 a.m. the couriers worked their way through the city, installing 90 10-foot crocodiles in various high-traffic locations.

The stunt was a success and even garnered attention on the local Fox affiliate. The firm's apt handling of a difficult and unusual project earned it respect, not only with MGM, but also with other area businesses who have now started calling on CourierGuy to handle their extraordinary courier needs.

FOCUS ON TECHNOLOGY AND THE FUTURE

Unusual jobs are not all that CourierGuy handles, though — far from it, in fact. The firm is building a solid, more traditional client base through adherence to basic business principles: give the customers what they want, when they want it and make the process as easy as possible.

This philosophy is what drove Miner to develop his software in the early days. Using Visual Basic 6, a Microsoft Access database and HTML, Miner created the back-end software that allows him to administer his company's rapidly growing business and the front-end software — the CourierGuy.com Web site — that provides his customers with an easy-to-use interface for placing and tracking their orders.

Miner is quick to point out that the CourierGuy software is still in its early stages and is undergoing constant development. For clients this means that what is easy today will be even easier tomorrow. Miner hopes to leverage this technology into a nationwide business. His plan includes franchising CourierGuy.com locations in cities throughout the country or partnering with existing courier companies to provide a nationwide courier service that is easily accessible through one Web site.

CourierGuy.com's commitment to improving its existing technology and solid plans for future growth should allow the firm to grow and achieve Miner's vision of a nationwide, Internet-based courier service in very short order.

(Far left) "It is our vision to be known for our superior service, customer dedication and industry innovations. We continuously strive to be the leader in our field," says President Michael Miner.

Vice President Tammy Mayfield is shown here organizing an unusual delivery job.

NETWORKS

𝒟ALLAS TRANSPORTATION, COMMUNICATIONS AND ENERGY COMPANIES KEEP PEOPLE, INFORMATION AND POWER CIRCULATING THROUGHOUT THE REGION.

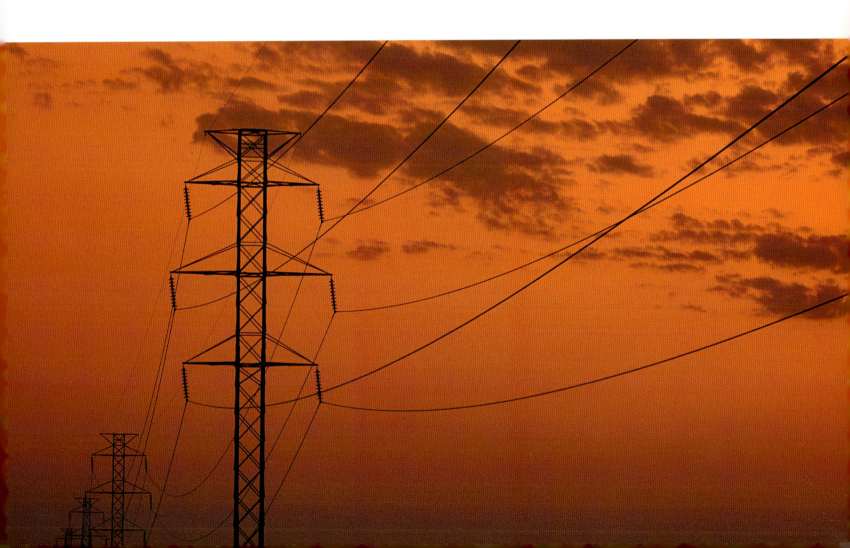

AMERICAN AIRLINES

AMERICAN AIRLINES' JETLINERS ROAM THE world, serving travelers from Europe to Japan to deepest South America. But the airline's people call Dallas/Fort Worth home.

American has come a long way since Charles Lindbergh piloted the first rattling DH-4 biplane loaded with mail for a predecessor company. But since its inception almost 80 years ago, the airline has planted deep roots in the one-time prairieland of north Texas.

Despite the economic slowdown and September 11th terrorist attack that forced airlines around the globe to cut back, today's American Airlines remains the industry leader. It is the world's largest airline, flying the world's largest fleet of modern jetliners. Together with its regional carriers, American Eagle and American Connections, the AA network serves more than 250 cities in 41 countries with some 4,400 daily flights.

The 2001 acquisition of Trans World Airlines, a proud but failing air transport pioneer, gave American additional jets, talented employees and a strong connecting hub in St. Louis. That merger has been described as the largest and most complex, yet smoothest, integration ever undertaken in aviation.

Through the **one**world airline alliance, American and seven international partners serve 575 destinations in 135 countries. With more than 8,500 flights each day, **one**world boasts an aircraft taking off or landing somewhere in the world every five seconds.

Notwithstanding its size and scope, American has always emphasized quality rather than quantity. Safety and customer service have been top priorities since American Airways emerged in 1930 from the air-mail companies cobbled together by an investment company called the Aviation Corporation, or AVCO.

Today, AA's commitment to customer service under Chairman and CEO Don Carty is exemplified by its More Room Throughout Coach program. By removing an average of two rows from virtually every jetliner in its fleet, and spreading the remaining rows, it can offer more personal space and leg room to every coach passenger. Since the program was introduced early in 2000, employees have reconfigured more than 850 aircraft and removed nearly 10,000 seats — the capacity of a good-sized sports arena.

AA's leadership in safety and service have been supported by innovative marketing, such as the 1981 introduction of the world's first travel rewards program. Today's AAdvantage program counts over 45 million members worldwide. Nearly half of the miles accrued on AAdvantage each year are earned through hundreds of partner airlines, hotel companies, car rental agencies and others who recognize the drawing power of AAdvantage miles, "the nation's second currency."

AAdvantage, along with numerous marketing and operating innovations, was made possible by the computing wizardry of the Sabre system. Sabre, launched in the early 1960s to help with reservations, was spun off as an independent company in 2000 but still provides much of American's computing power.

American, American Eagle and other subsidiaries operate under the corporate umbrella of the parent AMR Corp. But in the eyes of Dallas residents, American belongs to them. It is their hometown airline, with its headquarters, its largest hub and about 30,000 people working at Dallas/Fort Worth International Airport and neighboring corporate campus.

American's presence dates to 1928, when the predecessor Texas Air Transport sent its first open-cockpit mail planes aloft to begin scheduled service at Dallas' Love Field as well as Fort Worth and nearby cities. Those flights marked the beginning of nearly eight decades of continuous service to the DFW area.

Texas Air, which evolved into Southern Air Transport, became American Airways' Southern Division in 1930. It would become a model for the new airline under the legendary Cyrus Rowlett ("Mr. C.R.") Smith, who would later guide AA itself for four decades.

Despite his leadership in making American the nation's leading airline by the late 1930s, Smith disappointed his fellow Texans by moving the company's headquarters first to Chicago and then, in 1939, to New York's new LaGuardia Field. They weren't pacified even by AA's introduction of Dallas Love Field's first service with such aircraft as the Douglas DC-3 and DC-6, the Convair 240, — or the Boeing 707, which added the community's first jet service between Dallas and New York in 1959.

It wasn't until 1979 that CEO Al Casey brought the expatriate company and more than 900 employees home to a rolling, wooded complex just south of the new DFW Airport. Casey was motivated by more than nostalgia. In the wake of the deregulation of the nation's airline a year earlier, American's survival depended on building a fortress hub at a central airport.

Besides, AA already maintained its training center for pilots and flight attendants near the airport and planned a huge Southern Reservations Office on the same complex.

In January 1979 American stunned competitors by inaugurating service over 19 new routes out of DFW. It was the forerunner of the "growth plan" of the 1980s, guided by Casey's aggressive successor, Bob Crandall. That expansion was built around a system of connecting hubs that today include Chicago, Miami and San Juan.

American began adding service from DFW and Chicago to Europe in the 1980s and today also uses DFW as a gateway to Japan and cities throughout the Western Hemisphere. About 530 American flights depart DFW every day, a vast operation supported by capital improvements such as a $1.1 billion international terminal. But the airline's presence is felt throughout the community in ways unrelated to air travel.

It is as visible as Dallas' downtown sports arena, American Airlines Center, where the NBA's Dallas Mavericks and professional hockey's Dallas Stars have been playing since 2001. The arena bears American's name through a 30-year sponsorship agreement. AA presence also manifests itself in the support the company and individual employees provide to numerous charitable and cultural organizations.

But AA's primary job remains carrying people safely, conveniently and dependably from one point to another, as CEO Don Carty reminded employees recently. "Our mission is simple," he said. "We bring people and cultures together from around the world. "We spread the joy of flight, and do so in the absolute safest way we know how. And," he added, "it is noble work."

ASSOCIATED AIR CENTER

ASSOCIATED AIR CENTER, HEADQUARTERED IN Dallas for over 50 years, is known worldwide for its expertise in handling all types of corporate and commercial airplane modification and maintenance.

The company's corporate facilities are composed of a 50-acre fixed base operation and over 400,000 square feet of hangar and support facilities. As a FAA/JAA Class IV-rated facility, Associated Air Center is equipped to provide major overhauls, structural modifications, avionics installations and heavy maintenance on practically any transport category business aircraft. It has performed more aging aircraft assignments than virtually any other completion center, including mandatory inspections, service bulletin incorporation and necessary modifications. It is the single-source provider, handling all the details from start to finish, on time and within budget.

Associated Air Center's reputation for unsurpassed quality was a major factor in its being designated a Boeing Business Jets Completion and Service Center. Associated Air Center is also the completion center for Airbus Industries, the European aircraft-manufacturing consortium.

Whether it is a Boeing 737, Airbus A320 or MD-80, new or old, Associated Air can convert it to being a home or an office in the sky for heads of states, corporate executives, sports teams and entertainers. No detail is too small, no safety feature too cumbersome for the almost 600 employees who take responsibility for all aspects of the conversion.

Associated Air Center understands all the regulatory aspects of conversion processes. The company supports a full staff of degreed structural, electrical and systems engineers who have significant aircraft experience and specialize in finding new solutions to maintenance and modification problems. The engineering staff is supported by experienced draftsmen, quality control inspectors and FAA licensed supervisors to ensure that strict quality control measures are followed. Moreover, everything — every nut and bolt, every slight or major alteration — is tracked and filed for internal or government reference. If a procedure has been performed at Associated Air Center, it is well documented.

In keeping with their commitment to current technology, the staff is equipped with the latest in specific aircraft design, analysis, diagnostic and service equipment, providing a unique ability to respond to customer design, engineering and fabrication requirements. The staff is experienced in all phases of aircraft certification procedures and can meet customer requirements up to and including complex STCs, installations and field approvals.

Associated Air Center, however, is more than just an aircraft mechanic's dream. It is also a place where clients

Boeing 757-200 head-of-state conference room

Boeing 757-200 corporate lounge

can dream up the interior that most suits their personal and work requirements. The company's designers, working along with a designated full-time project manager, handle all the details for a simple or luxurious interior.

Clients can choose from thousands of fabrics, leathers, carpeting, cabinetry, finishes and fixtures. In addition, virtually any amenity can be incorporated into the airplane's interior design. If a client wants state-of-the-art audio/video equipment, business computers, satellite phone, fax, secure voice and security systems, then that is exactly what the client will get. Associated Air also installs fully equipped galleys with cook tops, dishwashers, trash compactors, microwaves and executive lavatories, often outfitted with showers, sinks, bidets — even Jacuzzis.

Along the design path, Associated Air will recommend materials and configurations for an interior that affords maximum comfort, durability, payload, soundproofing, space utilization and ease of maintenance while meeting or exceeding all FAA/JAA safety requirements. Associated Air also can create special applications including the incorporation of emergency air ambulance units, environmental control units, auxiliary fuel systems, auxiliary power units, air stair doors and more. At Associated Air Center customer satisfaction begins with understanding exactly what the client wants in the aircraft.

With Associated Air Center's computer-aided design (CAD) technology and experienced design professionals, a client can explore a full range of interior design possibilities with tremendous speed, flexibility and cost efficiency.

While the interior is prepared, Associated Aircraft's experienced technicians can install the latest avionics, including complete electronic flight instrument systems, flight management systems and the latest state-of-the-art communication systems. Their engineers will also work with client pilots to determine the position of avionics equipment for enhanced access and visibility.

Associated Air Center understands that these custom modifications and enhancements done correctly take time and that time is precious for clients who need their airplanes in action. Lost airtime means money. Therefore, to minimize an aircraft's downtime and facilitate maintenance, Associated Air technicians will often prefabricate the avionics system and all interior work in their facility before installing it in the plane. Moreover, Associated Air Center's technicians work around the clock seven days a week to get the job done quickly.

Another way Associated Air Center minimizes airplane down time is with its "Probe 1" computer-enhanced automated data collection and job tracking system. It is a network system that communicates with Planning, Production, Purchasing, Quality Control and Invoicing and provides a system of checks and balances to ensure the efficient delivery of a quality product. This allows constant, up-to-the-minute tracking at the touch of a button.

Located at Dallas' Love Field Airport, Associated Air Center is easily accessed from all regions of the country, which can save time and money when planes must be flown in for service. This is no ordinary gas station. During a maintenance or refueling visit, clients have access to clean, air-conditioned offices near the airplane and a host of comfortable amenities, including conference rooms, restaurant, flight planning center, catering, rental cars and nearby support service to handle any need.

Associated Air Center began with much more modest beginnings. Back in 1949, it was a small three-man operation that installed radios in surplus military aircraft. Today, it is the recognized leader as a one-source center for modifying, maintaining, enhancing and servicing fixed wing aircraft. Along the way, Associated Air Center has helped Dallas become a booming transportation center, a magnet for avionics and a perfect place to land.

Boeing 737-300 sports team lounge

WRR CLASSICAL 101.1 FM

Henry "Dad" Garrett, noted Dallas inventor and founder of WRR radio

WRR's Fair Park studios c. 1957

HENRY GARRETT'S PIONEERING efforts to develop a radio transmission system in order to communicate with firemen in the field evolved into Texas' first licensed radio station known as WRR. Garrett and colleagues constructed a custom-made 20-watt radio transmitter, and Dallas residents with crystal sets tuned in to classical recordings, jokes and weather reports between emergencies. On August 5, 1921, the city of Dallas' Police and Fire Signal Department, of which Garrett was superintendent, received the second commercial license ever issued in the United States for a radio station. WRR officially began transmitting on March 13, 1922, the first municipally owned U.S. broadcasting station furnishing regular entertainment programs.

First located in the Dallas Central Fire Station, WRR moved into new Fair Park studios in 1937 and relocated to a new facility in 1973. In 1948 WRR AM acquired a "sister frequency," and WRR Classical 101.1 FM was launched. In April 1978 WRR AM was sold to Bonneville Broadcasting Co. and assumed different call numbers.

Eighty years after its first transmission, city-owned WRR 101.1 FM still broadcasts under its original call letters. WRR is not only one of the leading classical stations in the United States but is to Dallas what the National Portrait Gallery is to Washington, D.C. — a treasured cultural icon. Fads come and go, even among radio stations, but WRR is a Dallas mainstay institution offering back-to-basics radio programming to aficionados of classical music.

Dallas residents have a great sense of ownership and pride about WRR. Because it's attuned to the interests and needs of its dedicated local listening audience, WRR has shaped the future for many organizations that rely on ticket sales, radio advertising and exposure for their continued success.

WRR's reputation has drawn renowned conductors from Europe to Dallas' excellent concert halls, and WRR has aired great orchestra concerts. Yet WRR has not remained static, having moved forward to create an Internet presence that has earned it a worldwide audience. In a heartbeat, classical music lovers from Hamburg to Hanoi and Joplin to Johannesburg tune in to WRR by computer to learn of Dallas' symphony, opera and ballet, and an ethnic culture specific to the Dallas way of life. WRR is the voice of Dallas' cultural life, an oasis of music on the airwaves.

WRR also stretches its audience's horizons. It plays both great classical music of bygone eras and the work of new composers, and showcases local talents through its Music of the Metroplex program. WRR reflects its local ownership by funneling a portion of its profits back into the community; it has contributed $1.5 million in the past five years to local arts groups. WRR employees are passionate about good music and exposing their listeners to it; in leaving WRR in better shape than they found it; in passing on a great heritage to the next generation; and continuing to give back to the Dallas-Fort Worth community that has made WRR a community treasure.

Dallas Public Library

PROFESSIONAL *Services*

*A*ttorneys, accountants, architects, engineers and advertising professionals provide essential services to the Dallas area.

AGUIRREcorporation

AGUIRRE is particularly proud of its work on the Dallas Area Rapid Transit (DART) system; shown here is DART's Mockingbird Light Rail Station in Dallas.

(Below) The Moises E. Molina High School, part of the Dallas Independent School District, is another favorite AGUIRRE accomplishment.

PEDRO AGUIRRE, FAIA, FOUNDED AGUIRREcorporation in 1960. AGUIRRE is a professional services corporation specializing in the development and application of facility systems. The firm provides strategic planning, architectural/engineering design, facility management, construction services and general contracting. Its strength is in building solutions that help clients achieve their visions.

AGUIRRE has gained an excellent reputation for providing quick, successful responses to the fast-paced high-tech industry, where lost minutes could mean the loss of millions of dollars. An example is AGUIRRE's participation in the design and construction of telecommunications facilities and several television stations. AGUIRRE has completed projects across the United States in the commercial, education, criminal justice and health care markets. AGUIRRE's clients include private industry as well as local, state and federal agencies.

Among the myriad of projects that AGUIRRE has completed over the years, the company is particularly proud of its design for the Dallas Area Rapid Transit system, the Dallas Independent School District, and the Student Center and Fine Arts Complex for Texas A&M International University's Laredo campus. The Student Center and the Fine Arts Complex were designed to help establish a new entrance to the campus while blending with the existing architectural theme of the campus.

AGUIRRE has received two substantial contracts from the North Texas Tollway Authority for work on the President George Bush Turnpike. In 2000 work was completed for the operations building, counting facility and command center, which monitors traffic and turnpike security. AGUIRRE provided the architectural design, interior architectural, and electrical and mechanical engineering for the project. AGUIRRE also designed and developed construction documents for 36 toll plazas on the turnpike, including five main-lane toll plazas, each of which is connected to an operations building by a tunnel.

Over the years AGUIRREcorporation has garnered many honors, but 2000 and 2001 proved to be banner years for the company. AGUIRRE won two national awards from Associated Builders and Contractors (ABC), a national trade association representing more than 23,000 contractors, subcontractors, material suppliers and related firms across the country. One of the award-winning projects was AGUIRRE's design-build work for the new 61,000-square-foot SandStream Communications & Entertainment Corporate Headquarters and Networks Operations Center. AGUIRRE played a key role in the success of this one-of-a-kind facility, which blends communications, broadcast and corporate offices. ABC's North Texas Chapter honored AGUIRRE with its First Place Award of Excellence for the SandStream project, which also qualified it for entry into the ABC National Competition. AGUIRRE was extremely proud to then accept the first place Eagle Award in the "interior build-out" category of the National ABC Excellence in Construction (EIC) Awards. Again, in 2002, AGUIRRE received the top ABC National honor in the "specialty, interior build-out" category, winning its second Eagle Award. This recognized AGUIRRE's exceptional interior work for the BillMatrix Corporate Headquarters in Dallas. AGUIRRE provided architecture, engineering and general contracting services

for the new 26,500-square-foot, high-tech headquarters for BillMatrix, a leading provider of comprehensive electronic bill payments solutions.

Also in 2000 and 2001, AGUIRRE was recognized by *Hispanic Business Magazine*. AGUIRRE was ranked as one of the 500 largest Hispanic-owned companies in the United States, reflecting its continued success as a leader in the industry.

Pedro Aguirre, FAIA, the corporation's founder, chairman and CEO, is a Dallas native whose lifelong residence and career have contributed to Dallas' growth and quality of life. Although Aguirre's personal and professional accomplishments are certainly too many to list, some must be highlighted. He was elected to the Dallas City Council in 1973. He was appointed by President Richard Nixon to the board of directors of the Center for Housing Management and served from 1974 to 1980. While serving on this board, he participated in establishing national guidelines for the Management of Assisted Housing. Aguirre became the first architect to be elected president of the National Bankers Association in 1985; received a presidential citation for private-sector initiatives by President Ronald Reagan in 1986; was listed as one of the "100 Influential Hispanics in America" by *Hispanic Business Magazine* in 1988; was appointed by Texas Gov. Ann Richards to serve as Chairman of the Texas Board of Architectural Examiners; and currently serves as vice chairman of the DFW International Airport board of directors. Among Aguirre's many outstanding accomplishments, the most cherished honor is that of receiving the Outstanding Alumni Award from Texas A&M University's College of Architecture in April 2001.

Pedro Aguirre considers his business to be unique in the marketplace. It grew from a one-man operation into a nationally recognized firm in Dallas, where the business was developed and where the community shares in the company's prosperity. In addition to Dallas, AGUIRRE has recently completed design, construction and design-build projects from Boston to San Francisco, and is licensed to perform work nationally. In 1999, a year before AGUIRRE celebrated its 40th anniversary, the company adopted a concept called Shared Values® in order to develop a new image and management style. By sharing the same core values, the staff develops and mentors rather than managing relationships, which heightens employee morale and ultimately provides better customer service.

AGUIRREcorporation's commitment to the Dallas community does not begin or end with Pedro Aguirre, however. AGUIRRE president and COO Gary Roden is a past president of the North Texas Chapter of ABC, is a national vice chairman of ABC and serves on the board of Wednesday's Child Benefit Corporation. John V. Nyfeler, FAIA Vice President and manager of AGUIRRE's Austin office, is president elect of the Texas Society of Architects, and Frost E. Gardner, PE, a partner at AGUIRRE, is president elect of the Dallas Chapter of the American Society of Heating, Refrigeration and Air Conditioning Engineers. Peter Aguirre, Pedro's son, is a member of the Dallas Hispanic Chamber of Commerce, and most AGUIRRE vice presidents and management personnel serve on various local and national boards.

Throughout its 42-year history, AGUIRRE has chosen to approach challenges and successes in the same manner — with "The Can-Do Spirit that Gets the Job Done®." With this spirit, AGUIRRE's future will always be a bright one.

AGUIRRE designed the Student Development Center for Texas A&M International University, Laredo, Texas, to establish a new campus entrance and also blend with existing architecture.

The Texas Cable News (TXCN) facility for A.H. Belo Corporation in Dallas is an example of AGUIRRE's design of several television stations.

BARON & BUDD, P.C.

BARON & BUDD, P.C. IS THE LARGEST LAW FIRM in the United States that exclusively represents victims of exposure to asbestos and other toxic substances. From the day the firm was founded, Baron & Budd has fought hard to accomplish twin goals — to seek fair compensation for people who suffer disease as a result of exposure to hazardous substances and to prevent future misconduct that may cause similar harm to others. The firm is recognized in the legal community as a leader in this area of the law.

Because Baron & Budd limits its practice to representing individuals, each client receives individual attention. Although many Baron & Budd lawyers and staff dedicate their energy to representing victims of asbestos-related diseases, they also represent victims of disease caused by numerous other toxic substances such as lead, water pollutants, radiation and other chemicals. The firm also represents those who have suffered injuries caused by dangerous drugs.

The firm's focus on justice for toxic substance victims, its fight to educate the public on environmental hazards and its work to deter worker exposure to toxic substances can be easily traced to the founding member's personal philosophies. A lifelong advocate for the environment, consumers and working people, Frederick M. Baron graduated from the University of Texas School of Law in 1971 following a summer where he worked on a project for consumer rights advocate Ralph Nader in Washington, D.C.

Baron was inspired by Nader's philosophy — "do well by doing good" — and in 1973, while working for a small Dallas firm that handled civil rights and labor cases, Baron represented his first client with an asbestos-related illness.

Asbestos litigation captivated Baron. When his firm was unenthusiastic about four asbestos cases referred to him, Baron decided to strike out on his own and formed his own firm in 1975. In 1979, Russell W. Budd, who was just out of law school, teamed up with Baron. Together they built the nation's largest law firm exclusively representing victims of toxic injury.

Baron & Budd has become a powerhouse in the U.S. courts. Its legal victories have earned the law firm the distinction as a national leader in the fight for environmental justice. As a trial firm, Dallas-based Baron & Budd has won verdicts on behalf of hundreds of victims of disease caused by asbestos and other toxic substances and has successfully settled thousands of cases.

Notable cases include representation of 1,600 residents of Tucson, Arizona, who became sick because of their exposure to TCE-contaminated water; more than 400 West Dallas children who lived in a neighborhood polluted by a lead smelter; several hundred Costa Rican farm workers who became sterile from exposure to the pesticide DBCP; and residents of the towns

(Far right) Russell W. Budd had just graduated from law school when he teamed up with Fred Baron in 1979.

A lifelong advocate for the environment, consumers and working people, Fred Baron founded his firm in 1975.

of Apollo and Parks Township, Pennsylvania, who were exposed to radioactive emissions from an area nuclear plant.

The firm has garnered some valuable verdicts for its clients. A 47-year-old client who developed malignant mesothelioma as a result of his exposure to asbestos as a construction worker was recently awarded $55.5 million. A jury awarded more than $17 million to seven foundry workers who developed asbestosis as a result of exposure to asbestos. The family of a union pipe fitter who died of colon cancer as a result of his occupational exposure to asbestos products was awarded $10.4 million, and $9.1 million was awarded to an aircraft mechanic who developed malignant mesothelioma as a result of exposure to asbestos at two Texas airports.

Baron & Budd is justifiably proud of its considerable pro bono work, especially regarding constitutional issues and environmental regulatory issues, and its partnership with public interest and environmental groups. Brent Rosenthal, a Baron & Budd partner who oversees the firm's substantial appellate caseload, is one of several firm attorneys who have received national recognition. Trial Lawyers for Public Justice awarded Rosenthal its Public Justice Award in 1993 for his pro bono work representing the National Wildlife Federation in the infamous Exxon Valdez case. Rosenthal, who became an attorney "because of the opportunity to change the world for the better through reason, debate and persuasion rather than financial might or violence," is an adjunct lecturer at Southern Methodist University School of Law.

In 2000 *The National Law Journal* named firm founder Fred Baron as one of the "100 Most Influential Lawyers in the U.S." for his work to protect the rights of victims of asbestos and other toxic substances. Baron's work in helping shape 20th-century law led to his inclusion in a *Texas Lawyer* commemorative publication, *Legal Legends: A Century of Texas Law and Lawyering* (2000).

Lisa A. Blue, Ph.D., who has represented hundreds of victims of asbestos and other toxic substances for Baron & Budd, has received several important honors for her accomplishments in U.S. trial courts. The Texas Chapter of the American Board of Trial Advocates named her Trial Lawyer of the Year in 1999, and *The National Law Journal* named her one of the top 50 women litigators in the United States in 2002. Blue is also a licensed psychologist and published author. *D Magazine* named Blue and Baron as two of Dallas' best lawyers in 2001.

Baron & Budd has made a lasting mark in its work to defeat collusive class-action settlements for resolving grand-scale catastrophes. The firm won two landmark cases — *Amchem Products v. Windsor* (1997) and *Ortiz v. Fibreboard Corp.* (1999) — by convincing the U.S. Supreme Court to decertify nationwide class-action settlements involving the "future claims" of asbestos-related injuries or claims from people who later develop asbestos-related illnesses. The result guaranteed that injured victims can redeem their legal rights individually rather than as unwilling members of a large, national class action.

Environmental hazards will continue to be a significant part of American life, but Baron & Budd is bringing a great deal of legal expertise to the relationships between science and epidemiology and hazardous waste and disease. The firm has effected positive changes in laws regarding exposure to toxic substances. Fred Baron's founding philosophy — "do well by doing good" — endures.

Not certified by the Texas Board of Legal Specialization.
Results obtained depend on the facts of each case.

Baron & Budd, P.C. is the largest U.S. law firm to exclusively represent victims of exposure to asbestos and other toxic substances.

Lisa A. Blue, Ph.D. has represented hundreds of victims of asbestos and other toxic substances for Baron & Budd, and has been named one of the top 50 women litigators in the United States.

HUGHES & LUCE, LLP

HUGHES & LUCE HAS A HISTORY OF DEVELOPING innovative and lasting alliances with its clients. The firm pursues "first-ever" results that enable its clients to compete aggressively and to achieve their business objectives. The firm's strongest asset is the reputation it has for helping its clients succeed.

Hughes & Luce represented Hillwood in its development of the American Airlines Center and surrounding Victory project in Dallas.

Hughes & Luce has been providing outstanding legal representation to clients ranging from start-ups to worldwide leaders since its formation over 30 years ago, and has gained increasing recognition along the way. Its clients include industry leaders such as EDS, Ericsson, IBM, Wal-Mart, Perot Systems, Southwestern Bell, Dean Foods, American Airlines and Dell. The firm has represented several of these clients from their inception through their emergence among the most successful and innovative companies in the world. Gregg Engles, Chairman and CEO of Dean Foods, agrees: "Hughes & Luce has been with us every step of the way. Our company wouldn't be where it is today without them."

The firm understands that its success relies on its ability to provide exceptional service and dependable advice. Gil Friedlander, General Counsel of EDS, commented: "Hughes & Luce delivers for EDS again and again." As a result of its client focus, Hughes & Luce was ranked number one among Texas-based firms and seventh nationally in a client service survey conducted in 2001 by the BTI Consulting Group, an independent national market research and management-consulting firm. *The Survey of Client Service Performance for Law Firms* identified the 30 firms that are the "cream of the crop" in client service. In interviews with over 200 corporate counsel of Fortune 1000 companies, Hughes & Luce ranked as one of the firms that "have truly differentiated themselves in the eyes of their clients." Hughes & Luce's client service score was 83 percent higher than the second-place Texas-based finisher and almost four times better than the average score of all law firms nominated by clients. The firm's Managing Partner William McCormack states: "We are pleased with this recognition by Fortune 1000 companies of our commitment to superior service. We work with client teams to solve business challenges efficiently, and we try to bring more value to the client relationship than clients expect."

Hughes & Luce lawyers are at the top of their game. They are consistently recognized as "go-to" lawyers in Texas, the U.S. and, occasionally, beyond:

• Six Hughes & Luce lawyers are named in the 2002 edition of *Best Lawyers in America*, a semi-annual listing of lawyers chosen by their peers.
• The firm is listed in the 2002 edition of *The World's Leading Lawyers*.
• The *American Lawyer* recently cited the firm as one of the "Firms to Watch" in the U.S.

- Martindale Hubbell, a leading legal publication, lists Hughes & Luce in its current *Bar Register of Preeminent Attorneys.*
- *Texas Lawyer* named two Hughes & Luce attorneys as "Go-To" Lawyers in Texas in its 2002 survey.
- *D Magazine* ranked seven Hughes & Luce lawyers among the "Best Lawyers in Dallas" in 2001.
- Four Hughes & Luce associates are listed as "Best Lawyers Under 40 in Dallas" in a *D Magazine* peer survey.

The firm is known for its academic excellence and was one of the first law firms in Dallas to recruit nationally, starting in the early 1970s. The firm has continued its tradition of building a strong practice and firm culture from the bottom up. Its entering lawyers are generally viewed as among the best and brightest in the U.S.

Hughes & Luce lawyers have also served as visiting professors at the Kennedy School of Government at Harvard, at The University of Texas School of Business, at the law schools of The University of Texas, Baylor, Southern Methodist and other institutions. Its lawyers are frequently published and quoted in legal, industry and trade journals and other publications.

Hughes & Luce lawyers and alumni include federal and state trial court judges, the Chief Justice of the Texas Supreme Court, an Associate Justice of the Texas Supreme Court, the Texas Attorney General and Democratic and Republican candidates for governor. Additionally, the firm has provided leadership to national, state and local bar organizations; the firm's ranks include a former President of the State Bar of Texas, three former Presidents of the Dallas Bar Association, members of the Board of Governors and House of Delegates of the American Bar Association, members of the Boards of Directors of the State Bar of Texas and Dallas Bar Association and Section leaders and committee chairs for all of these organizations.

Hughes & Luce continues its long-standing tradition of public service and recently won the President's Award of the State Bar of Texas for *pro bono* service, the Bar's most prestigious award. This was the first President's Award honoring a firm rather than an individual lawyer in the 60-year history of the award. The American Bar Association has also given the firm national recognition, and the Dallas Bar Association recently named Hughes & Luce as "Law Firm of the Year" for its *pro bono* activities. The firm's commitment to community service is substantial, with lawyers serving as founders, board members and officers of leading community, arts and cultural organizations and other charities.

Hughes & Luce operates in eight formal Practice Groups: Business Reorganization and Bankruptcy, Corporate and Securities, Labor and Employment, Outsourcing and Technology, Public Policy, Real Estate, Tax, and Trial and Dispute Resolution. The firm also combines the expertise of its lawyers into multi-disciplinary client and industry teams designed to identify legal and business needs and to develop service strategies that provide exceptional support to the client. The firm's multi-disciplinary teams include: Antitrust, Business Fraud, Construction and Architecture, Employee Benefits, Environmental, Energy and Natural Resources, Estate Planning, Hospitality and Hotels, Insurance, International, Intellectual Property, Internet and E-Commerce, Land Use, Probate, Professional Liability, Property Rights, Securities Litigation, and Technology-Based Business.

Hughes & Luce's clients count on the firm for several things: its entrepreneurial spirit and innovative problem-solving, its expertise and knowledge of the clients" businesses, and its dedication to their success. Jay Fitzsimmons, Treasurer of Wal-Mart commented: "Nothing is too complex for them." Hughes & Luce places its clients' objectives first and always seeks to deliver the solutions they need.

Not certified by the Texas Board of Legal Specialization.
Results obtained depend on the facts of each case.

HUITT-ZOLLARS, INC.

WHEREVER YOU GO IN DALLAS YOU'RE LIKELY to touch or be touched by the work of Huitt-Zollars, Inc. If you travel by train, plane, bus, automobile, or even by trolley, you'll witness an example of a Huitt-Zollars project. If you live, shop or work in uptown, downtown or suburbia, you'll encounter the firm's design influence on everyday life.

The idea for Huitt-Zollars began from a friendship born more than 30 years ago. While working for the same engineering firm early in their careers, Larry Huitt, a structural engineer, and Robert Zollars, a civil engineer, became respected colleagues. Although they initially pursued different career paths, their shared business values and a mutual love of golf soon developed into a partnership that would launch this Dallas-based engineering and architecture firm.

When Huitt and Zollars decided to form their own company in 1975, they composed a set of core values to build their business around — values that continue to be the backbone of the company today. Values that focus on employee and client satisfaction guide the daily operations of the firm through quality, integrity and uncompromised personal service.

Today, Huitt-Zollars epitomizes the vision of its founders. From day one, the company has followed this vision unerringly and has grown into one of the largest, most respected engineering firms in Texas. The company's reputation for quality performance has made it the recipient of a large number of repeat assignments, a key indicator of client trust.

CORPORATE GROWTH

In the early years, Huitt and Zollars concentrated on civil and structural engineering. Business was slow in the United States, and the firm decided to seek work overseas in Nigeria, Africa. The new entrepreneurs gained valuable experience on contracts and learned quickly how to pursue and work on large projects. They gained invaluable experience working with people from different cultures. There were some business perils in working outside of the United States. Nigeria was so far behind technologically that the engineers had to import a suitcase full of calculators because none were available in the area.

By 1977 the economy had improved and the firm was again concentrating on work in the United States. Land planning was added to its list of services. Huitt-Zollars began to expand in the 80s, adding services and opening new offices. The company's growth was generally premised on moving into a new area to support a current client's project in that area. In that way, Huitt-Zollars provided outstanding service to its clients, while guaranteeing that its new offices would be self-supporting before they were started.

The firm opened an office in Houston in 1981. The following year the firm branched into public sector work. Between 1983 and 1988 Huitt-Zollars opened offices in Fort Worth, Phoenix and Tustin, California. In 1985 the firm won a significant multiyear contract with DFW International Airport, beginning a trend that would see the company become significantly involved in transportation in the D/FW Metroplex.

In 1989 the firm converted its profit-sharing plan, established in 1981, to an Employee Stock

Dallas Area Rapid Transit

Ownership Plan so employees could share in profits and in the growth of the company through the benefits of ownership.

In 1990 the firm won the contract for the Dallas Area Rapid Transit Light Rail Starter System. The contract involved development of a 20.5-mile, $905 million LRT rail transit system, an 11-mile commuter rail system and related transit mobility projects. Its work would eventually win the company many local and national awards, including a U.S. Department of Transportation Honor Award, which represents the highest quality of design based on international standards. Through the years, the firm has won many design awards including the Eminent Conceptor Award in 1997 given by the American Council of Engineering Companies for the best project in Texas. This award was yet another prestigious honor for its lead role in the DART project.

Huitt-Zollars made its first major acquisition in 1993, purchasing Yandell and Hiller, Inc., merging the new company with its existing Fort Worth office. The acquisition added architecture, mechanical engineering and electrical engineering to the firm's repertoire and expanded the company's involvement with federal contracts.

By decade's end, Huitt-Zollars had opened offices in El Paso, Denton, and Austin, Texas; Albuquerque, New Mexico; and Seattle and Tacoma, Washington. An acquisition of two offices in California furthered Huitt-Zollars' expertise in land development, giving the firm entrance to the master-planned community market in southern California. This allowed Huitt-Zollars to better serve clients throughout the country in this growing field.

CIVIC ACTIVITIES

Longtime believers that individuals should contribute to the communities in which they live and work, both Zollars and Huitt are active in many civic and professional organizations. Additionally, the two are active with local charities, both on a personal level and through their company. Huitt retired in 2001 but remains involved in the company as a member of its board of directors.

Huitt-Zollars has endowed scholarships at the alma maters of Huitt (Texas A&M) and Zollars (SMU) to assist engineering students with financial commitments. The firm also contributes to many other organizations, including the American Cancer Society, Bryan's House, American

DFW International Airport

Diabetes Association, Junior Achievement of Dallas and the Dallas Museum of Art.

PROJECT HIGHLIGHTS

Dallas-area projects include DART, DFW International Airport, President George Bush Turnpike, McKinney Avenue Trolley and public infrastructure design work for the Uptown/McKinney Avenue area, State-Thomas Neighborhood and the Central Business District.

Throughout Texas and the western United States, examples of Huitt-Zollars' work are plentiful and have greatly improved the quality of life for local citizenry. Throughout the years adherence to the company's core values has yielded significant returns in the local landscape through projects ranging from public works and transportation-oriented projects to urban/suburban mixed-use developments.

State-Thomas Neighborhood

RTKL

RTKL STRIVES TO CREATE GREAT URBAN DISTRICTS with animated public spaces and street life. The firm's reputation for urban design, architecture and mixed use planning is evidenced by a portfolio of projects that meld retail, entertainment, residential hospitality and health care uses into holistic environments. RTKL's work celebrates the aspirations and inclinations of the consumer, addresses the need for social interaction and capitalizes on the vitality of an enriched environment and experience.

These attributes are nowhere more true than at Mockingbird Station, acclaimed by David Dillon, architectural critic for *The Dallas Morning News*, as "An Urban Space that Sings." As part of its further efforts to revitalize Dallas, RTKL is converting The Mercantile Complex into a residential/retail project to help animate Main Street with 24/7 activity. RTKL's commitment to creating places where people want to be is demonstrated over the greater Metroplex area in Legacy Town Center, the Charles W. Eisemann Center for the Performing Arts, and the transit-related development plans for Galatyn Park, the Northwest Corridor and Las Colinas Urban Center.

RTKL's commitment to downtown Dallas is seen in the firm's move into Republic Center. A vacant bank lobby became a highly animated space teeming with ideas generated by more than 200 highly creative individuals. The Dallas location, RTKL's first regional office, was established in 1979.

Archibald Rogers and Francis Taliaferro founded RTKL in Annapolis, Maryland, in 1946. Rogers provided the guiding vision by articulating a broad concern for community development based on an open, rational process and community involvement. Taliaferro complemented these concerns by paying close attention to each client's unique needs. By the late 1950s Rogers had gained regional attention on planning matters and agreed to head the Baltimore business community's effort to rebuild the deteriorating city core. The small firm developed an expertise in designing schools, libraries and other small-scale buildings. In 1949 the firm joined with Charles Lamb, whose strong design sense established the aesthetic underpinnings for the firm's architecture. George Kostritsky joined shortly thereafter as its fourth partner. A talented urban designer, this charismatic Harvard professor recruited a cadre of talented architects and planners who were to become the firm's next generation of design leaders.

RTKL became recognized as an innovative leader in planning and urban design, resulting in commissions for downtown centers for Cincinnati, Hartford and more than a dozen other cities across the United States. What had begun as a modest architectural practice based on educational work evolved during the 1970s into a nationally recognized planning and urban design firm. It was also a decade in which the firm was able to diversify into new areas that ultimately would become the core of its practice.

Diversification was a key management strategy to achieve growth and stability in

John Castorina, Wayne Barger, Bill Persefield, Mark Lauterbach, Tom Brink, Curt Whelan, Todd Lundgren, Brad Barker, Lance Josal, Paris Rutherford, Tom Witt. Not pictured: Don DeBord, Randy Stone, Jeff Gunning

Dynamic Dallas: An Illustrated History

an inherently cyclical industry. After RTKL diversified its services and building types, the firm began to expand geographically to become a national and international firm. The company's strategy for regional expansion was to select areas of the United States with high growth rates and in which existing clients desired a presence. RTKL created core teams of key principals and staff committed to the company's management and design philosophy to establish the new offices.

For over 50 years RTKL has played a lead role in the revitalization of cities around the world, beginning with Baltimore's Charles Center in the 1950s. An international, knowledge-based firm serving a global, idea-driven industry, RTKL has grown and adapted its broad spectrum of integrated services to meet and anticipate client needs. Today's market demands specialization and expertise. RTKL anticipated this trend and restructured itself in the mid-1990s into specialized design divisions that include retail/entertainment, residential, hospitality, corporate, health care and public/institutional. Each of these divisions provides RTKL's clients with expertise typically associated with a small, boutique design firm yet draws on the large company's resources to provide a full range of services within each specialty.

"Our ever-changing world requires strategic thinking and ideas that respond to economic, political and social forces," says Lance Josal AIA, director of RTKL's Dallas office. "There's renewed interest from the public sector in investing in downtown cultural resources, entertainment and sports venues, and neighborhoods. Young professionals want to cut down on commuting time and both live and work in an urban pedestrian-oriented environment. Suburban empty-nesters are returning to the city. Suburbs are perceived as soulless, and smart-growth initiatives that resonate with the environmentally aware are cropping up throughout the U.S."

RTKL is partnering with clients to create the next generation of new urban districts, mixed-use developments, new concept retail/entertainment destinations, live/work environments and traditional neighborhood developments. The "big picture" ideals of urban planning are the backbone of the firm's design philosophy. It's a mindset that takes buildings beyond isolated objects in space and considers how they fit into the broader context.

Interior, Dallas office

Responding to demand for urban and suburban development, the firm is collaborating with private developers, city and suburban governments, transit agencies and new urban warriors to create 24/7 environments that promote a sense of community and pride of place. The highly successful and award-winning Addison Circle north of Dallas is an example of RTKL's ability to create financially sound, sustainable and enjoyable environments.

The firm's work with clients worldwide — Disney, Hyatt, Marriott, Forest City, Simon, Daewoo, Mitsui and Kajima to mention a few — together with its partnerships with cities and towns throughout the United States, illustrates that RTKL is focused on creating sustainable places that are based on financial, political and social success through a solution-oriented approach grounded in creativity, market reality and client/stakeholder input.

RTKL is an ideas-based creative firm that offers the most comprehensive integrated end-to-end planning and design services available in the market today, providing trend-setting ideas in urban districts.

Interior, Dallas office

SNELLING AND SNELLING INC.

MORE THAN A HALF-CENTURY AGO, SNELLING and Snelling Inc. began as a small mom-and-pop staffing firm in Philadelphia, Pennsylvania. There was no sophisticated technology to perform the work necessary to match the candidates with jobs; just lots of paper and elbow grease.

It was 1951 when Lou and Gwen Snelling first opened the doors of the business. There were no computers to ease the job. There were just a lot of filing cards that contained the company names and specific skills of the employees they were seeking, as well as those that contained the candidates and their skills. The company started out by placing everything from clerical to professional. It all started with the vision of helping others achieve the success they desire by putting America to work and becoming one of the largest staffing companies in the country.

Shortly after the business was formed, Gwen Snelling called her sons, Bob Snelling Sr. and Ray Snelling, to help run the business. Lou Snelling's health was failing, but the desire to keep the business in the family gave an early birth to the second generation's involvement. Bob Sr. left his engineering studies at Penn State, and along with Bob's young bride, Joan, and brother, Ray, they helped build the business.

Within a year or two after the business began, Snelling created an innovative concept of specialty desks. Employment counselors, as they were called back then, would specialize in placing people within a particular field. There were counselors who ran sales desks, manufacturing desks and clerical/manufacturing desks, among others.

Snelling and Snelling Inc. quickly grew to become a nationally recognized household name as the company began franchising its proven successful system to those seeking to become independent business owners. The first franchise was sold in 1956.

During its first 50 years, the company would ultimately bring millions of prospective employees and companies together. Today, Snelling Personnel Services ranks among the largest staffing firms in the nation, with a network of more than 300 offices across the country.

In 1990 five third-generation family members joined the business and remain actively involved in the company's leadership and day-to-day operations. This family commitment is one of the keys to the family-owned company's 50th anniversary celebration in 2001.

When Bob Snelling Sr. began making his plans to transition into retirement, the third-generation of Snellings were already helping with the business. The family decided at that time to move its corporate headquarters from Sarasota, Florida. After an extensive relocation study, Dallas was selected for many reasons. The business infrastructure in Dallas was attractive. It was a move to accommodate all of the company's traveling field employees more efficiently, as well as to experience the synergy of the prosperous business community that Dallas offers. Snelling maintains a rich presence in Dallas, with 14 offices in the Dallas-Fort Worth area and more than 100 employees working in the corporate offices. The company's goal is to continue to provide the

Snelling and Snelling Inc. marked its 50th year in business in 2001. Snelling's board of directors includes (left to right) Tim Loncharich, Rick Spragins, Bob Paulk, Linda Paulk, Bob Snelling Jr. and Rusty Crews.

very finest in staffing services, maintaining the strength of its brand name and the reputation that the company has built.

"Snelling has grown into one of the only true full-service staffing companies offering a diverse range of services from career placement, temporary, temp-to-hire, contract, payroll and other consulting services in the area of human resources," says Linda S. Paulk, President of Snelling and Snelling Inc.

One of Snelling's greatest assets is the strength of its extensive training resources, providing a thorough understanding of the Snelling system. Whether by logging on to the Snelling Virtual Classroom in cyberspace or attending Snelling University in Dallas, Snelling's staffing professionals are provided with the most up-to-date training available in the industry.

From its state-of-the-art facility in Dallas, Texas, Snelling University provides basic and advanced operations and leadership training for all employees when they first join Snelling as well as offering refresher courses and continuing education. This kind of top-of-the-line training promotes consistent service for all of its client companies.

Because Snelling is committed to using technology to maximize the level of success, it is the only company in the industry to offer an online virtual classroom for interactive training. This classroom can be accessed 24 hours a day, seven days a week for further review of the archived informative sessions. Such leading-edge training is a valuable benefit to the client companies since they can be assured that when working with Snelling they are working with knowledgeable professionals who are prepared to provide insightful, modern staffing solutions.

"At Snelling, our vision of building upon the rich history of our brand name and proven operating system is realized by the artful blending of innovation, experience, technology and ethics. Our passion is to provide an outstanding service experience to each client and employee we bring together," says Bob Snelling Jr., Snelling's chief information officer.

In today's tight labor market, Snelling recognizes that a company needs the right tools to find the right people. Snelling designs its solutions to meet the specific needs of its clients as well as finding the right employees or the job. Snelling serves businesses of all sizes, from large to small.

Snelling has succeeded because its progressive environment attracts high-caliber candidates. State-of-the-art systems, dedicated customer service, strict ethical standards, professionalism, team spirit and enthusiasm are among the many factors that contribute to Snelling's renowned reputation.

"When I think of the effect this company has had on America, sometimes I just sit and I shake my head. To think that this could all come from that tiny office in Philadelphia — who would have imagined my parents' business would have such an impact on so many people?" says Robert O. Snelling Sr., retired chairman of the board.

The Snelling family's original commitment to helping others achieve success remains at the very core of Snelling services. To that end, the company and its employees are actively involved in the support of local charities including the Children's Cancer Fund, American Cancer Society, Children's Advocacy, local food banks, the Crystal Charity Ball, Bryan's House, The Family Place and Captain Hope's Kids.

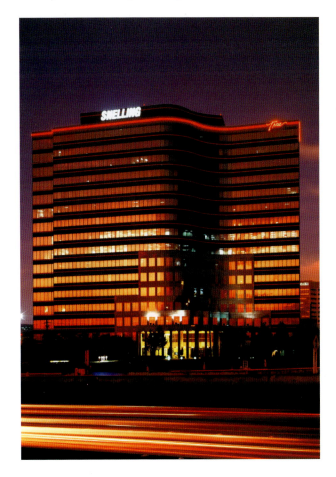

The national headquarters for Snelling and Snelling Inc. has been in Dallas since 1992.

STRASBURGER & PRICE, L.L.P.

HENRY W. STRASBURGER AND HOBERT PRICE, with three other associates, withdrew from their then-current firm in 1939 to form Strasburger, Price, Holland, Kelton & Miller. The new firm began its practice on the 10th floor of downtown Dallas' noted Magnolia Building in January 1940. Over 60 years later the firm has grown to over 220 attorneys serving clients in more than 30 practice areas in offices in Dallas; Austin; Houston; San Antonio; Washington, D.C.; and Mexico City. The practice began primarily as an insurance defense firm and now provides Fortune 1000 companies and corporate and institutional clients litigation, transactional and corporate legal assistance.

Mr. Strasburger and Mr. Price both graduated from the University of Texas Law School in 1921. Thomas, Milam, Gormley & Touchstone immediately hired Price. The same firm hired Strasburger a few months later. The two attorneys had contrasting styles, with Hobert Price using a steel-trap memory to swing decisions by instantly citing case precedents, and Henry Strasburger taking the more theatrical approach in the courtroom. The combination of Strasburger & Price's approach to law drove the firm's growth from the original seven to the size of the firm today.

Two of the firm's original founders from 1939 were Philip L. Kelton and Mark Martin. Kelton was a graduate of Harvard Law School, and his progressive thinking led to the creation of the firm's business practice in the 1950s. Mark Martin developed a nationwide reputation defending lawsuits and serving as counsel for insurance companies. His tireless work with the insurance industry is credited with building the firm's defense practice to the largest of any Texas firm. Martin was president of the Dallas Bar Association, chairman of the board of the State Bar of Texas and an official in the American Bar Association.

Early in the history of the firm, Henry Strasburger, Phil Kelton and Mark Martin developed a firm philosophy that included a code of fair dealing with opposing counsel. The Strasburger philosophy has been to defend its client's position, but to always do so with courtesy to the other parties, to make agreements with opposing counsel whenever possible, and to build a firm where every lawyer's reputation is above reproach. Phil Kelton once said, "The firm's word is its bond."

Strasburger & Price boasts 12 members of the American College of Trial Lawyers, four past presidents of the Dallas Bar Association, two former presidents of the Texas Association of Defense Counsel and two that served on rules advisory

David Kitner, David Meyercord, Jerry Beane, Gary Crapster, and Robert Thomas (seated)

panels to the Texas Supreme Court and the U.S. Court of Appeals for the Fifth Circuit. These accomplishments illustrate the firm's leadership in the legal community.

The firm values community service and expresses this belief through pro bono legal counseling, financial support, volunteerism, event sponsorship and membership on local boards of directors. Organizations the firm supports include the Susan G. Komen Breast Cancer Foundation, for which it provides pro bono counsel on matters such as advice on intellectual property issues. Strasburger & Price sponsors the Greater Dallas Community Relations Commission's Thomas C. Unis Valuing Diversity Award, an award named for Tom Unis, a later partner of the firm who founded the commission in 1969. Strasburger & Price is the title sponsor of a Family Violence Prevention Services/San Antonio Battered Women's Shelter event that raises critical funds for the shelter.

In honor of its 60th anniversary in 2000, the firm was a corporate donor in the project to restore the Pegasus that graced the top of the firm's first building, the Holtze/Magnolia building in downtown Dallas. The city of Dallas sold the building in 1979 but retained ownership of the Flying Red Horse, a symbol of Dallas and a beacon to travelers when it towered 400 feet above street level in 1922. Strasburger & Price donated to the restoration project to celebrate its 60th year and to restore the Pegasus to its place, soaring atop Strasburger & Price's first office building.

From humble beginnings, Strasburger & Price has taken flight and expanded its legal services not only in Dallas, but nationally and internationally as well. Firm members are constantly pursuing new horizons on behalf of their clients while holding fast to their rich heritage in the city of Dallas.

Tom Unis

Henry Strasburger

Not certified by the Texas Board of Legal Specialization.
Results obtained depend on the facts of each case.

HALFF ASSOCIATES, INC.

DRIVE ALONG THE MAIN ARTERIES OF Dallas-Fort Worth and it is impossible to escape the influence of Halff Associates, Inc. The company's name may not be plastered on signs, but look deeper into some of the area's grandest business parks, largest waterways and intricate highways and it is apparent that Halff Associates has left its mark on North Texas.

Founded on December 4, 1950, by Albert H. Halff, the first office was a one-man operation located at Dallas' Snyder Plaza. Halff is considered a pioneer, opening an environmental engineering firm nearly 20 years ahead of its time. The company has since developed into a multi-disciplinary firm offering a range of services, including civil engineering, infrastructure/site development, transportation engineering, architecture, MEP engineering, structural engineering, subsurface utility engineering, planning/landscape architecture, right-of-way acquisition, construction management, surveying and water resources.

Halff has grown from its modest beginnings to serve the mightiest of the public and private sector in the United States, Central America and the Caribbean from offices in Dallas, Fort Worth, Houston, Austin and McAllen, Texas. Some high-profile clients include FEMA, Corps of Engineers, Department of the Navy and Texas Department of Transportation.

The American Airlines Center, home of the NHL's Dallas Stars and the NBA's Dallas Mavericks, has Halff Associates' stamp all over it. From demolition to site clean-up, utilities to tree-lined streets, Halff worked on all aspects of the arena site, converting it from an old railroad yard and electrical generating plant to a showplace for the city. Halff Associates was awarded the Environmental Protection Agency's Region Six Phoenix Award, a national award for Brownfields clean-up, for the arena site works.

Other noted Dallas-area projects include the civil infrastructure for the consolidated rental car facility at DFW Airport, construction management for the President George Bush Turnpike, and design of the Cole Park Detention Vault, which can hold 650 million gallons of storm water underground.

Halff's current floodplain studies include re-mapping Houston after the disastrous year 2000 floods and design of real-time flood protection systems for the Lower Colorado River in Texas. Halff's Implementation Plan for the Dallas Trinity River Corridor, talked about on the national level, proposes unprecedented development of major lakes and recreational amenities within the Trinity Floodway in the shadow of downtown Dallas.

Halff Associates has grown steadily through the past two decades and into the early 2000s. The firm is consistently ranked in *Engineering News Record* magazine's list of the top 500 design firms in the United States and is ranked by *Dallas Business Journal* as the second-largest engineering firm in the Dallas-Fort Worth Metroplex. With 12,000 major projects in its portfolio, Halff Associates is ready to meet the challenges of a rapidly changing world. By offering a comprehensive range of services and embracing a philosophy that emphasizes integrity, technical knowledge and commitment to client service, the company intends to remain the first choice for clients with unique needs.

The Cole Park Detention Vault prevents flooding by storing stormwater.

Dallas Public Library

QUALITY OF *Life*

*M*EDICAL, EDUCATIONAL AND RELIGIOUS INSTITUTIONS, AS WELL AS RECREATION-ORIENTED COMPANIES, CONTRIBUTE TO THE QUALITY OF LIFE ENJOYED BY DALLAS RESIDENTS AND VISITORS TO THE AREA.

BAYLOR HEALTH CARE SYSTEM

A Century of Healing

WITH THE PHRASE "CARING FOR GENERATIONS, a century of healing," 2003 marks 100 years of Baylor Health Care System providing nationally recognized health care for the people of Dallas and the entire north Texas area.

In 1903, with major support from such men as George W. Truett, D.D., the pastor of the First Baptist Church in Dallas; Charles M. Rosser, M.D., the founder of the Baylor College of Medicine; and Col. C.C. Slaughter, a respected businessman and cattle baron; as well as a commitment from the Baptist General Convention of Texas to support and administer the hospital, the Texas Baptist Memorial Sanitarium opened in a 14-room renovated house on Junius Street near downtown Dallas. And from that hospital, now Baylor University Medical Center, emerged Baylor Health Care System.

Baylor Health Care System's mission includes the same commitments as the mission of that first Baylor hospital when it began caring for patients a century ago: "Founded as a Christian ministry of healing, Baylor Health Care System exists to serve all people through exemplary health care, education, research and community service."

The Baylor system was formally established in 1981, and its corporate offices are located on the campus of Baylor University Medical Center. Baylor University Medical Center was the first hospital to be part of the system, but Baylor Medical Center at Ennis and Baylor Medical Center at Grapevine were added soon afterward. Baylor Medical Center at Waxahachie joined the system in 1983. Since that time Baylor Health Care System continues to steadily grow and now has owned, leased or affiliated hospitals in Dallas, Fort Worth, Garland, Grapevine, Irving, Coppell, Denison, Waxahachie and Sulphur Springs. Baylor Health Care System's most recent addition is All Saints Health Care System in Tarrant County, which joined the Baylor system in January 2002.

Anchored by Baylor University Medical Center, located near downtown Dallas, Baylor Health Care System includes 15 hospitals in North Texas and 32 primary care, family health and senior health centers. It also encompasses physician centers and practices, specialty centers, rehabilitation clinics, ambulatory surgery centers and the Baylor Research Institute.

Baylor Research Institute conducts more than 300 active, experimental research protocols annually. Research programs currently are underway in the areas of cardiology, oncology, organ transplantation, metabolic disease and others.

Baylor Institute for Rehabilitation serves as the hub for physical rehabilitation services for the system, providing a specialized inpatient and outpatient rehabilitation program for persons who have experienced a

Texas Baptist Memorial Sanitarium's three founders, staff and supporters gathered in 1904 outside the original hospital for a groundbreaking ceremony for a new building. Col. C.C. Slaughter, the hospital's major donor, turned the first spade of dirt. Dr. George W. Truett, who challenged the citizens of Dallas to build "a great humanitarian hospital," is seated on the left end of the bench. Dr. Charles M. Rosser, the young physician who had the vision for a modern hospital for Dallas and enlisted others to make it a reality, is shown standing in the middle of the back row.

traumatic injury to the spinal cord or brain. It also offers rehabilitation services for people who have had a stroke, joint replacement, or other orthopaedic and neurological impairments that require physical rehabilitation.

With more than 20 years in health care management, Joel Allison came to Baylor Health Care System in 1993. In 2000 he was named president and CEO. As Allison leads Baylor Health Care System into the 21st century, his primary responsibility is to help Baylor attain its vision of becoming the world's "most trusted source of comprehensive health services." And to do so, he continues to develop Baylor as a patient-focused health care delivery system and clinical enterprise offering prevention and wellness, physician, outpatient, acute hospital and other services that are geographically dispersed, yet efficient and fully coordinated.

In 2001 Baylor Health Care System had more than 74,000 admissions, including newborns, 227,000 emergency department visits and 444,000 outpatient visits that contributed to a total operating revenue of $1.2 billion. The community benefit preliminary report in 2001 to the state of Texas stated the system provided community programs and activities valued at $133 million. These statistics represent the programs developed to support the mission of Baylor Heath Care System — to serve all people through health care, education, research and community service.

BAYLOR UNIVERSITY MEDICAL CENTER

"Is it not now time to build a great humanitarian hospital, one to which men of all creeds and those of none may come with equal confidence?"

—George W. Truett, D.D., 1903, co-founder of Baylor University Medical Center

Baylor University Medical Center began with just 25 beds in 1903 as Texas Baptist Memorial Sanitarium. When its new 250-bed hospital was completed and opened to patients in 1909, it was often referred to as the Johns Hopkins of the Southwest because of its modern facility.

The hospital's name changed to Baylor Hospital in 1921 when Baylor University, a Baptist higher-education institution in Waco, Texas, accredited all the schools that were on the hospital's campus. Those schools included Baylor College of Medicine, Baylor College of Dentistry,

Joel T. Allison, FACHE
President and CEO

Baylor University School of Nursing and Baylor School of Pharmacy. In 1959 the name of the hospital changed for a final time to Baylor University Medical Center to better reflect the multiple hospitals, specialty centers and services of the downtown campus.

By continually providing innovative health care, Baylor has earned a national reputation for many medical firsts. In 1929 the nation's first prepaid insurance plan was developed and implemented at Baylor Hospital as "the Baylor Plan," the predecessor of the "Blue Cross Plan." In 1938 a physician at Baylor invented the ADTEVAC machine that dried blood plasma so it could be stored for later use without refrigeration. This medical invention saved thousands of U.S. soldiers' lives during World War II. Baylor also was the founding place of the American Association of Blood Banks in 1947.

In 1980 Baylor developed a plan called "Two Days Alternative" to help ease the shortage of nurses impacting the medical center at that time. The plan allowed nurses to work two 12-hours shifts on the weekend and get paid as a full-time employee. It brought Baylor attention from hundreds of other hospitals in the United States and many hospitals in other countries wanting to copy Baylor's plan.

Texas Baptist Memorial Sanitarium's new building had 250 beds in six wards and 114 private rooms and was considered the most modern medical facility in the city when it opened in 1909.

Florence Nightingale Maternity Hospital was built in 1937 on Baylor's campus, but due to the "baby boom" after World War II, it was torn down in 1956 to make room for the construction of a larger women's and children's hospital. In 1959 that new hospital, now Hoblitzelle Hospital, opened.

Other medical firsts that brought prominence to Baylor University Medical Center include: implanting the Southwest's first pacemaker (1960), performing North Texas' first marrow transplant (1983), performing Texas' first liver transplant (1984), performing Texas' first unrelated donor bone marrow transplant (1988).

Surgeons on the medical staff at Baylor University Medical Center performed the world's first extracorporeal perfusion (bridge to transplantation) using a genetically engineered pig liver (1997).

Baylor also has garnered local and national recognition because of the wide range of medical and specialty services and centers it offers.

One specialty center, the James M. and Dorothy D. Collins Women and Children's Center, offers gynecology, obstetrics, pediatrics, prenatal diagnosis, high-risk pregnancy care, gynecologic oncology, breast care and reproductive services. This area also encompasses a Family Resource Center offering classes on a variety of topics. The Prenatal Diagnostic Center in this area offers obstetric genetic services like screening, counseling, amniocentesis, ultrasound and percutaneous umbilical cord sampling. The Neonatal Intensive Care Unit gives premature and seriously ill newborns advanced life-support services and technologies.

Our Children's House at Baylor is a 35-bed specialty care center offering a palliative program for children with chronic or terminal illness. It serves as a cost-effective bridge between acute care and release from the hospital for children in a rehabilitation program or in need of ventilator assistance, as well as a transitional program to train families in care giving before returning home.

Baylor University Medical Center is recognized across the United States for its heart and vascular programs. In 2001 Solucient recognized the center as one of the top 100 cardiovascular programs in the country. Its facilities include the largest cardiac catheterization laboratories in the Dallas area performing the most procedures in North Texas, and a cardiac transplant program. Baylor's vascular surgeons perform procedures such as complex renal surgery, complex extracranial cerebrovascular surgery and complex aneurysm surgery.

Baylor began a heart transplant program in 1986. In 1996 Baylor and the University of Texas Southwestern Medical Center formed the Baylor-UT Southwestern

Heart and Lung Transplant Program. Since 1999, these programs have achieved a 90-percent-or-better one-year survival rate.

The Baylor Regional Transplant Institute is one of the nation's top transplant facilities and has provided care and treatment for more than 5,500 transplant recipients since 1983. The transplants include blood, marrow and solid organ including liver, kidney, heart and lung.

The Baylor-Charles A. Sammons Cancer Center opened in 1976 and treats all forms of cancer with an emphasis on breast and prostate cancer, and blood and marrow transplantation. The cancer center participates in many clinical trials, which gives patients access to advanced cancer treatment, including new immuno therapies and gene therapy trials. The W.H. and Peggy Smith Baylor-Sammons Breast Center provides a range of services for patients with breast cancer and those with benign breast health concerns.

In 1998 Baylor established the limb salvage program, another specialized program. This program treats patients with complex orthopaedic injuries and conditions, such as severally crushed bones, severed limbs and hands, fractured bones that won't heal due to infection or osteoporosis, and bone malignancies and limbs that healed in incorrect positions.

Since 1993 Baylor University Medical Center has been recognized by *U.S. News and World Report* in the "America's Best Hospital" guide. The year 2002 marked a decade of national recognition with Baylor named in the guide and ranked among the top 50 hospitals. In 2002, for the third year Baylor Health Care System was named one of the nation's "most wired" hospitals and health systems in the *Journal of the American Hospital Association, Hospitals and Health Networks.*

Dallas-area residents voted Baylor University Medical Center the most preferred hospital and hospital with the best image and reputation in a 2001 poll conducted by the National Research Corporation. In the same poll, the medical center ranked first

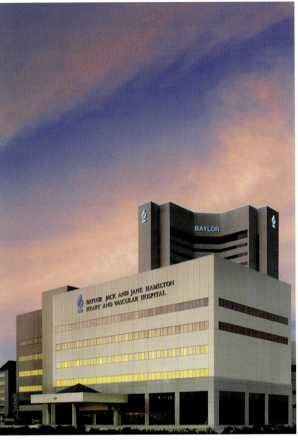

The Baylor Jack and Jane Hamilton Heart and Vascular Hospital at Baylor University Medical Center opened in April 2002 as a 50-bed specialty hospital dedicated to heart and vascular care.

and was described as having the best doctors and nurses in the city of Dallas.

Baylor is proud of its reputation for quality care and its employees, who go above and beyond what is required, to provide quality care to its patients and the community it serves.

Baylor University Medical Center's campus, located two miles east of downtown Dallas, encompasses six hospitals and several specialty centers.

Quality of Life

DALLAS COUNTY COMMUNITY COLLEGE DISTRICT

REMEMBER THE 1960S? LOVE BEADS AND GO-GO boots... the age of drugs, sex and rock' n roll... war protests, peace marches and assassinations... space exploration, the New Society and — yes — the Dallas County Community College District.

Thirty-five years ago, during the turmoil and triumphs that enthralled a nation, Dallas-area leaders envisioned a city, community and county of well-educated, productive citizens who would lead the metroplex into the next century. They knew that progress, profit, culture and expansion would depend on an educated work force, and their top priority was access: schools close to all residents; educational opportunities that would take students from where they were to where they wanted to go in their careers; and links to additional education, employment, work force development and lifelong learning.

More than 1 million students later, DCCCD serves people of all ages from all walks of life who simply want to succeed both personally and professionally. Since 1965 the district's campuses have welcomed high school students and adults whose common goal is to earn a degree or a certificate and to use that knowledge to better themselves and their communities. DCCCD — formerly the Dallas County Junior College District — celebrated its 35th anniversary in 2000-2001 and continues to expand as the needs of its students continue to grow.

Students on campus

Multimedia technology

FIRST STEPS

During the 1960s, when the United States underwent a cultural, environmental and political revolution of its own, Dallas-area leaders knew what they wanted: to establish a system of colleges that would meet the educational needs of the people who lived in Dallas and Dallas County. A virtual "Who's Who" of Dallas supported the establishment of the Dallas County Junior College District — individuals like R.L. Thornton Jr. and Margaret McDermott, who eventually served as the first chair and vice chair of the district's board of trustees, respectively.

The district was founded in May 1965 after citizens voted to create DCJCD and approved a $41.5 million bond package to finance it. During its first seven years the district welcomed students to four campuses, beginning with El Centro College in downtown Dallas. After an additional $85 million in bonds were sold in 1972, DCCCD'S other three campuses were added. That same year the district adopted a new name and became a community college system to reflect its philosophy that all seven colleges were community institutions. Throughout its formative years the district received critical support from the business and civic communities, and leaders scouted the entire country for the best people and locations as DCCCD established itself and its mission to educate citizens.

DCCCD's purpose is to offer educational opportunities in several forms: an associate's degree in either arts or sciences that comprises freshman and sophomore courses and which enables students to transfer to other colleges and universities; one or two-year technical career programs with certification; and adult education programs that include work force development, continuing education, and literacy and other basic skills programs for adults.

While the seven colleges in DCCCD offer a variety of programs and options, they each focus on creating an educational program designed for the individual student. With the help of taxpayers and funding from the Texas Legislature, the district continues to keep tuition rates low to help reduce financial barriers to higher education.

ACCESS CONTINUES TO BE THE DRIVING FORCE FOR DCCCD.

SEVEN SOLUTIONS TO LEARNING

From urban sidewalks to natural habitats, DCCCD's seven colleges throughout Dallas County provide a unique set of learning environments and educational programs. There's something for everyone at a Dallas County Community College.

Take El Centro, for example — the district's first college — which opened in 1966 and offers residents and downtown employees an opportunity to take classes near work or close to home. From nursing and allied health programs to urban education and fashion design, students can prepare for successful careers in a number of fields. Located near the West End entertainment district, the college is housed in a turn-of-the-century building that features both the courses and technology that students demand today. And they can DART (Dallas Area Rapid Transit) to class by bus or light rail.

Campus expansion began in earnest in 1970 with Eastfield College in Mesquite and Mountain View College in Oak Cliff. Built on 244 acres of prairie, Eastfield College now is surrounded by development and residential areas as Dallas expands east. The campus is nicknamed "the village" and boasts national championship teams in baseball and golf. Students seek to enroll in the school's acclaimed interpreter training program, which teaches students American Sign Language, qualifying them to serve as interpreters for the deaf.

2001 senior adult graduate

Eastfield also offers the only auto body technology program in the district.

Mountain View College offers a natural setting for students and area wildlife in suburban Dallas neighborhoods. As students move from class to class, they enjoy a winding creek through the center of campus, large sculpture pieces and clusters of trees, and they can visit a declared natural habitat, too. Among Mountain View's noted programs are the Teacher Training Academy, which "grows" teachers from high school to community college to a four-year university and back to the classroom; e-commerce, vital to business growth and development; a senior citizens' day program that offers informational classes, lunch and opportunities for socializing; visual and performing arts; aviation; and more.

Richland College, part of Garland in north Dallas since 1972, enrolls DCCCD's largest number of students on a single campus. Many students earn associate's degrees and then transfer to four-year institutions, where they pursue a bachelor's degree. The campus offers academic programs in areas such as fine arts, business

Music and the arts

Small business seminars at the Bill J. Priest Institute

and science, as well as technical programs in fields like semiconductor manufacturing. Nontraditional students — such as displaced homemakers or senior citizens — can prepare for new careers through Richland's Adult Resource Center and its Emeritus program, respectively.

After more funding was secured in 1972, both Cedar Valley College and North Lake College opened in 1977, and Brookhaven College opened in Farmers Branch (north Dallas) the following year, completing the current seven-campus district. Cedar Valley, located in Lancaster, treats students to the view of a 17-acre lake and rolling hills as they fire pottery, paint, act and learn about sound in the Commercial Music Studio, where future sound technicians, engineers and musicians receive training. The college offers a noted veterinary technology program and a Law Enforcement Academy.

Located in Irving, North Lake College is a mecca for students who learn on a campus that is terraced and a place to enjoy. North Lake partners with many hi-tech and corporate groups in the Irving/Las Colinas business corridor, and students pursue studies in areas as diverse as visual arts and history to construction, real estate, mortgage banking, Microsoft systems engineer certification and other types of technology. North Lake also partners with the community and welcomes residents to a new library and the Academy of Irving ISD on its grounds.

Study group

In Texas, studying geoscience is a natural, and Brookhaven College provides that opportunity to seasoned professionals who travel from throughout the southwest and around the world to learn more at the Ellison Miles Geotechnology Institute. From science to the arts — the Center for the Arts, that is — and child development classes and facilities, Brookhaven offers a range of programs that prepare students for successful careers. And the college partners with major automobile manufacturers to train students in state-of-the-art automotive technology classrooms and facilities.

Each of the seven colleges in DCCCD is accredited individually by the Commission on Colleges of the Southern Association of Colleges and Schools to award the associate's degree.

BRICKS AND CLICKS

Economic development and distance learning are critical to students and their future employers as well as to businesses and corporations whose leaders want employees to continue their education throughout life and work. DCCCD set the pace for distance learning in 1972 and is nationally recognized for development, production and distribution of courses delivered by television, videotape and the Internet. The heart of this distance learning operation is the R. Jan LeCroy Center for Educational Telecommunications, and the Dallas TeleCollege offers more than 100 courses that are pre-recorded and offered at scheduled times through public broadcast or cable. Students also can earn an associate's degree online. And online classes are even more convenient because they meet students' hectic schedules; they also can interact with professors and other students in real time. Education is changing, and DCCCD is leading the way.

DCCCD and 30 other educational institutions created a virtual institution called the Western Governors University. The district was WGU's pilot institution for Texas and is the only community college system in the state that participates in the virtual university. WGU's institutions offer approximately 500 courses and more

than 30 degree programs. The district also is involved with the Southern Regional Electronic Campus, the University of Phoenix, Starlink and the Virtual College of Texas. DCCCD is a national leader in online and distance learning.

Created in 1989, the Bill J. Priest Institute for Economic Development opened to provide business counseling and training opportunities for individuals and businesses in the Dallas area. Assessments, short- and long-term training, and programs like the Customer Service Call Center, the Small Business Development Center and the Business Incubation Center offer opportunities to learn and grow as an employee, a business and an entrepreneur. The institute also provides staff training in the areas of computer software, leadership, communication and quality principles to companies.

OPPORTUNITIES FOR EVERYONE

Students are DCCCD's top priority, and the district continues to provide educational opportunities for a diverse population. One of its top recruitment programs is Rising Star, which ensures graduating Dallas County high school seniors the financial support to further their education. The program, which started with high schools in south Dallas, includes all Dallas County public high schools. High school seniors who earn a "B" average and exhibit financial need can become a Rising Star.

With a dropout rate of 40 percent in Dallas County and an even higher 60 percent rate in Dallas ISD, the need for the Rising Star program is critical to the future of employers, employees and communities in the area. And Rising Star students have a choice concerning their educational program. They can enroll in an associate's degree program, or they can choose to pursue any one of more than 120 occupational training or professional certification programs offered by the DCCCD.

Access to higher education is the key to success, and the district seeks to eliminate financial barriers for students by offering scholarships, grants, loans and other programs.

FUTURE PLANS, PAST PRIDE

With steady enrollment growth and a focus on access and "students first," DCCCD and its seven colleges will continue to meet the needs of students, employers and the community as it looks toward future anniversaries and accomplishments. More than 50,000 credit students and 27,000 continuing education students continue to take classes, earn degrees and certificates, and pursue technical careers as the district grows. Technology, changing needs and future trends will shape the future, but DCCCD will continue to offer higher education opportunities at affordable costs to those who wish to succeed.

Visual communications

LIVE AND LEARN AT DCCCD

- Founded: 1965
- Colleges/Locations: Brookhaven; Cedar Valley; Eastfield; El Centro; Mountain View; North Lake; Richland; Bill J. Priest Institute for Economic Development; R. Jan LeCroy Center for Educational Telecommunications
- Enrollment: approximately 50,000 credit students and 27,000 continuing education students per semester
- Annual budget: approximately $300 million
- Funding sources: local taxes, state of Texas appropriations, tuition
- Fact: DCCCD is one of the largest institutions of higher education in Texas.
- Focus: access for all students
- Key areas of learning: freshman and sophomore classes leading to an associate's degree and transfer to four-year institutions; technical programs and certification; continuing education, work force and adult education
- Number of students enrolled during its 35-year history: more than 1 million

AMERICAN GOLF CORPORATION

Making a Difference

WITH OVER 250 GOLF COURSES WORLDWIDE

under its management, American Golf Corporation (AGC) is recognized as the leading operator of Public Golf Courses and Private Country Clubs in the United States and beyond. As American Golf continues its third decade in the golf industry, it looks forward to upholding the time-honored traditions of golf's rich heritage while at the same time embracing new traditions that make the game more affordable and accessible for a broad spectrum of people to enjoy.

The Santa Monica, California-based company supports charitable efforts and initiates player development programs in the communities it serves. American Golf's *Adopt-a-Charity Program* has raised more than $300 million for local grass-roots organizations since the program's inception in 1985, while national partnerships within the industry have helped to raise funds and awareness for a variety of causes. American Golf's environmental programs have helped to beautify communities, conserve natural resources and preserve wildlife habitats.

Through our unique *Nike Golf Learning Centers,* which aim to make golf more fun and less intimidating, as well as our many player development programs for juniors, women and inner-city youths, American Golf has introduced thousands of new golfers to the great game — an endeavor it looks forward to building upon into the foreseeable future.

AGC IN TEXAS

A number of American Golf's finest facilities at both the public and private level are located in the state of Texas. American Golf offers a wide array of public (16) and private (13) golf properties designed by some of the industry's most acclaimed golf course architects with 14 in the Dallas/Fort Worth Metroplex.

Created by acclaimed architect Tripp Davis, the Scottish-themed *Tribute Golf Club* on the shores of Lake Lewisville in The Colony pays magnificent homage to the birthplace of golf and its rich traditions. The club's spectacular par 72, 6,972-yard links-style course was designed with the influence of great holes from such renowned Scottish links as St. Andrews, Muirfield, Troon and Prestwick. A host of outstanding amenities complete this unique golf experience.

Designed by Tom Weiskopf and Jay Morrish, *Buffalo Creek Golf Club*, located in Heath/Rockwall, takes full advantage of native terrain, creating a unique golf experience for every player. Buffalo Creek Golf Club challenges the best golfer while providing an enjoyable experience for the average player as well. In 1998 it was rated "The #1 Public Golf Course in Texas" by the *Dallas Morning News*.

The Trails of Frisco Golf Club, bold with its vision, design and expanse, has attracted most of the area's attention since its opening in 2001. Designed by one of the region's fastest-rising stars, Jeff Brauer, the par 71 course offers one of the best examinations of a golfer's skills, daring and ability. What once were seemingly a limitless trail of land, woods and endlessly waving wheat, Frisco is now the fastest-growing community in all of North Texas.

Eldorado Country Club in McKinney is nestled along Comegy Creek amidst

(Below right)
The Tribute Golf Club,
The Colony

Nike Golf
Learning Center

hundreds of tall Oak trees and rolling terrain. Renowned architect Gary Roger Baird designed the scenic 6,770-yard, par 72 layout, which features tight, tree-lined fairways and well-bunkered greens with two lakes coming into play throughout. With over $750,000 in clubhouse and golf course enhancements the last few years — the final piece of a $8.7 million renovation — now complete, the new Eldorado is open and waiting for players to discover its newest treasures.

For the *Great Southwest Golf Club* located in Grand Prairie, designers Byron Nelson and Ralph Plummer set out in 1964 to sculpt a track that would consistently provide an inspiration for the most discriminating golfer. The vision still holds true today. This historic Texas course features 6,706 yards of mature, tree-lined fairways, plush Champions Bermuda greens and enough water hazards and bunkers to challenge even the best golfers in the Metroplex.

AGC has also worked to create additional options for golfers in cluster markets that create options which allow members to experience the privileges of membership at multiple courses. Many of these programs have been launched in Texas, and they've proven to be a huge success! Programs like the Texas Trail Golf Club and the Metroplex Alliance have allowed golfers to transcend the traditional limitations of membership and maximize their privileges at courses and clubs throughout the Lone Star State.

Public golfers across the state of Texas will find what they're looking for in American Golf's *Texas Trail Golf Club* membership. From municipal courses to resorts, members enjoy discounted golf privileges and a variety of services at 16 courses statewide. Texas Trail Golf Club

AMERICAN GOLF DALLAS/FORT WORTH FACILITIES
Private Country Clubs
Eldorado Country Club, McKinney
Thorntree Country Club, Desoto
Diamond Oaks Country Club, Fort Worth
Woodhaven Country Club, Fort Worth
The Trails of Frisco Golf Club, Frisco (semi-private)
Great Southwest Golf Club, Grand Prairie

Public Courses
The Tribute Golf Club, The Colony
Buffalo Creek Golf Club, Heath
Waterview Golf Club, Rowlett
Mesquite Golf Course, Mesquite
Twin Wells Municipal, Irving
Riverside Golf Club, Grand Prairie
Riverchase Golf Club, Coppell
Ridgeview Ranch Golf Club, Plano

Members enjoy premier amenities including green and cart fee discounts, a USGA Handicap, a one-year subscription to *Golf Digest*, special savings on golf shop merchandise, eligibility in tournaments held at Texas Trail courses, e-mail specials and more. Another wonderful aspect of this membership is the great service and hospitality members enjoy at the Clubs they visit.

AGC's private club members in Dallas/Fort Worth enjoy the expanded privileges of The *Metroplex Alliance*. The core of the program is the ability of its Members to have additional access to several private country clubs, golf clubs, dining facilities and fitness facilities within the area. One of the unique and most attractive aspects of membership is its private *concierge*. The concierge acts as a one-stop shopping outlet with access to tee times, dinner reservations, theater, concerts, sporting events and much more.

As steward's of golf's future, AGC is honored to play a role as the world's largest golf course management company and work alongside the United States Golf Association, PGA of America, PGA Tour, Ladies Professional Golf Association, Tiger Woods Foundation and other industry groups in writing the next chapter in golf's storied history.

(Above)
Trails Golf Club, Frisco

Eldorado Country Club, Mckinney

ATI CAREER TRAINING CENTERS

CAREER SUCCESS THROUGH EDUCATION MAY be found in the halls of two-year and four-year colleges, universities or private career colleges and schools. More and more in Texas, graduates of private career institutions are making a major impact in the employment marketplace and contributing to the economy of Texas. Private career institutions focus on giving the student the most relevant, up-to-date job skills in the shortest amount of time. The Dallas Fort Worth Metroplex is lucky to have three campuses of one of the nation's top private career institutions, ATI Career Training Center.

Congressman Dick Armey presents the President's Award for Outstanding Community Service to Mr. Dung "Dennis" Pham (right), a computer-assisted design graduate from ATI Career Training Center in Dallas, Texas.

President and CEO Joe Mehlmann with corporate executive directors and school directors

"Employability of ATI graduates is the bottom line," says ATI President Joe Mehlmann. "You can't teach something for the sake of teaching it. It has to be a current skill for the job marketplace." This philosophy has guided ATI since Mehlmann purchased his first school in 1985, the American Trades Institute on Maple Avenue near Love Field in Dallas. American Trades Institute, which provided the acronym for the education corporation, had operated in Dallas since 1965 and had 120 students studying automotive, welding, refrigeration, air conditioning/heating and offset printing when it was purchased. Since 1985 ATI has grown to eight campuses in three states that have a total enrollment of over 3,000 students and annual revenues in excess of $40 million.

Mehlmann's family immigrated to the United States in 1958, when Mehlmann, a native German, was just a teen-ager. Typical of first-generation citizens, Mehlmann's father worked hard in a power tool manufacturing plant to provide a future for his children. The junior Mehlmann earned a bachelor of arts degree from Illinois Benedictine College and a bachelor of science degree in mechanical engineering from the University of Notre Dame, where he captained and starred on the soccer team. He first entered the field of postsecondary education when he was hired by Lincoln Technical Institute in Chicago as a sales representative in 1973. He advanced quickly, as he developed a love of education and respect for the private career sector, which provided an avenue to success for those not college bound.

After his initial success with American Trades Institute, Mehlmann kept a constant eye on the job marketplace in the surrounding community, adding programs with a high potential for postgraduate employment, a practice continued today. His company grew explosively, opening two more campuses in the Metroplex under the name ATI Career Training Center, then purchasing four schools in South Florida and one in Phoenix, Arizona, with plans for further expansion in the works.

While American Trades Institute continues to successfully train students in its original trade programs, ATI Career Training Center campuses on Technology Boulevard in Dallas and on Loop 820 in Hurst offer programs in medical and dental assisting, business administration technology, computer-assisted design (CAD), graphic illustration, electronics technology and information technology and network administration (ITNA). The Dallas campus also offers a two-year degree in respiratory therapy.

ATI's curriculum is market-driven, to assure students the best potential for getting jobs in their chosen fields. To achieve this, ATI conducts research to improve existing programs and unearth potential new programs with job market demand. Programs like business administration technology, graphic design, CAD and ITNA are constantly evolving to include new software and technology developments. In planning a new program based on research results, ATI forms an advisory committee composed of industry members to guide ATI in curriculum development. This careful work results in programs that prepare the ATI graduate with the entry-level skills needed to enter the marketplace and an ATI student career placement rate of over 90 percent.

Mehlmann endorses management guru Zig Ziglar's philosophy that if you help enough other people be successful then you will be successful. That philosophy is even evident in the award-winning Student Association at ATI campuses, which focuses on community involvement, working with the Texas Adopt-a-Highway program, the Ronald McDonald House and Buckner Children's Home. Students are also encouraged to volunteer for the Salvation Army and Scottish Rite Children's Hospital, and blood drives take place regularly on ATI campuses.

The future looks bright for ATI schools and their graduates. The trends in work-force needs continue to point to the kinds of programs ATI offers, and new trends will be incorporated along the way. Joe Mehlmann, his staff and instructors succeed with many by serving the ATI mission: "Helping people achieve a better lifestyle by preparing them, through education, for a career in their chosen field." Many happy ATI graduates agree that the school has succeeded with them.

ATI Career Training Center in Dallas, Texas

ATI Career Training Center in Hurst, Texas

BUCKNER BENEVOLENCES

BUCKNER BENEVOLENCES BEGAN IN DALLAS IN 1879 when Dr. Robert Cooke Buckner, a Baptist pastor, wanted to put the Christian principles of charity into practical action. He began by founding Buckner Orphans Home for three orphan children and ended up shaping the history of non-profit social services in Dallas with Buckner Benevolences.

Buckner Orphans Home was established to provide care for Dallas children who were orphaned after the Civil War. After the Civil War, African-Americans were free and needed education, so Dr. Buckner founded their first high school in North Texas. He also established the Dallas Humane Society for abandoned animals. Then in 1894, Dr. Buckner founded Children's Hospital in Dallas and became the driving force behind the opening and operating of the Baptist Memorial Sanitarium, which is now known as Baylor Healthcare System.

Over the years, Buckner Benevolences kept up with the changing needs of the people of Dallas by expanding its social outreach to the growing population of elderly, to families in crisis, to foster care, as well as local and international adoption. Buckner saw each expansion as an opportunity to serve God in different ministries.

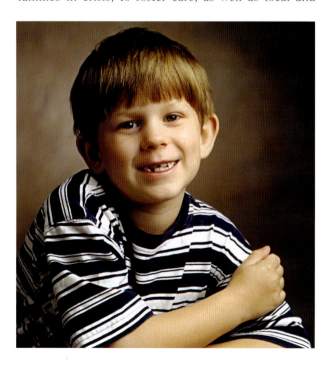

Buckner Benevolences is the umbrella organization for its four major service ministries.

Buckner Children and Family Services evolved from the original Buckner Orphans Home and in 2000 oversaw the reconstruction of the original East Dallas site to new state-of-the-art facilities. Buckner also reaches outside of Dallas to include a network of community and residential services around Texas. In addition to these facilities, Buckner Children and Family Services also offers parenting classes, family counseling, a statewide network of foster care and transitional housing programs.

Buckner Retirement Services began with a row of houses on the edge of the original orphanage to provide a place for retired pastors and missionaries, who served as grandparents for the children living at the home. As Dallas grew, so did Buckner Retirement Services, and in 1954 it opened the Mary E. Trew Home, which developed over the years into Buckner Retirement Village. Now there are five retirement communities with locations in Dallas, Austin, Longview, Houston and Beaumont that give loving, attentive, certified care. For those senior adults living independently there is Buckner ElderCare Services, which delivers services directly to senior adults in their own homes.

Buckner Adoption and Maternity Services evolved from Buckner's first adoption in 1884. It is a state-approved, licensed adoption agency that also works with women in crisis pregnancy situations as well as pre- and post-adoption counseling. Buckner's strong reputation for integrity and compassion through the adoption process led to the opportunity to expand to international adoptions and the creation of one of the strongest support networks for adoptive families of international children.

Buckner Orphan Care International began in 1995 to respond to the millions of children living in orphanages around the world. In 2000 alone, Buckner Orphan Care International served 175 orphanages, 41 children in international foster care and distributed $2.75 million in humanitarian aid. It also collected and distributed 500,000 brand new shoes through Shoes for Orphan Souls, an annual program that collects shoes for orphan children around the world. Shoes for Orphan Souls is a multi-state humanitarian aid program that uses volunteers, businesses and churches who pull together to collect, bag and distribute these shoes internationally, nationally and locally in Dallas.

In Dallas and around Texas, Buckner Benevolences has reached out in a myriad of ways, touching the lives of thousands. Whether it is a community center with a flourishing after-school program, partnerships with churches to provide social services to low-income apartment complexes or working on the Texas-Mexico border to handle the high rates of poverty, unemployment and teen pregnancy, Buckner is there to help.

Buckner is one of the largest, most diversified social care agencies of its kind in the nation. Thousands of volunteers are coordinated as the agency seeks to restore and heal individuals and families of all faiths and backgrounds. In the process these volunteers are enriched by the charity work they are doing in the name of the Lord. They meet lifelong friends and know the comfort and satisfaction of belonging to a community that deeply cares.

The mission statement of Buckner states that all services of the organization are to be ministered with professional competence. In this case, competency means efficiency. It is with pride that Buckner takes every cent — 100 percent of every donation — and applies it directly towards its service ministries. All administrative services are provided through a trust fund, and the organization has consolidated all administrative functions at corporate headquarters.

The mission statement also promotes the strict adherence to Christian principles in all Buckner work. The Christian ethics and attitude pervade Buckner in all its outreach efforts and the spirituality and dedication of the mission is apparent in each of the ministries. In all its operations and services, Buckner holds to the policies, principles and doctrines of the Baptist faith.

As one of the most influential leaders in Baptist history, Dr. R.C. Buckner's establishment of Buckner Benevolences remains a constant call to Texas Baptists to become individually involved in living out their Christianity for the betterment of humanity. It was Dr. Buckner's foundation of social awareness, concern and action that made Buckner Benevolences a historically honest and dependable leader in the Dallas non-profit arena.

Buckner Benevolences began with one man passing a hat to collect enough money to build a home for orphans. Now every year more than 80,000 people in Dallas and around the world are touched by Buckner programs.

With more than a century of contribution to the people of Dallas and around the world, Buckner never rests on its accomplishments. With its dignified approach to ministry, Buckner continues to work tirelessly to meet new needs and to give sustenance and hope.

CANDLEWOOD SUITES

BUSINESS TRIPS AREN'T ALWAYS FUN. BUT Candlewood Suites in north Dallas is out to change that. That's why it has worked so hard on each room. Candlewood Suites knows that business travelers have specific needs, especially when they are staying a week or longer.

Candlewood Suites are built to give the business traveler privacy and comfort. Each suite is designed to bring out the best in short- and long-term hotel living. The beds are comfortable, the kitchens are spacious and the work areas are larger than many home offices.

Moreover, every Candlewood Suite has a full kitchen complete with a microwave and full-size refrigerator. There are proper utensils for light cooking in the microwave and on the stove top, can-openers and silverware. The kitchen is designed for the quick meal that is so common in the business traveler's schedule.

As a business traveler, work is paramount. That is why Candlewood Suites has made sure each room has an oversize executive desk to spread out papers on and a stress-busting chair to make those long desk hours more comfortable. All rooms are completely equipped for high-tech travelers who must have 24-hour access to the telephone, e-mail and Internet services on their portable computers.

At Candlewood Suites, each room has two separate phone lines so guests can work on the Internet and talk on the phone just like in the company office. It is a small detail to provide two phone lines instead of one, but it is amazing how many hotels forget this feature. Moreover, knowing that local calls are often a necessity for business travelers needing to make local arrangements, all local phone calls are free. That is a quite a difference from other hotels, whose local call costs can add up quickly. Candlewood Suites even has a low-priced long-distance service for guests to use. This can be a lifesaver when a phone card is forgotten and long-distance calls must be made.

The front desk also provides the executive services guests may need fast, like needing to send a fax or make a few copies or staple a report at the last minute. Candlewood Suites understands that all in business is not predictable, and it makes sure it is prepared for the needs of its business guests.

All guests at Candlewood Suites are ensured the privacy necessary for relaxation. Guests do not need to dread that early morning knock on the hotel door that is

Candlewood Suites

Candlewood Suites

Dynamic Dallas: An Illustrated History

ritual for most hotel housekeeping staffs. Candlewood Suites housekeepers clean rooms only once a week so guests are not disturbed when working during the day in the hotel. In addition, all guests have free use of washers and dryers so they need not worry about laundry — it is available, laundry detergent and all, for a guest's extended stay needs. For those guests requiring dry cleaning, Candlewood Suites offers same-day dry cleaning. Hotel staff can arrange pick-up and delivery of suits, shirts and other items. Generally, during the work week, clothing dropped off by 8 a.m. may be claimed at the front desk by 6 p.m.

Unlike many hotels, the front desk is closed between 11 p.m. and 7 a.m. This does not affect the service though, because the night manager is on site, available to guests, working behind the scenes. In this way, any night questions or requests are taken right to the top and dealt with quickly and professionally. This goes for late night check-in, too. Candlewood Suites has a convenient late-night check-in procedure designed for the weary late night traveler. Check-in is easy, fast and hassle-free, just the way it should be.

When guests check-in, Candlewood Suites gives each something extra with their key. Each guest receives a quarter, which is enough to buy a first soda in the Candlewood Cupboard™. This well-stocked convenience store is not your typical hotel gift shop. In the Candlewood Cupboard™, guests may purchase food, snacks and sundry items at fair, not hotel-inflated, prices.

In addition, the Candlewood Cupboard™ is on the honor system because at Candlewood Suites guests are trusted and respected. Guests can pick out what they want, when they want it. There is no cashier. Guests just leave their money in the designated place. Since business

Candlewood
One-Bedroom Suite

travelers can get hungry at some odd hours, this makes it easy to always find something tasty to eat.

Moreover, this little in-house grocery makes it really easy on an out-of-town guest who doesn't know where the local grocery stores are located, much less want to take the time to get there, go shopping and return to the hotel. These guests don't want to dine out every meal either. The goal is meal convenience, and Candlewood Cupboard™ achieves it with style. The Candlewood Cupboard™ is stocked so that guests can fix a great meal right in the suite's kitchen.

For many business travelers, exercise is just as important as food. That is why each Candlewood Suites has a fitness center that is fully equipped with workout machines and mats. It is open during the day and evening so that even the busiest business traveler can find time to exercise.

When it is time to relax in room, Candlewood Suites makes sure each room is comfortable. Each suite has an overstuffed recliner that is just right for relaxing while watching the television or listening to the radio. If guests prefer listening to a CD or watching a video, they can do that, too. Guests can bring their own videos or CDs or borrow one at no charge from the varied collection available at the front service desk.

Candlewood Suites is not a traditional hotel and that is the best part for business travelers. It has concentrated on what is important for a busy guest with work demands. It has prepared for the business traveler's requirements for comfort, quiet, space and good value. Candlewood Suites doesn't nickel-and-dime expense-account travelers to debt. Candlewood Suites gives them more of what really matters.

Candlewood
One-Bedroom Suite

DALLAS CAN! ACADEMY

APHORISMS SUCH AS, "IF YOU CAN CONCEIVE it and believe it, you can achieve it!" and, "You've got to get out of bed to get ahead!" can pack a lot of truth in a few words.

Dallas Can! Academy students use the two simple statements above in their Winner's Circle pep rallies for motivation, and the statements neatly summarize the program. Dallas Can! Academy is a non-traditional educational program that gives young Texans a second chance to complete high school by earning a high school diploma or a General Educational Development (GED) certificate. The program reaches out to youth between the ages of 16 and 21 who have dropped out or are at risk of dropping out of school — those that might be heading for a wrong turn in their lives. Dallas Can! Academy has an open-entry policy that gives students the opportunity to begin classes at any time during the school year.

Site of first Dallas Can! Academy

Ambassador Program students look over campuses on College and Career field trip.

The origins of Dallas Can! Academy can be traced back to 1976 and Grant East, a successful systems analyst and head of his own company. East decided to give back to the community by helping young people in prison develop positive outlooks and skills. He established Freedom Ministries, a nonprofit organization working with adult and juvenile prisoners. This program led East to the idea of helping at-risk youth *before* they ended up on the wrong side of the law. He realized that keeping them from dropping out of school by providing an alternate education experience was one way to make a difference.

That difference was created in 1985 when Dallas Can! Academy was founded. The program began in a borrowed farmhouse east of downtown near Mesquite. It later moved to the campus of the old Dallas Bible College before moving to its permanent facility on the eastern edge of downtown in 1990. The academy added a second building in Oak Cliff in June 2000 to house both academic programs and administrative offices.

In 1996 the program received one of the first charter school designations in Texas, allowing Dallas Can! Academy to award high school diplomas in addition to preparing students for GED certification. The Dallas Can! model has since been replicated across Texas with two Fort Worth Can! Academy campuses, Houston Can! Academy, San Antonio Can! High School and Austin Can! Academy. Under the administration of TEXANS CAN!, these programs have helped more than 25,000 students. Ninety-five percent of these students are minorities, almost all are considered economically disadvantaged and at risk, and many are high school dropouts. These students need individual attention and are more successful in the smaller classes TEXANS CAN! schools provide. Dallas Can! Academy is funded by a combination of local fund-raising efforts and state and federal sources.

The youth served by Dallas Can! Academy may have special needs, but the program follows three simple principles that well serve any educational setting:

— *"Discipline in Private, Reward in Public."* Shame and humiliation lead to alienation and failure; recognition and reward lead to achievement.

— *"Rules without Relationships Breed Rebellion."* Today's youth reject what they don't respect. Caring adults who take the time to form meaningful relationships create an environment in which discipline and structure have meaning.

— *"Behavior is Based on Need."* A young person's anti-social behavior can almost always be traced to an unmet family, social, emotional or psychological need. The program's trained counselors deal with behavioral problems by dealing with their root causes.

One special program offered at the Oak Cliff campus is Families for Learning. Students who are already mothers or pregnant qualify for Families for Learning; along with GED preparation, they take a curriculum designed to enhance their quality of life. Classes include parenting, nutrition, self-esteem building, etiquette, domestic violence, breast cancer awareness and pre-natal care. Families for Learning began in 1992 with a grant from the National Center for Family Literacy and is designed to help break the cycle of poverty and illiteracy across generations.

Another program is the Ambassador Program where students' lives are shaped by volunteer community mentors. Among other skills, the mentors help students with career selection, interviewing skills and creating resumes. In addition, the SMU Work-Study Tutoring Program has become an important part of Dallas Can! Academy. Students from Southern Methodist University devote many classroom hours helping students with their daily classwork and prepping them for the Texas Assessment of Academic Skills (TAAS) tests. All students in Texas must reach satisfactory performance on the exit level TAAS tests (TAKS test in spring 2003) in reading and math to receive a high school diploma.

On designated Fridays the academy holds Winner's Circle, an activity where students get recognition for their accomplishments. The hour-long program includes a motivational speech from a local community leader. The awards and recognition include perfect attendance, academic advancement, positive attitude and citizenship. Winner's Circle lets the students end the week feeling good about continuing their education and about themselves.

At the end of the day, or the school year in this case, the bottom line remains *results*, and Dallas Can! Academy doesn't disappoint. In 2001 Dallas Can! Academy received an honors report card from the Texas Education Agency, reporting that the program far exceeded state accountability goals. Three areas in particular were higher than expected: retention of recovered dropouts, students completing their courses and seniors who met diploma requirements. This year the number of students with passing TAAS scores was *225 percent above state requirements*. More than 60 percent of Dallas Can! students are continuing their education at junior colleges, traditional four-year colleges and universities, vocational training schools, or entering the military services.

Of course, considering all that Dallas Can! Academy offers at-risk youth, its success and the success of so many of its graduates is not all that surprising. Dallas Can! Academy is considered the "premier charter school system" in Texas, and its teachers, faculty and staff are more than life-changers — they set the standard for excellence!

At the weekly Winner's Circle, students are recognized for their accomplishments.

The reward of great accomplishment... graduation day!

Through the Families for Learning program, Dallas Can! Academy helps students, who are already mothers or pregnant, obtain their GED.

Quality of Life

DALLAS VA MEDICAL CENTER

DALLAS VA MEDICAL CENTER (VAMC) BEGAN providing health care to area veterans before World War II and has developed an outstanding reputation for medical research and teaching. In 1996, Dallas VAMC and Fort Worth Outpatient Clinic (FWOPC) integrated with Sam Rayburn Memorial Veterans Center in Bonham to become VA North Texas Health Care System (VANTHCS), serving 38 counties in north Texas and two in southern Oklahoma. VANTHCS handles over 10,000 admissions and approximately 685,000 outpatient visits annually. With an operating budget of $328 million, VANTHCS employs approximately 3,100 with 1,300 volunteers. As the tertiary referral center, Dallas VAMC provides every level and type of care except transplants.

Nocturnal dialysis

Dallas VAMC is located in east Oak Cliff, an area formerly known as Lisbon. In 1940, the hospital known locally as Lisbon VA opened its first group of buildings. Surrounded by open fields on one of the highest elevations in Dallas, the complex consisted of nine separate buildings, including the main building still referred to as Building 1. Though plans were developed for a new VA hospital near The University of Texas Southwestern Medical Center at Dallas (UT Southwestern), veterans fought and won the battle to keep it in southern Dallas county. Housed on an 84-acre campus, Dallas VAMC includes a 300-bed acute care hospital, multi-specialty outpatient clinics, 116-bed Transitional Care Unit, 40-bed Domiciliary, 30-bed Spinal Cord Injury Center, 60-bed Psychiatric Residential Rehabilitation Treatment Program and Comprehensive Homeless Center.

In 1955, Dallas VAMC added Building 2, then a 515-bed facility with state-of-the-art closed-circuit television facilities and many modern health care innovations. The Nursing Home Care Unit (now called Transitional Care Unit) was built in 1984, and a Magnetic Resonance Imaging facility was added in 1991. The Spinal Cord Injury Center opened in 1996, and a Clinical Addition was dedicated in the fall of 1998 with state-of-the-art pharmacy, laboratory, radiology services and critical care units. Through a collaborative project between Dallas VAMC, City of Dallas and Dallas Area Rapid Transit, the VA Community Center was built in 1999. The VA Community Center provides meeting facilities for campus groups and veterans service councils and also includes a Wellness Center that promotes health and fitness and the Child Care Center to provide on-site child care services. The One VA Mall opened in 2000, offering one-stop shopping to customers, including the Veterans Canteen Service Retail Store, Blue Bell Ice Cream and Starbucks Coffee service, Café VA and One VA kiosk. The One VA Service Center provides offices for Veterans Benefits Administration,

Dallas VAMC today

National Cemetery Administration, Texas Veterans Commission and Disabled American Veterans.

Dallas VAMC was chosen to house a regional research center in 1947. One of the primary roles for the center was to conduct medical research with an emphasis on enhancing the quality of life for veterans. The opportunity to conduct research is a powerful recruiting tool used to attract outstanding health care professionals, and many have been honored for their work. Roger Unger, MD, was selected for membership in the National Academy of Sciences, one of the highest honors awarded a scientist in the United States. He was the first investigator at Dallas VAMC to receive VA's prestigious William S. Middleton Award for outstanding medical research in the field of diabetes. Other recipients of the Middleton Award include Paul Srere, PhD, in 1974 for his work in carbohydrate and fat metabolism; Sami Said, MD, in 1981 for his discovery of vasoactive intestinal peptides; and Kosaku Uyeda, PhD, in 1984 for his work in glucose metabolism. Dr. Uyeda has received attention recently for identification of the protein that translates excessive carbohydrate intake into body fat. Other research accomplishments include development of the mesh implant for fractures in 1973 by George Hahn, DDS; original research for the stomach ulcer drug, Tagament™; and Mevacor for treatment of high cholesterol. Other protocols include the use of microbubbles as a delivery system for medication or gene therapy; studies of sleep deprivation and the aging process; and investigations exploring the transport of lipids in the body. Through its partnership with UT Southwestern, Dallas VAMC is a major teaching and research center, training physicians,

Veterans Day program

dentists and associated health students from over 110 other training programs.

The community served by Dallas VAMC has broadened beyond the mandate of only veterans. Now active-duty and retired military and their spouses under the TriCare program, and survivors of military members who die on active duty or survivors of veterans who died of service-connected disabilities are eligible for health care.

Alan G. Harper, director since 1991, states, "The commitment of our employees to serve this community is unfailing. We work together to provide the highest quality health care, improve access to care, and be an employer of choice. We participate in community projects, including painting local houses, raising funds for the Combined Federal Campaign and conducting health screenings in various locations. Dallas VAMC could not achieve its goals without dedicated people who love veterans and remember the past sacrifices they made for our freedom today. I am proud to be the leader of these outstanding employees."

Original hospital, 1940

Quality of Life

EPISCOPAL DIOCESE OF DALLAS

The Rt. Rev. Alexander Charles Garrett, first bishop of the Diocese of Dallas

St. Matthew's first church house, which became the first cathedral of the district of North Texas in 1875

THE EPISCOPAL DIOCESE OF DALLAS COMPRISES 77 member churches in 25 counties — an area of 17,000 square miles. But Dallas was only an untamed frontier outpost when Bishop Alexander Garrett arrived on December 31, 1874, during a "blue norther." Garrett booked a room for his family above a downtown saloon, but the windows would not close. Cold blasts chilled the family and led to son Tommy's death from exposure. Nonetheless, the good priest quickly went about the business of conducting worship services, visiting the sick, marrying and burying people, and keeping up the spirits of the often-dispirited people of God on the edge of the frontier. Within just a year of Garrett's arrival, Dallas' St. Matthew's parish was deemed a cathedral church of the Episcopal Church.

Bishop Garrett's wobbly, horse-drawn carriage was a common sight as he roamed throughout North, Central and West Texas, planting the seeds of the kingdom of God in what Garrett called "The Big Pasture." On October 22, 1895, the Episcopal Diocese of Dallas was established with 13 parishes.

Garrett was bishop of the diocese for 50 years, a Dallas civic leader and one of the most powerful voices in the national church. When he died at age 92 in 1924, the diocese contained 54 churches; St. Matthew's Home for Children; St. Mary's College, at that time a major educational institution in Dallas; and All Saints Hospital in Fort Worth.

The growth of the diocese was a major success story for the Episcopal Church in the late 19th century. The church was the dominant denomination on the eastern seaboard, but Garrett's success showed that Anglican worship was needed on the partially civilized frontier. The second Bishop of Dallas, The Rt. Rev. Harry Tunis Moore, was an able administrator both locally and nationally during a period when the national church worked to strengthen its mission and presence nationwide. Moore established youth fellowships in every parish, developed summer camp programs and guided the diocese through the 1920s' economic inflation, the Depression and World War II. The saga of St. Mary's College demonstrates Moore's challenges. In 1917 the college incurred a debt of $250,000 when it built Garrett Hall. The stock market crash of 1929 all but eliminated the chance of retiring the debt, and because of this, combined with competing colleges, St. Mary's was forced to close. The cathedral left its downtown Dallas Gothic structure for the former college grounds, where it remains today.

The Rt. Rev. Charles Avery Mason, who succeeded Moore, took full advantage of the post-World War II growth. Fired with evangelistic zeal, Mason started 100 missions in northeast Texas and confirmed 20,000 new members during his episcopacy, the greatest growth period in the diocese's history. It was a time of building, not just of large structures and parish halls, but also Camp Crucis and St. Philip's School and Community Center in South Dallas, which serves the African-American community.

The Rt. Rev. A. Donald Davies was consecrated as fourth bishop in 1970 and set about reorganizing and strengthening the business infrastructure in order to better support the diocese's ministries. During Davies' episcopate, major new buildings were added to Camp Crucis and the Bishop Mason Retreat and Conference Center; two retirement centers were developed; the Anglican School of Theology and the Episcopal School of Dallas were established; and an important Hispanic ministry was begun. In 1983, when the diocese was divided into the dioceses of Dallas and Fort Worth, Davies became the first Bishop of Fort Worth. Bishop Donis Dean Patterson, who served from 1983 until 1992, successfully reorganized the Dallas diocese and helped establish a fiscal organization to hold church properties in trust and administer diocesan funds. The Rev. Gwen Langdoc Buehrens, the diocese's first woman priest, was ordained in November 1985.

Christ Episcopal Church in Plano is the fastest-growing Episcopal church in the United States.

The sixth diocesan bishop, the Rt. Rev. James Monte Stanton, was consecrated in 1993. Known for his work with the National Episcopal Cursillo movement, Stanton has a deep interest in church growth and evangelism. As a result, the diocese is committed to establishing and building churches, working for justice, supporting education and ministering to disenfranchised persons, especially to the homeless and abused women. At his first diocesan convention, Bishop Stanton introduced a radical idea — that convention attendees commit themselves to a project, resulting in two houses being built through Habitat for Humanity. The diocese has paid for building more than a house per year for Habitat projects ever since.

Schools within the diocese, such as The Episcopal School of Dallas and The Canterbury Episcopal School in Southwest Dallas County, provide alternative choices for top-tier private education in the Dallas area. The Church of the Transfiguration's new middle and high school, The Parish Episcopal School, opened in August 2002 in a 337,000-square-foot, state-of-the-art building designed by I.M. Pei. The 50-acre site makes it one of the largest independent school campuses in the Dallas area.

Since 1971 the Anglican School of Theology, a graduate-level educational institution of the Diocese of Dallas, has served the diocese in nurturing, maintaining and continuing the Episcopal Church's tradition. The school offers a full theological curriculum, three degree plans and specialized courses to fulfill licensing requirements for certain lay ministries. Courses are also open to adults interested in fulfilling personal spiritual needs.

The Episcopal Diocese of Dallas is deeply committed to its youth. Dances, retreats, community service activities and weekends are designed to give church youth a greater sense of God's love. Youth and camp conferences offer venues for spiritual growth and service and finding ways to alleviate youth violence.

The Episcopal Diocese of Dallas appears to be on the threshold of a third major growth period, particularly due to the Baby Boomer generation seeking spiritual nourishment as it matures. Existing parishes have shown considerable numerical growth; several new mission churches have been established; and the diocese has bold, ambitious plans to establish 10 new churches and 40 new faith communities within the next five years. It is clear that Bishop Garrett's pioneering vision — to establish churches and see them grow — continues apace in North Texas.

KINDRED HOSPITAL DALLAS

LOCATED IN CENTRAL DALLAS, KINDRED Hospital Dallas — a 110-bed facility — is widely known as "the hospital that doesn't look like a hospital." Kindred is licensed by the state of Texas as a general, acute care hospital and is accredited by the Joint Commission of Health Care Organizations. The hospital is also certified by Medicare.

Opened in 1987, the hospital moved to its current location in 1998. It features a six-bed intensive care unit with hemodynamic monitoring capability, two operating room suites and six special negative airflow isolation rooms. Key physicians at the hospital have been listed on *D Magazine*'s "100 Best Doctors in Dallas Fort Worth." Kindred Dallas has approximately 200 physicians on staff with specialties including cardiology, pulmonary, wound care, physical medicine and rehabilitation, gastroenterology, general surgery, internal medicine, nephrology, ophthalmology, orthopedics, pain management and urology, among many others. Additionally, Kindred has a strong nursing program that features 24-hour care with appropriate nurse-to-patient ratios.

Kindred provides acute care for patients generally requiring extended treatment and recovery time. The hospital has expertise in acute cardiac and pulmonary medicine, surgery, dialysis, wound care, infectious disease and rehabilitation. The main focus of the hospital's programs is on medical and surgical services to pulmonary and ventilator-dependent patients who require long-term hospitalization. The hospital is well known in the community for its outstanding success rates in weaning patients from ventilators and is renowned for its success with acutely ill patients. Kindred has also developed an outpatient surgical program that offers cosmetic and reconstructive surgery procedures.

The hospital's vision is to be the premier integrated health care service company in the greater Dallas and northeast Texas area. It provides all levels of care throughout the continuum of medical need and specializes in respiratory, catastrophically ill and medically complex patients. Kindred's commitment to quality is at the forefront in the delivery of health care to its patients. Its goal is for patients to return to their pre-hospitalization quality of life or fullest potential. The acute and medically complex patients admitted to Kindred Hospitals are transferred or referred from other health care providers such as general acute care hospitals, intensive care units, managed care programs, physicians, nursing centers and home care settings.

Kindred's mission is to provide non-discriminatory access to care, encompassing a broad continuum and comprehensive array of services to the catastrophically ill and medically complex patients. It hopes to achieve optimum results by following its core values of quality and excellence, patient-focused approach, cost-efficient care through resources management, customer service and teamwork. The hospital respects the rights of each

Kindred Hospital, Dallas

patient and recognizes that each patient is unique with individual health care needs. Kindred respects each patient's personal dignity and right to privacy; the hospital feels it is important to provide considerate, respectful care.

The skilled and experienced staff at Kindred is dedicated to providing quality care to its patients while offering a unique blend of services to optimize each patient's chance for recovery from illness or injury. The high-quality medical staff supervises the patient care in conjunction with the interdisciplinary team.

The hospital also offers state-of-the art respiratory services; comprehensive laboratory services; a pharmacy with therapeutic drug monitoring; radiology services and physical, occupational and speech therapy. Kindred also has a team of licensed dietitians who provide patients with nutritious, appetizing meals. The hospital's social workers provide excellent social work services and discharge planning. Other top-level services at the hospital include its internal case management and psychosocial services — including spiritual support. Patient/team conferences are held regularly.

The hospital also has a strong program of social and spiritual services and case management. Social workers provide a range of services including counseling, discharge planning, referrals to community agencies, arrangements for home health visits and assistance in securing medical equipment for home use. An on-site family support group is also available. The hospital chaplain is available for religious needs and the hospital will also make arrangements to contact personal ministers, rabbis, priests and other spiritual leaders at the request of the patient.

Kindred Hospital Dallas is a subsidiary of Kindred Healthcare, Inc. Kindred's Hospital Division is the largest long-term acute care operation in the United States. In many ways, the hospitals closely resemble large intensive care units, primarily focused on caring for medically complex patients. Most of these patients suffer from multiple systematic failures or conditions, including neurological disorders, head injuries, brain stem and spinal cord trauma, cerebral vascular accidents, chemical brain injuries, central nervous system disorders and developmental anomalies. Kindred has a core competency in treating patients with pulmonary disorders.

Kindred has developed a number of programs to improve the quality of care in its hospitals. It maintains

Lobby and reception area welcomes visitors and family members.

Intensive care unit for acutely ill patients

an integrated quality assessment and improvement program for patient care, encompassing utilization review, quality improvement, infection control and risk management. Kindred's electronic medical record system, ProTouch,™ enables real-time multiple user access to patient clinical data. Quality initiatives are directed by Kindred's chief clinical officer and a medical advisory board composed of physicians associated with Kindred's facilities from across the country.

An integral part of the dynamic Kindred Healthcare family, Kindred Hospital Dallas is a leading health care provider in Dallas and east Texas. With the resources of its parent company at its disposal, in tandem with a staff of top-quality physicians and other medical professionals, Kindred Dallas will continue to work toward its vision of being the premier integrated health care service company in its region.

PARKLAND HEALTH & HOSPITAL SYSTEM

Bluitt-Flowers Health Center, a part of the Community Oriented Primary Care program.

FOR MORE THAN A CENTURY, PARKLAND Health & Hospital System has served the health care needs of Dallas County. Over the last eight years, Parkland has ranked among the best hospitals in the United States in *U.S. News & World Report's* annual survey. For the 2001 survey, the hospital was recognized in 11 categories: rheumatology, endocrinology, gynecology, urology, otolaryngology, geriatrics, kidney disease, neurology/neurosurgery, gastroenterology, orthopedics and heart. Parkland was named as a 100 Top Hospital by HCIA-Sachs in 2000 for superior financial and clinical performance. In 1994, it earned the Foster G. McGaw Award for Excellence in Community Service and the John P. McGovern Humanitarian Medicine Award to Parkland's President and CEO Dr. Ron J. Anderson. Parkland earned the Public Service Excellence Award from the Public Employees Roundtable in 1996.

The awards and accolades punctuate years of dedicated service to the community; a tradition of service to the poor and the belief that health care should be made available to everyone. Although Parkland has all these attributes, it may be best known as the hospital to which President John F. Kennedy was transported and in which he died after his assassination in 1963. Over a 48-hour period, Parkland became the temporary seat of the U.S. government, the site of the death of the 35th president and the site of the death of Kennedy's accused assassin, Lee Harvey Oswald.

Parkland Hospital, the core of Parkland Health & Hospital System, was established in 1894 by the city of Dallas to care for the city's poor. In 1954, the hospital moved into a new, larger building and began accomplishing a series of medical "firsts." That same year, Parkland became the first civilian hospital in Texas to use an artificial kidney machine. The hospital developed one of the first nuclear medicine labs in the nation in 1956 and three years later began the first medical service in Texas specializing in pediatric infectious diseases.

The Regional Burn Center was established in 1962 and has treated more burn patients than any civilian burn center in the world. The burn center pioneered skin graft techniques, infection control and nutritional support for burn patients. To aid survival from severe burns, Parkland created a skin bank that grew to become the largest in the United States and then expanded furnishing corneas, bone, cartilage, tendon and other

Parkland Hospital

tissues for transplant. The tissue bank is one of the largest U.S. banks for transplantable tissue. In 1964, the hospital performed the first kidney transplant in Texas and continues to boast a mortality rate among the lowest in the nation.

Parkland's Community Oriented Primary Care program was established in 1989 to create health care outreach centers for underserved neighborhoods, bringing preventive medicine to indigent residents and alleviating the problem of long waits for service at the hospital. The program immunizes children and brings medical care to the homeless through mobile medical vans at city shelters. Nine centers are now located in strategic areas of Dallas County, and many of the locations have social service agencies located under the same roof with health care professionals to provide an additional layer of support to communities in need.

Parkland Health & Hospital System is able to provide the finest and most up-to-date medical care available to its patients through its affiliation with The University of Texas Southwestern Medical Center at Dallas. Parkland's research component is the UT Southwestern Medical School, participating in over 600 research protocols each year. Parkland is the teaching hospital for the medical school. That fact, coupled with the research, keeps the hospital on the cutting edge of medicine.

Parkland has many Centers of Excellence that are recognized around the world including burn treatment and research, epilepsy, trauma care, kidney/pancreas transplant, cardiovascular services, diabetes treatment, gastroenterology, radiology, neonatal intensive care and high-risk pregnancy. The hospital also delivers more babies than any other U.S. hospital — more than 16,323 in fiscal 2001. Parkland delivered the Davis quintuplets in 1975, the Zuniga quintuplets in 1998 and a set of naturally conceived quadruplets in 2000.

Parkland's Emergency department handles more than 119,500 patient visits each year and the hospital was the first Level I Trauma Center in the region. The community health centers and outpatient clinics average close to 1 million visits each year. Parkland was named the hospital for contagious diseases by the Centers for Disease Control in Atlanta. The North Texas Poison Center is located in the hospital and is the area's only certified regional poison center. The center receives 250 emergency calls each day for its team of specially trained registered nurses, pharmacists, paramedics, physicians and a board of more than 60 expert consultants.

As the Dallas County hospital serving indigent patients, Parkland Health & Hospital System has served as a safety net since 1894. Over those 100-plus years, Parkland has gone beyond a simple safety net to bring health care out to needy patients through the Community Oriented Primary Care program and to become, and remain, a facility on the cutting edge of medicine through its affiliation with UT Southwestern Medical Center. The primary mission of Parkland is to make health care available to all residents of Dallas County. Parkland has achieved its mission and continues to accomplish much more.

Maternity Ward

PRESBYTERIAN HOSPITAL OF DALLAS

THE ROOTS OF PRESBYTERIAN HOSPITAL OF Dallas go back to 1955, beginning at the Dallas Country Club. During a round of golf, Frank H. Kidd Jr., M.D. and Dr. William M. Elliot Jr., pastor of Highland Park Presbyterian Church, discussed creating a new hospital that would be affiliated with the church. Highland Park Presbyterian Church member Toddie Lee Wynne Sr., and Roderic Bell, who would become the hospital's first administrator, completed the key players in the hospital's founding. The vision of these men became reality in 1966 when Presbyterian Hospital of Dallas opened with 300 beds, 200 physicians on the medical staff and 155 employees. By 2002 Presbyterian had grown to 934 licensed beds, 1,335 physicians on the medical staff and 4,200 employees, and it continues to operate under its service mark, "It's all in the way we treat you."

The founding group located a site for the new hospital. The land was just east of Central Expressway, an area that was considered "far North Dallas" at the time, and it had been the home of Reynolds Presbyterian Orphanage, which had moved to Waxahachie. The purchase of this land was made possible by a pledge from Algur H. Meadows, which spurred a $4 million fund-raising campaign. In 1960 the Presbyterian name was released to the hospital by the North Central Texas Presbytery and ground was broken in 1963. Presbyterian Hospital of Dallas opened to the public on May 3, 1966, as the fifth general hospital in Dallas and the first major general hospital built in the area since 1927.

The hospital expanded during the 1970s with the openings of Professional Building I in 1970 and Professional Building II in 1978. Presbyterian Hospital of Kaufman became the second hospital in the Presbyterian system in 1979. A third facility, a full-service retirement community, Presbyterian Village North, was added to the system in 1980.

A major addition to the hospital, the Margot Perot Women's and Children's Hospital, was dedicated in 1983. The facility provides advanced health care services in obstetrics, gynecology, ambulatory surgery and newborn services. The hospital, now known as the Margot Perot Center for Women and Infants, includes labor-delivery-recovery suites where the mother goes through the entire birthing process in a homelike atmosphere. The center's ARTS program, Assisted Reproductive Technology Services, performed the first laparoscopy for the retrieval of oocytes in 1984 and currently provides a range of fertility treatments including in-vitro fertilization.

The mid-1980s were busy years for Presbyterian Hospital of Dallas. A new hospital, Presbyterian Hospital of Winnsboro, opened in 1985, and in 1986 Presbyterian Healthcare System became the official name of Presbyterian's expanding organization of health care facilities. The system has continued to grow since that time, adding a number of affiliates including additional hospitals and health services.

Presbyterian Hospital of Dallas provides technologically advanced care and a high degree of personal service.

In 1986 the Presbyterian Healthcare Foundation was chartered as a nonprofit foundation to provide volunteer and fund development programs in support of the system. The Foundation plays an important role in Presbyterian's mission of providing high-quality health care within and outside the hospital walls as it works to protect the long-term fiscal viability of the Presbyterian Healthcare System. Along with the Foundation, Presbyterian has an extensive and effective hospital volunteer program. Volunteers provide a wide range of services to the hospital including escorting patients to their rooms from the admitting office, staffing information desks, delivering flowers to patient rooms and helping materials management stock operating room supplies. They also assist in the recovery room by acting as liaisons to the family, filling ice buckets, stocking blanket warmers and conducting other important tasks.

Presbyterian Healthcare System continued its growth by joining forces with Tarrant County health care leader Harris Methodist Hospital System to form Texas Health Resources in 1997. Adding Arlington Memorial Hospital to the family made Texas Health Resources the largest nonprofit health system in Texas. Presbyterian Healthcare System remains a part of Texas Health Resources.

Into the 2000s Presbyterian Hospital of Dallas has moved from being a large community hospital to becoming a regional referral center known for providing care for complicated cases with a high degree of personal service. Many innovative, minimally invasive procedures are performed at Presbyterian Hospital of Dallas including osteochondral cartilage transfer for orthopedic patients and Gamma Knife, a non-invasive procedure for lesions in the brain.

Presbyterian Hospital of Dallas is best known for women's and infants' services at the Margot Perot Center. For its continued excellence in obstetrics services, readers of *Dallas Child* magazine have named Presbyterian Hospital of Dallas the "Best Place to Have a Baby" for the past decade. Along with its birthing suites and respected fertility program, the facility has a 47-bed Level III Neonatal Intensive Care Unit (NICU) with advanced technology and board-certified neonatologists on its medical staff. The center's 21-bed Special Care Nursery provides care for infants who have improved and graduated

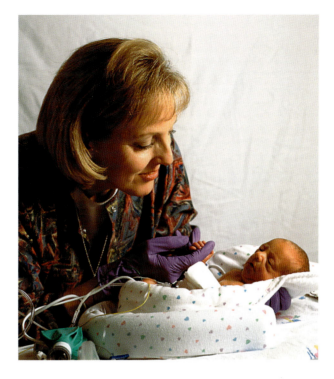

Presbyterian's Margot Perot Center is known for its exceptional care of women and infants. Its NICU cares for premature infants and other newborns with special needs.

from the NICU but may still need extra care. Care for high-risk obstetrics cases and cancer in women is also offered at the Margot Perot Center, which is also home to the Women's Diagnostic and Breast Center.

The advanced care offered at Presbyterian Hospital of Dallas stretches beyond care for women and infants. Its Cardiovascular Services are a crucial part of the care provided for patients with complicated conditions. From the Ross Procedure for repair of damaged heart valves, to clinical trials aimed at the study and treatment of heart disease, Presbyterian Hospital of Dallas is at the forefront of cardiac care. Patients with neurological disorders will find a host of specialized services including care for Parkinson's, epilepsy and stroke. Orthopedic surgeons on the medical staff offer comprehensive care that addresses joint replacement, hand and upper extremity disorders as well as orthopedic oncology. Other areas of focus include gastrointestinal services, rehabilitation and oncology. Patients find many specialized programs as well, including the Arthritis Consultation Center as well as the Eating Disorders and Asthma Management Programs.

These and many other services are offered at Presbyterian Hospital of Dallas in a patient-focused environment of high-quality care where each patient is treated as more than a health care case but also as a whole person — mind, body and spirit.

THE SALVATION ARMY

THE SALVATION ARMY IS AND WILL ALWAYS BE first and foremost about hope — hope for the destitute and the poor, the hungry and the homeless, the lonely and the confused. The Salvation Army is about second chances and changing lives. It is about the love of a merciful God. It is about the blessing of serving God by giving to others and about preserving the dignity of each individual being served.

The Salvation Army has been serving the needs of the people of Dallas for more than 100 years. Its services have always been wide and varied, meeting the unique challenges of the decades. In the 21st century it is a model of non-profit outreach providing social services literally from before birth to death. It has met human needs throughout the years with an impeccable reputation for integrity and efficiency that has made Dallas an innovative leader for Salvation Army work nationally and internationally.

A perfect example of how the organization makes a difference in thousands of lives daily in Dallas is The Salvation Army Carr P. Collins Social Service Center. The 172,000-square-foot complex focuses on helping individuals and families resolve life's immediate challenges. Each individual or family that comes for help is assigned a case worker to help sort out their particular issues using the multitude of resources available.

At the Carr P. Collins Center there is a Men's Shelter that houses up to 132 men per night and a Women's Shelter that houses up to 40 women, with day care being provided for those with children. Residents are helped with finding permanent employment and shelter. The center also provides life-skills classes, a substance abuse program and nutritious meals. More than 500 families per month are provided emergency services that include financial assistance to pay rent and utility bills and to meet other emergency obligations. A domestic violence shelter offers abused women, many with children, continual security, legal assistance, emotional support and counseling. A homeless prevention program, as well as The Salvation Army's trademark spiritual counseling and chapel service programs, are also available.

The Salvation Army has also responded to the particular challenges of the citizens of impoverished neighborhoods in the Greater Dallas Metroplex by providing services through 10 major community centers. A vast array of programs for youths through seniors is offered, including: church services, scouting-type programs, choirs, senior citizens' groups, athletic teams, day care, Bible studies, after-school tutoring, libraries, computer training, summer day camps, neighborhood safety meetings, life-skills classes and musical band programs. In addition to all of these key programs for stabilizing and revitalizing low-income neighborhoods, the centers also provide social service needs like food, clothing, and rent and utility bill assistance.

The Salvation Army is particularly in the public eye during the Thanksgiving and Christmas seasons. The familiar bell ringers with Salvation Army Red Kettles collect money at more than 250 locations to support local community programs. Bags of groceries are collected and distributed and more

than 1,000 Christmas dinners are served. The Angel Tree program allows shoppers at malls and donors at corporations and organizations the chance to buy specific Christmas gifts for underprivileged children and seniors. More than 200,000 Angel Tree gifts are distributed annually.

Also targeting youth is The Salvation Army's Project Tomorrow program, which provides up to 18 scholarships for middle and high school students at Salvation Army Community Centers to attend a private, Christian-based college preparatory school.

When Salvation Army founder William Booth began preaching hope and salvation in 1865, thieves, prostitutes, gamblers and drunkards were among his first converts to Christianity. More than 150 years later, the Adult Rehabilitation Center in Dallas serves 130 male alcoholics in its program of counseling, work therapy, recreational activities and spiritual counseling. This center is directly supported by the sale of items that have been donated to the Army's popular thrift stores. These thrift stores help low-income people buy goods at prices they can afford.

One of the most important efforts of The Salvation Army is visitation among the poor, lowly and the sick. This cause is embraced by the League of Mercy program in Dallas, which consists of women officers who coordinate groups to spread comfort and cheer to the lonely and suffering in nursing homes, VA hospitals and to the home-bound.

The Salvation Army may concentrate on the needy, but it is a wellspring of salvation and rejuvenation that thousands of volunteers from all walks of life feel after helping out at The Salvation Army. Volunteering has provided many with a sense of purpose in life and a way to thank God by serving those who are less fortunate. Whether these volunteers have given money, time, in-kind gifts or prayers, their generosity and love have inspired generations.

The reason The Salvation Army's donors have been so supportive throughout the years is because they know when they contribute to the Army they are giving their money where it will do the most good. Out of every dollar donated, 87 cents goes directly to meeting needs. Moreover, all Salvation Army administrative services are handled with both frugality and humility.

The organization's supporters are many and varied. They include countless individuals, an array of major corporations, and even Dallas' professional sports teams and celebrities. These compassionate individuals and groups fulfill a desire to positively affect their world by contributing monetary and in-kind gifts, as well as by serving as volunteers and hosting special events.

All of the operations of The Salvation Army are supervised by trained, commissioned officers who undergo two years of intensive formal education at Salvation Army Schools for Officer Training, plus five years of required continuing education. These men and women have dedicated their lives, skills and service to God.

For more than 100 years The Salvation Army has responded to the immediate needs of people and the long-term health of communities. It has provided the physical necessities of life as well as the emotional and spiritual grounding that allows individuals and families to prosper. The Salvation Army continues to turn help into hope.

Quality of Life

THE UNIVERSITY OF TEXAS AT DALLAS

IN THE COMPETITIVE WORLD OF HIGHER education, colleges across the country often move at frenetic paces. Eager to stay one step ahead of its rivals, or one notch above each other on ever-present rankings lists, a school might lure prospective students with a nationally ranked football team, or even offer pop-culture courses on Madonna or Oprah. These tactics might catch the eye of many an impressionable 17- or 18-year-old; however, appealing to incoming students' lowest common denominator isn't what The University of Texas at Dallas (UTD) is about. Offering a top-quality education in the sciences, business and liberal arts is. It's the crux of what the school calls its "strategic intent."

The university was founded only 33 years ago, but through the years, U.T. Dallas' enrollment has grown at an impressive clip. In 2001, more than 12,500 students attended UTD, which is one of the fastest-growing public universities in the United States and is home to *the* fastest-growing engineering school in the country. Students and professors at the school are tops in their respective roles, too: average SAT scores at UTD are consistently in the 1200 range, among the highest in Texas; and the school counts among its faculty and researchers a Nobel Prize winner and numerous experts in their respective fields.

It's not uncommon for school administrators to talk strategy. And frequently, the game of chess figures prominently (both literally and figuratively) in the school's business model. In June 2001, UTD was named "Chess College of the Year" for its top-ranked chess team, which had won the "Final Four" of chess earlier that year. And fittingly, school officials say the game speaks to UTD's current mentality. "We view chess as a metaphor for intellectual rigor and academic excellence," explains UTD President Dr. Franklyn G. Jenifer.

True enough, the school's evolution does seem to parallel moves on a chessboard. Steady and deliberate, calculated and methodical, with more than a few flashes of brilliance, The University of Texas at Dallas has taken a decidedly unique road to its current prominence.

Unlike most other universities, the school was built from the top down. The concept was the brainchild of a trio of men who had founded North Texas-based Texas Instruments (TI) in the 1950s. Eugene McDermott, Erik Jonsson and Cecil Green had a problem back then — they couldn't find enough qualified people locally to work for TI. But they weren't content simply to keep hiring out-of-state talent. They felt strongly about the need to create an educational forum where people could be trained and then stay in the area and put what they had learned to work.

In 1961, the three visionaries started what came to be known as the Southwest Center for Advanced Studies (SCAS). Later that decade, the state Legislature grew to share the trio's vision that there needed to be an educational institution in North Texas dedicated to fostering science-based learning. McDermott, Jonsson and Green then donated the SCAS and the lands surrounding it to The University of Texas System; and in 1969, the state officially recognized the resulting entity as The University of Texas at Dallas.

At that point in the school's history, UTD offered only graduate degrees. Slowly, however, the university began to make its move. By the mid-1970s, junior- and senior-level undergraduates were admitted, and in 1990 UTD matriculated its first freshman class. Enrollment at U.T. Dallas soon began to grow, but wisely, the university didn't forfeit quality for quantity. To this day enrollment standards at UTD are high: almost two-thirds of entering freshmen are in the top 25 percent of their graduating class. The popular barometer on grading schools, *U.S. News and World Report*,

President Franklyn G. Jenifer

Dynamic Dallas: An Illustrated History

consistently has ranked UTD as one of the three best public universities in the state and has rated some of its programs, such as audiology, among the best of their kind in the country.

The University of Texas at Dallas, located in the city's northern suburb of Richardson, revels in the obvious benefits that come with being affiliated with the University of Texas System, including comparatively low tuition. Students may pay a state-school price, but in return they receive a high-quality education. "At UTD, we sometimes say that you get a private school education at a public school price," says President Jenifer. "We try very hard to be a cut above."

The school seems to be one step ahead, too. UTD officials note that their institution "doesn't try to be all things" to all students. The mother lode of the curriculum is heavy on the sciences: computer science (UTD ranks second in the nation in computer science grads), engineering, chemistry, mathematics and molecular biology are among the offerings. But alongside these degree programs, the school also affords students a strong liberal arts program and features an excellent School of Management. "It is critically important that we remain focused on the things that we do well," Dr. Jenifer says.

Clearly, the university is doing better than "well," especially in the area of research. The school that was founded by researchers is now, more than 30 years later, making a name for itself as a first-class research facility.

Three projects that researchers at the university are working on are lately garnering much attention. In fall 2001, two pioneers in the cutting-edge science of nanotechnology joined the school's faculty and established an interdisciplinary UTD NanoTech Institute on campus

(nanoscience is the study of materials smaller than 100 nanometers — or 1/100th the width of a human hair strand). With their expertise, they hope to achieve breakthroughs that could revolutionize such fields as electronics and medicine.

A second research project, aided by a $10 million grant from the National Aeronautics and Space Administration (NASA), is aimed at figuring out how to predict weather in outer space. And a third involves the establishment of the U.T. Dallas Sickle Cell Disease Research Center on campus to find better treatments and ultimately a cure for sickle cell disease, a serious blood disorder whose victims are primarily African-Americans.

The caliber of this research mirrors the top-tier level of the students and faculty at UTD. "Cream of the crop" is an expression that would fit. Or, as one official at the school is fond of saying: "Cream of the cream."

The opportunities on the horizon for UTD seem endless. The school's burgeoning popularity with educators and students alike is resounding. Excellent students, a strong faculty, innovative research programs and a curriculum targeted to 21st century needs have combined for a (theoretical, of course) checkmate.

UTD was named "Chess College of the Year" in 2001. Shown in photo is team captain Yuri Shulman, who is majoring in computer science

The UTD Mall

URSULINE ACADEMY OF DALLAS

URSULINE ACADEMY OF DALLAS IS A PRIVATE Catholic college-preparatory high school for young women in grades 9-12. Founded in 1874, the academy is the oldest continually operating school in Dallas, offering a values-based education in a caring Christian environment.

At Ursuline each student is encouraged to develop her individual talents, interests and potential through programs focused on academic excellence, spiritual formation, physical development, leadership, community building and service. Ursuline Academy, with its valued traditions, prepares young women to think critically and act responsibly in a global society.

The mission and rich heritage of Ursuline Academy are rooted in the vision of St. Angela Merici, who founded the Order of St. Ursula in Brescia, Italy, in 1535. At a time when the talents and abilities of women were largely forgotten, Angela realized the crucial role of women in the church and the world, as witnessed in her writings: "Love your daughters equally; do not prefer one more than another, because they are all creatures of God. And you do not know what He wants to make of them."

Angela's vision and mission quickly spread throughout Europe, and the education of girls became a primary ministry of the Ursuline order. The first religious order to reach North America, the French Ursulines founded a school in Quebec in 1639. They opened a convent and academy in New Orleans in 1727 and built their Galveston, Texas, house in 1847.

In 1873 Monsignor Claude M. Dubuis, Texas' first Catholic bishop, determined that the fledgling city of Dallas needed the Ursulines. On January 28, 1874, six Galveston Sisters, led by Mother St. Joseph Holly with $146 in their common purse, arrived in Dallas by train to establish a school in the frontier town. Their luggage had been lost and they had not been able to sleep. Incredible hardships lay ahead. It was an unusually severe winter and the four-room frame house Bishop Dubuis had built for them supplied little shelter from the weather. Water froze indoors and broke the pitchers on the washstands; rain and snow dripped through the roof, soaking the beds, bedding and other furniture; and only one room had a stove. Nonetheless, the Sisters set about their work. On February 2, less than a week after they arrived, the Ursulines opened their school with seven day students.

By the end of the first term Ursuline Academy had grown to 50 students, and the Sisters borrowed money to erect a better two-story building. By 1875 the Ursulines were able to establish their new convent and a day and boarding school. But they would still have to deal with and transcend the hot Texas sun, which had burned the vegetables in the ground that summer; the bitterly cold winter that followed — so cold that the rock foundation crumbled and had to be replaced — and the nationwide economic depression of the 1870s. In 1882 the Sisters began construction of their third building on a 10-acre site in East Dallas. In 1883 work was completed on the handsome Gothic structure designed by Nicholas J. Clayton, who had planned many of Galveston's beautiful structures.

News of the Ursulines' presence in Dallas had now spread to other areas, and newspapers praised the academy and its curriculum. In 1878 Ursuline Academy of Dallas

The Ursuline Academy of Dallas Class of 1943

"Old Ursuline" — the main section of the academy's beautiful Gothic building was completed in 1883. The Sisters' original four-room frame house is seen to the left.

was chartered by the Texas State Legislature. By 1890 the academy was drawing students from many states and Mexico, as well as from some of Dallas' most prominent families. The Ursuline Academy Alumnae Association was formed in 1899.

In 1950 Ursuline moved to a new building on Walnut Hill Lane in North Dallas, site of the present-day campus. Growing steadily over the years, the academy's expanded facilities now include 16 buildings beautifully situated on nearly 28 acres in the parklike setting. Today, Ursuline Academy continues its long tradition of academic excellence, innovation and service to the community. The diverse enrollment of nearly 800 young women students is about three-fourths Catholic. All students participate in programs for spiritual formation including schoolwide liturgies, class retreats and peer ministry.

The rigorous curriculum is built on strong core courses in English, math, science, social studies, theology and foreign language. Students also choose from a rich variety of electives in areas ranging from computer science and journalism to visual and performing arts. Physical education and athletics are important elements of student life.

Ursuline Academy has been an important part of the Dallas community in many ways. The Ursuline motto is *Serviam*, Latin for "I will serve." A key goal is for students to embrace a lifelong commitment to community service. Ursuline alumnae have earned an excellent reputation for service to the community, not just as students but also later in life. When students gain a sense of their heritage, they become aware of the academy's relationship with the larger world. By considering questions such as, "What makes life meaningful?" and "What is my contribution to life on this planet?" students prepare for future roles as active members of society. Often a service program will help a student find her life's work.

Progressive methods of education are characteristic of the Ursuline tradition. Today, students at the academy use technology as a tool to help them learn. Every student has a laptop computer, an approach that has broadened the educational venture in and out of the classroom. In 1996 Ursuline was one of six schools in the United States to pioneer the "Anywhere, Anytime Learning" program in partnership with Microsoft and Toshiba. Through *e-Serviam*, student teams create Web sites for nonprofit agencies that do not have funds to develop their own.

Sharing Gospel vision and values, Ursuline educators around the globe empower their students to be a transforming presence in today's world. With strong support from parents, alumnae and friends in the community, Ursuline Academy of Dallas continues its mission to prepare young women to be strong Christian leaders.

St. Angela Merici's dictum — to treat each young woman individually — is still the time-honored approach to education at Ursuline Academy.

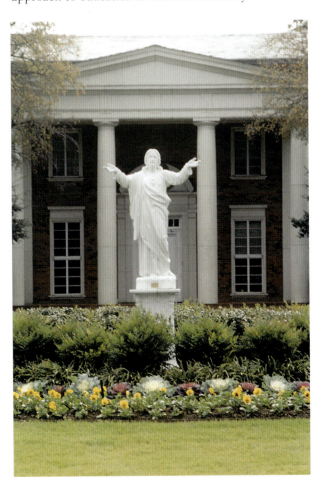

Ursuline Academy was among the first schools in the United States to integrate laptop technology into the curriculum.

In December 1950 the entire academy relocated to a new building in North Dallas on its Walnut Hill Lane property, site of the present-day Ursuline campus.

Quality of Life

CATHOLIC DIOCESE OF DALLAS

ON JULY 15, 1890, THE ROMAN CATHOLIC Diocese of Dallas was established by Pope Leo XIII. It included the entire northern portion of the State of Texas from Texarkana on the east to El Paso on the West, a distance of over 800 miles. The new diocese was carved out of the Diocese of Galveston and embraced 108,000 square miles, an area slightly larger than the state of Colorado. The estimated Catholic population was about 15,000.

By 2002 the Diocese of Dallas was reduced to 7,523 square miles, slightly smaller than the state of Delaware. In the process, all or portions of the dioceses of El Paso, Lubbock, Amarillo, Fort Worth, Tyler, Austin and San Angelo were carved from territory of the Dallas Diocese. Although downsized in area, the Catholic population of the present Diocese of Dallas is estimated in excess of 843,000.

Dallas Catholics were first served by circuit riding priests from Nacogdoches, the oldest city in Texas. Catholic history in Texas owes much to France, from whence came the clergy, bishops and religious who served in the pioneer days of the republic and early statehood. Under Spanish rule and the Republic of Mexico, particularly in the time of the missions in the 18th century, the Catholic faith was established by Franciscan missionaries.

The coming of the railroads in the 1860s and 1870s established Dallas as a commercial center. When the panic of 1873 caused the Texas and Pacific Railroad to temporarily halt its westward thrust at Dallas, the city became the railhead that shipped the millions of hides of the great buffalo herds wiped out by hunters eager to meet the demand for their fur.

A small clapboard church that served as Dallas' first cathedral was replaced in 1902 by Sacred Heart Cathedral, a neo-gothic building of red brick designed by early Texas architect Nicholas Clayton. It was one of the first churches to be built with electric lights, which were used in abundance with all the vaults of the apse lined with light bulbs. The effect was brilliant, but the maintenance was a nightmare. The cathedral, which was renamed Cathedral Santuario De Guadalupe in 1987, celebrated the centenary of its dedication on October 26, 2002.

As Dallas grew, the Catholic population increased with immigrants from the North and Midwest and from the South and Southeast. Many settlements were made by immigrants from Germany, Poland, Czechoslovakia, Ireland and other European countries. Others came from Mexico and Latin America, resulting in a confluence of cultures that has been enriched even more in past decades by an influx of immigrants from Asia and the Middle East.

The multicultural Catholic presence of 2002 includes 65 parishes and 10 missions, with liturgies celebrated regularly in eight languages other than English. Catholics are served by 209 priests, 152 deacons, 12 religious brothers and 154 women religious, 180 professional lay ministers and hundreds of volunteer lay ministers.

Catholic primary and secondary schools and religious education programs serve some 60,000 students. Two Catholic universities and one seminary serve the higher education needs of the diocese.

Chief pastors are Bishop Charles V. Grahmann, D.D., sixth Bishop of Dallas and Bishop Joseph A. Galante, D.D, J.CD. Coadjutor Bishop, of Dallas.

Dallas Catholics celebrated the centenary of the dedication of historic Cathedral Santuario De Guadalupe on October 26, 2002.

CATHOLIC EDUCATION OF DALLAS

FAITH AND KNOWLEDGE MEET IN DALLAS' Catholic schools. Dedicated to academic excellence, passing on Christian values and service to the community, the 41 Catholic elementary and secondary schools of the Diocese of Dallas serve 15,000 students.

Catholic education in Dallas dates back to the arrival of a group of Ursuline nuns from Galveston in 1874. Within a few years they had established two parochial schools and Ursuline Academy, which still serves the community. Other orders of women religious, including the Sisters of St. Mary of Namur, the School Sisters of Notre Dame, the Daughters of Charity of St. Vincent de Paul, the Holy Cross Sisters and others dedicated themselves to providing Catholic education to early settlers in northern Texas. Many, like St. Mary's School in Jefferson, opened in 1869, survived only a few years; others, like Ursuline Academy, have served the community for over a century and a quarter.

Vincentian Fathers established the first Catholic college in Dallas. Established in 1910 as Holy Trinity College, it was later renamed the University of Dallas, but it closed its doors in 1929. The charter lay dormant until 1955 when the Sisters of St. Mary of Namur reactivated it to relocate and expand Our Lady of Victory College in Fort Worth. The effort was expanded into the present University of Dallas, which opened its doors in September 1956. Today, the university, located in Irving, Texas, has more than 3,000 students in a variety of undergraduate and graduate programs. A second Catholic university began operations in the Diocese of Dallas in 1993. Our Lady of the Lake University of San Antonio operates weekend undergraduate and graduate programs at its campus in Irving.

Holy Trinity Seminary, located on the University of Dallas campus, was established in 1955 and moved into its present building in 1966. College level and pre-theology students from nine dioceses are in formation at Holy Trinity.

Today, the majority of Catholic school teachers and administrators are professional lay men and women, although men and women religious are still involved in Catholic education. Times change, but what remains constant is the quality of academics, the dedication of teachers and administrators, and the integration of religious values into the overall curriculum.

Admission at all Catholic schools is open to students of any race, faith or national origin. Tuition and availability of financial aid varies from institution to institution.

Catholic education truly is where faith and knowledge meet.

> **Admission at all Catholic schools is open to students of any race, faith or national origin.**

> **Times change, but what remains constant is the quality of academics, the dedication of teachers and administrators, and the integration of religious values into the overall curriculum.**

Dallas' first Catholic school was opened in 1874 by the Ursuline Nuns in this simple cabin on the grounds of Sacred Heart Procathedral. *Jibeen Be Ling Drawing*

CITY OF PLANO

PLANO, TEXAS, IS A POWERHOUSE AMONG the suburbs of Dallas. It was an All-America City recipient in 1994. *D Magazine* named Plano as one of the "Best Places in the Metroplex" to live. The city was listed in the book, *50 Fabulous Places to Raise Your Family*, and was ranked as one of the top 25 Safest Cities in the U.S. with a population over 75,000. *Ladies' Home Journal* ranked Plano 3rd in a list of America's Ten Best Cities for Women in 2000, and the city has been the 5th-fastest-growing city in the United States with a population over 100,000.

The history of Plano dates back to the early 1840s as settlers moved west into the Republic of Texas. Collin County became a county in 1846 and Texas a state in 1845. Plano received its name around 1850 and incorporated in 1873, giving the town a mayor, five aldermen and a constable. The year 1872 brought a major change to the new city with the arrival of the Houston and Texas Railroad. Plano was the first depot by rail coming into Collin County from the south. The stagecoach had already arrived in Plano around 20 years before, linking the city to the rest of the state and the nation.

Plano schools date back to the early 1880s. After a vote the town assumed control of schooling and levied a 50-cent school tax. In 1899 Plano schools began operating under a board of education. The business community of Plano dates back to the city's earliest days, with a sawmill, gristmill, cotton gin and a store. Before the arrival of the railroad, raising livestock and farming were the principal business activities. The rail lines brought trade, and after the 1880s almost anything could be bought or traded in Plano.

In the 1960s, after close to a century of largely rural growth, Plano city planners began preparing for the influx of big business to the Dallas area. When the U.S. population began a historic shift to the area in the 1970s, Plano welcomed newcomers and became one of the fastest-growing cities in Texas and the United States.

Plano has become an attractive city in which to live and do business. Since the late 1990s over 10 million square feet of space has been developed in the Legacy business park. Legacy Town Center, a pedestrian-friendly development in the park, is a 150-acre mixed-use project including apartments, retail establishments, office space and a hotel. Legacy Town Center has an estimated buildout value of $500 million.

A 2001 "new urbanism" development is renewing downtown Plano with apartments, retail shops and office space. The development is adjacent to a planned Dallas Area Rapid Transit light rail stop and is the first step in creating a transit village, integrating residential, commercial, civic and cultural elements.

Plano's history reaches back to the wide open spaces of Texas' past, and it has grown to become an "All-American city."

Plano's Legacy Town Center complex viewed from the Post Legacy residential and retail complex in Legacy Park

The early days of Plano

DALLAS CHRISTIAN SCHOOL

DALLAS CHRISTIAN SCHOOL HAS BEEN IN THE business of educating young people for 45 years, but its mission is much broader than just teaching the basics of reading, writing and math. At Dallas Christian School, academics find a balance with spirituality; the school's mission is to prepare students for eternity as well as an earthly life.

Dallas Christian was chartered in 1957, founded by members of the Church of Christ, who were looking for a safe, nurturing and Christian environment to provide children a quality education. The sprawling campus includes buildings purchased from Christian College of the Southwest.

Dallas Christian offers classes from kindergarten through 12th grade. Parents can enroll students as young as 4 at W.W. Caruth Early Childhood Learning Center, which houses K-4 and K-5 programs, first and second grade, and a LEAP program for children too advanced for Kindergarten and not yet ready for first grade.

The school's trustees believe in laying the foundation for caring, productive lives early in a child's education. Elementary teachers focus on helping students integrate desirable character traits into their lives. By the time the student reaches middle and high school, each of them is ready to take on community service. The school emphasizes giving to those less fortunate by requiring all high school students to participate in service projects.

Teachers know each child by name, even though the student body is more than 800 strong. Discipline is a priority, uniforms are required, dress codes are enforced, campus police address safety issues and a campus minister is always available to the students. With open discussions and a spiritual bond, the staff and students interact much like family.

The nurturing environment inspires students to achieve excellence in both academics and sports. A number of graduates have been scholars and semifinalists in the National Merit Scholars program. Dallas Christian teams have been state champions 19 times in various sports since 1980, and numerous athletes have gone on to play at collegiate and professional levels.

The tenets of the Bible and Christianity are critical to the learning process at Dallas Christian, but children of many religious and ethnic backgrounds are enrolled at the school. Administrators believe diversity is crucial — they work to reach out to families from a variety of cultures.

The 100-acre campus is located among the rolling hills near the intersection of I-30 and I-635. The highway access makes the school convenient for families around Dallas-Fort Worth and beyond. Students come from as far away as Rockwall, north Dallas and Waxahachie.

Enrollment has been on the rise since the mid-1980s, requiring expansion. In the 1990s the school remodeled the junior high building and erected the Cox Event Center, a 27,500-square-foot multi-purpose complex that serves athletics, music, drama and other special events. The future will bring a new science and technology learning center that will include classroom labs for biology, science and computer studies.

Additions and expansions will change the look of the school by 2003, but administrators promise the spiritual core of Dallas Christian will never undergo any renovations, remaining a strong testament for generations.

DALLAS THEOLOGICAL SEMINARY

JUST EAST OF DOWNTOWN DALLAS, NEAR legendary Deep Ellum and not far from the historic Lakewood neighborhood, Dallas Theological Seminary sprouts not just deep Dallas roots, but national and international influence.

With its longstanding evangelical traditions, DTS is the world's second-largest interdenominational seminary — the only seminary that requires a study of all 66 books of the Bible. Dallas Seminary's high academic and theological standards draw students from all over the globe, many from impressive career positions. Students come eager to translate sharpened biblical knowledge into informed positions in academics, medicine, economics, politics, military, churches and Christian parachurch organizations, again, across the globe.

In 2001 DTS inaugurated its fifth president in 77 years: Dr. Mark Bailey. While the school is known for its faithfulness to conservative evangelical theology, Dr. Bailey entered the office excited about new technology, expansion, and using 21st century methods to provide training and leadership.

"Throughout our history Dallas Seminary has provided training you can trust," Dr. Bailey says. "Our founding president, Dr. Lewis Sperry Chafer, passionately modeled the pursuit of studying God's Word. Continuing in that tradition, I am convinced that we have one of the finest selections of degree programs to be found anywhere. Each program is a comprehensive quest to know the grace of God through His revelation. However, we offer more than programs. We are intent on equipping leaders who can be followed. Our faculty has stayed the course and is prepared to invest in the lives God entrusts to us. At Dallas Seminary, that model has captured our hearts."

Of Dallas Seminary's over 10,000 graduates worldwide, many are leading voices in evangelicalism. In the United States alone, DTS alumni head the *Ryrie Study Bible, The Living Bible* and nationally syndicated radio ministries such as Tony Evans' "Urban Alternative" and Chuck Swindoll's daily "Insight for Living," which reaches 131 countries. DTS alumni have published thousands of books and countless articles, and graduates also founded Young Life, Men's Leadership Ministries, FamilyLife, Rreach International and Walk Thru the Bible.

In 2001 the diverse DTS student body of over 1,600 assembled some 182 international students, 400 women and 302 minority students from 50 states, 56 countries and more than 55 denominations. Of the school's 10 degree plans, the master of theology has the bulk of the students, offering 11 tracks in such areas as chaplaincy, media arts and Bible translation. The five master of arts degrees are in counseling, Bible translation, education, cross-cultural ministries and general biblical studies. Other degree plans include master of sacred theology, doctor of ministry, doctor of philosophy and a certificate of graduate studies. DTS has campus extension sites in the Chattanooga/Atlanta, Houston, San Antonio/Austin and Tampa areas.

Dallas Theological Seminary, a worldwide cornerstone for evangelical Christianity, has exceptional students coming from everywhere and knowledgeable graduates heading for everywhere. Dr. Bailey explains the seminary's appeal: "Around the globe, people look to this school for its firm commitment to the Word of God in the work — past and present — of our professors and staff, students and alumni. DTS is known for commitment to the Bible, and people trust that."

FRISCO, TEXAS

THE CITY OF FRISCO, TEXAS, GREW RAPIDLY through the 1990s and into the 21st century. Its population of just over 6,500 in 1990 is expected to reach 300,000 by 2025. In 2000 Frisco was the fastest-growing city in Texas and the second-fastest-growing city in the United States with a population between 10,000 and 50,000. Anticipating this phenomenal growth, the Frisco Economic Development Corporation (EDC) was founded in 1991 to improve economic opportunities and quality of life for the citizens of Frisco.

The strategic vision for the corporation is to expand and diversify the local tax base, create job opportunities for all levels of employment, encourage responsible, diverse growth and development, and enhance Frisco's quality of life as an attractive and desirable place in which to live, work, play and grow. The Frisco EDC has developed dynamic partnerships with local and state governments as well as private developers to meet this challenge.

The city of Frisco in conjunction with the EDC, Frisco Community Development Corporation, Frisco ISD and the Southwest Sports Group brought a $300 million development to the city in 2001. The public/private development includes two sports facilities — a training facility for the Dallas Stars hockey club and a minor league baseball ballpark, and over 1 million square feet of new office, retail, residential, convention center and hotel space. The baseball park and hockey arena are scheduled to open in 2003, and the hotel and convention center will be started in 2004.

The corporation is also involved in a redevelopment project of an unused airport that faced turbulent times including litigation and bankruptcy. In June 2000 the Frisco EDC bought the property, which due to residential development could no longer function as an airport. The corporation has hired a professional consultant to develop a master plan to market the property and the surrounding 1,500 acres as a technology business park.

Another success story for Frisco is the 1.6-million-square-foot Stonebriar Centre shopping mall. The $200 million project was facilitated by an incentive package developed by the city, EDC, CDC and school district. Several retailers have chosen to break into the Southwest market at Stonebriar Centre, creating a unique shopping experience for visitors. A 126-acre power retail center, The Centre at Preston Ridge is located adjacent to the mall.

Frisco Square, located on 147 acres, will provide a 1920s vintage downtown business and residential district for Frisco. With more than 3 million square feet of planned office, retail, restaurant, entertainment and residential development, Frisco Square will also be home to Frisco's new city hall, library and heritage center.

The Frisco EDC markets the city of Frisco, recruits new business and through a contract with the Frisco Chamber of Commerce, works with existing businesses to further develop the City's economy. The city of Frisco is realizing phenomenal growth, and the Frisco Economic Development Corporation along with its partners is uncovering, promoting and maximizing the economic opportunity in that growth.

Fast-growing Frisco has new office, technology and business parks

Quality of Life

INTERNATIONAL LINGUISTICS CENTER

The worldwide faces of ILC's efforts

THE INTERNATIONAL LINGUISTICS CENTER (ILC) is a Dallas organization with a global reach. It was founded in 1971 and is located on a large campus in southwest Dallas. It is home to SIL International and its sister organization, Wycliffe Bible Translators. The campus includes the Graduate Institute of Applied Linguistics (GIAL), an adjunct campus for the linguistics program of the University of Texas at Arlington and the International Museum of Cultures.

SIL and Wycliffe trace their roots to 1934 and a two-student, two-faculty "school" begun in a northwest Arkansas chicken coop. Subsequently SIL has become one of the world's largest linguistics and literacy organizations. Its scientific linguistics expertise is applied toward the development of those people groups whose languages are not in writing. Once the languages are analyzed and committed to writing, people are taught to read and write. Primers, health books, folktales, the New Testament, portions of the Old Testament and finally a dictionary are translated into the focus language. Wycliffe supports SIL's work by providing personnel and funding from more than 30 countries.

SIL has completed 540 projects. Now about 40 million people have their own language in writing because of its work and millions have learned to read and write. Currently SIL is involved in 1,100 projects in 60 countries. For example, in early 2000 SIL dedicated its 500th New Testament, developed for the 60,000 Javanese people of Suriname.

The work of SIL is far from complete. Both SIL and other sources estimate that as many as 3,000 languages, representing about 400 million people, are not yet in writing. The development of a local written language establishes an educational foundation from which the people can make their own political, economic and spiritual choices. The ability to read and write is more easily developed in the mother tongue; then this new capability can be used to learn additional languages. SIL has become one of the world's largest non-governmental literacy organizations.

The Graduate Institute of Applied Linguistics offers courses in linguistics, sociolinguistics, literacy, language survey and anthropology year-round. It offers a certificate program in Applied Linguistics and two degree programs: master of arts with a major in applied linguistics and master of arts with a major in language development.

The International Museum of Cultures is an ethnographic museum with life-size and miniature exhibits portraying diverse people from around the world including people of Papua New Guinea in the South Pacific and jungle dwellers from Ecuador and Peru.

For over 30 years the International Linguistics Center has been the international focus of a program giving hope and educational opportunity to those without hope, those who do not even have their own language in writing.

The ILC campus

MEDICAL CITY DALLAS HOSPITAL

MEDICAL CITY DALLAS HOSPITAL HAS BEEN A part of the Dallas community since 1974, when a group of innovative, forward-thinking individuals set out to create a different kind of hospital.

These businessmen and physicians envisioned a medical community that could adapt to the continuing concerns of health care professionals, including the time constraints of doctors and the need for high-tech facilities to handle the demands of emerging specialty health care fields. The hospital they created to resolve these concerns has helped to shape the medical community in Dallas for over 25 years.

Medical City Dallas Hospital started a new generation of hospital complexes. Physician offices, diagnostic testing and support facilities are located within the physical plant in an environment unlike any other hospital. Here, atriums, fountains and landscaped open areas soothe the spirit even as the body is healed. Shops, restaurants and many other amenities are available to patients and guests alike.

But the focus remains on providing a level of patient care that is consistently outstanding. As a result, Medical City Dallas Hospital continues to be a magnet to attract physicians who are national and international leaders in their specialties.

Medical City is located in the heart of North Dallas at Central Expressway and Forest Lane. The 588-bed tertiary care center is home to the North Texas Hospital for Children at Medical City Dallas, the world-renowned Dallas Craniofacial Center and one of the top Transplant Centers in the country.

More than 1,300 physicians practice 85 medical specialties at Medical City. Patients come from all over the United States and 60 foreign countries to receive health care that is recognized on local, national and international levels.

Medical City Dallas Hospital consistently earns Accreditation with Commendation — the highest level of accreditation from the Joint Commission on Accreditation of Healthcare Organizations. In 1999 the Heart Transplant Program at Medical City was recognized as a top program in the country by the Department of Health and Human Services and today is one of the most active transplant programs in North Texas.

Physicians in the Cardiovascular Institute are at the forefront of cutting-edge technological innovations such as robotic-assisted microsurgery for optimum precision, beating heart surgeries and minimally invasive heart surgeries.

Medical City is one of the premier cancer centers in North Texas. Patients undergoing life-saving stem cell transplants stay in separate state-of-the-art facilities that are uniquely designed to give them the best chances for successful outcomes.

Women's Services offers a continuum of care for women in all stages of life. A full spectrum of services includes a state-of-the-art Labor and Delivery Unit, Intensive Care Unit, and Level III Neonatal and Pediatric Intensive Care Units.

The North Texas Hospital for Children at Medical City Dallas is a comprehensive children's hospital that serves as a regional referral center. Physicians from virtually every subspecialty are available, including pediatric cardiovascular, oncology and neuroscience services.

More than 25 years ago, Medical City Dallas Hospital began an innovative approach to health care by creating an environment that was aesthetically pleasing and practical for physicians and patients. In the process, Medical City has earned a sterling reputation for providing timely, efficient and effective medical care.

Medical City Dallas Hospital started a new generation of hospital complexes that has helped to shape the Dallas medical community for more than 25 years.

Quality of Life

OLD CITY PARK: THE HISTORICAL VILLAGE OF DALLAS

IN 1966 A GROUP OF CONCERNED CITIZENS, led by Mrs. Sawnie Aldredge, organized the Dallas County Heritage Society in order to save Millermore, the largest remaining antebellum mansion in Dallas. In 1967, after the Society received a charter as a nonprofit educational corporation, the city of Dallas allowed Millermore to be moved into City Park, the community's oldest public park, founded in 1876.

Millermore was reconstructed and opened to the public in 1969. In 1971 the Heritage Society asked the city to work with it to bring additional buildings of historic value to the park and develop a museum of architectural and cultural history focusing on the period 1840-1910. This proposal became Dallas's first official bicentennial project: Old City Park. Since then, the Heritage Society has moved nearly 40 historic structures to Old City Park, restored them, furnished them appropriately for their time period, and developed a series of living history educational programs designed to bring the past alive for both school children and adult visitors.

Old City Park: The Historical Village of Dallas is one of only five museums in the city of Dallas accredited by the American Association of Museums. Its educational programs and special events attract nearly 100,000 visitors each year who can watch a blacksmith at work, savor the smells of fresh food being prepared in the log kitchen, visit with an Hispanic interpreter telling the story of Mexican Americans in Dallas, participate in a hands-on crafts project, eat at the museum's 1876 farmhouse restaurant, or sit in one of several porch rocking chairs and enjoy the small-town atmosphere just minutes from downtown Dallas.

Dynamic Dallas: An Illustrated History

PRESERVATION DALLAS

IT IS AN IRONY OF THIS HIGH-TECH AGE THAT people have grown nostalgic for nostalgia. It seems the faster people plunge into change, the more they long for an anchor that ties them to the past. History and its markers take on renewed importance as they tether people to a pier of calm.

The phenomenal expansion of the 20th century left many American cities with new faces: the texture of sandstone and clapboard gave way to slick steel and glass. Parking lots paved over green spaces and a fluorescent glare whited out the warm glow of gaslights. As if squashed under the weight of a heavy, giant foot, cities spread to the outer limits of their suburbs. And all too often, the center did not hold. The historical centers and landmarks of many American cities atrophied and all but died in that century of rapid growth, expansion and change.

There were, however, in the city of Dallas a few voices that shouted out for help — help in preserving the past so as to strengthen the foundation as the city's structure stretched into ever-changing shapes and textures. Preservation Dallas, itself having changed and redesigned itself from its original identity as the Historic Preservation League founded in 1972, emerged as an advocate for preservation of the city's historic neighborhoods and buildings. Energized by its 1993 move into the Queen Anne-style Frederick Wilson House on Swiss Avenue, with the assistance of the Meadows Foundation, Preservation Dallas has provided leadership and advocacy in both preservation and revitalization.

Today, Preservation Dallas is a dynamic organization with membership in excess of 1,000 citizens who share and shape its vision and mission. The Preservation Center acts as a clearinghouse of information and resources about inner-city living opportunities. It offers assistance to neighborhoods interested in preservation and revitalization.

Preservation Dallas also offers broad educational opportunities such as architectural tours, seminars, Intown Outings and a Historic House Specialist certificate to area realtors. Working with local, state and national officials, Preservation Dallas is a highly visible advocate encouraging tax incentives for rehabilitation, designation of significant individual buildings and districts, and adaptive use of historic buildings in the central business district.

Preservation Dallas currently is working on the most ambitious project in its history, Discover Dallas! The project's purpose is to identify historic sites of architectural or cultural significance to Dallas so they can be used to stimulate private reinvestment and enhance the quality of life in the city.

Far from being a repository of a musty past, Preservation Dallas is a dynamic force in the present, keeping Dallasites ever aware of the city's roots, its anchor, its richly textured past. In Dallas, the old is new again.

Children playing at the Wilson House c.1910

The Wilson House, 1899, Wilson Historic District, 2002

RICHARDSON CHAMBER OF COMMERCE

IN ONLY FOUR DECADES THE CITY OF Richardson evolved from a rural village to an internationally acclaimed city of high technology, telecom companies and residential communities — a true "Telecom Corridor®."

Named after E.H. Richardson, a railroad contractor, Richardson was a mere crossroads along the North Texas landscape in 1873 dotted with cotton fields and small shops. That changed in the 1950s when two important technology companies, Texas Instruments and Collins Radio, established major operations in the area. This spawned an influx of engineers and professionals who settled nearby with their families. As a result, there was a dramatic increase in population and a concentrated effort by the city of Richardson to build outstanding schools, residential neighborhoods, parks and roads. In 1961 Texas Instruments executives helped found an institution of higher education that evolved to become the University of Texas at Dallas (UTD), specializing in engineering and computer science.

The list of companies settling in Richardson over the past 40 years mirrors the rise of the computer, telecom and technology industries in America. With the deregulation of the telecom industry in the 1980s, Richardson attracted the major telecom companies from around the world, including Nortel Networks from Canada, Alcatel from France, Fujitsu from Japan, Samsung from Korea and MCI/WorldCom from America.

In 1988, when Richardson's telecom industry was really booming, the *Dallas Times Herald* proclaimed Richardson as "The Telecom Corridor®." By 1992 *Business Week* named the Telecom Corridor® as "one of the hot spots for growth" and the name "Telecom Corridor®" was registered as a trademark by the Richardson Chamber of Commerce.

Obviously, the Telecom Corridor® is no anonymous office park on the prairie. The trademarked, T-shaped area includes all 28.3 square miles of Richardson. It straddles U.S. 75, north from IH 635 (LBJ Freeway) and extends along the east and west flanks of the new President George Bush Turnpike (State Highway 190). Within these boundaries are the offices of over 700 tech firms, half of which are in telecommunications. At the dawn of the 21st century, many consider the Telecom Corridor® to be the densest and most significant concentration of telecom companies in the world.

The critical elements that originally attracted so many corporations to the Telecom Corridor® and that continue to attract telecom and high-tech companies, including Cisco Systems, SBC Communications and Lucent Technologies, to Richardson have been consistent over the years. Richardson provides an excellent high-tech labor pool, a highly networked tech business community, a pro-business municipal government, superb K-12 and

Night view of Telecom Corridor® area along U.S. 75 looking north toward the President George Bush Turnpike

higher education systems, a moderate cost of living, and easy access to reliable domestic and international transportation systems.

The city of Richardson is an unusual combination of high-powered business sophistication and small town community. Richardson has been named the safest city in Texas, and the Richardson Independent School District has been honored as one of "America's 25 Best School Systems." The residential neighborhoods are brimming with beautiful, reasonably priced homes, local parks and recreation facilities. Clearly, Richardson offers a unique place in which to live and work.

THE BILL PRIEST INSTITUTE

THE BILL J. PRIEST INSTITUTE FOR ECONOMIC Development, established in 1989 to support economic development in Dallas County, was named for Dr. Bill J. Priest, founding chancellor of the Dallas County Community College District. The Institute's vision is to be the work force development and business performance improvement leader in Dallas. To this end, the Institute provides an array of services ranging from assessment, customized training, career training, business consulting and job placement to leased office space, small business start-up assistance and networking services. Assistance with patents, copyrights, trademarks, international trade, environmental compliance and government procurement is also available. The dedicated staff at the Bill Priest Institute strives to take customers to a level of world-class performance by valuing clients, acting with integrity, communicating openly and being accountable and adaptable.

The Bill Priest Institute is a small, nontraditional, nonprofit division of the Dallas County Community College District. Much of the Institute's focus is on developing the skills of the local work force and helping customers find gainful employment.

The Institute's contract/customized training for medium-to-large-sized businesses and community-based and government organizations provides a full range of business performance improvement services, from line training to leadership development — and everything in between. Corporate training services begin with a comprehensive organizational assessment, followed by customized curriculum development.

In supporting the city's efforts to expand and relocate businesses and create new jobs, the Institute employs innovative strategies to prepare individuals to meet employer needs throughout Dallas County. The Institute's qualified counselors train the under-employed and unemployed in classroom settings. Additionally, the Institute continually seeks to provide the leading-edge in training, including finding ways to blend online training with classroom training.

The Institute's Small Business Development Centers (SBDC), provided via a partnership with the Small Business Administration, help small businesses start or grow. SBDC programs have provided counseling to more than 75,000 area companies since their inception. The SBDCs offer low- or no-cost face-to-face counseling and training. Additionally, the Institute offers a Business Incubation Center, providing lower-than-market-rate rents for up to 60 businesses on site. To move into the center, fledgling companies must have approved business plans. Participating businesses can stay for up to four years, allowing them time to grow strong foundations before relocating.

As Dallas city leaders work to develop the economy, the Institute's location near downtown makes it ideally positioned to serve the work force training needs of individuals and companies in the area. The Institute's past accomplishments provide a strong foundation for future success.

The Bill Priest Institute, located near downtown, provides creative training strategies to prepare individuals to meet local employer needs.

DALLAS HISTORICAL SOCIETY

THE DALLAS HISTORICAL SOCIETY WAS founded at a dinner March 31, 1922, attended by 103 prominent citizens led by George Bannerman Dealey, publisher of *The Dallas Morning News*. The charter members elected attorney Rhodes S. Baker as the first president and approved a constitution and bylaws declaring the purpose of the organization to be "the discovery, collection, preservation, and publication of the history, historical records and data of and relating to the city and county of Dallas, Texas; and the cultivation of a taste for historic inquiry and study among its members."

For the next decade, the Society grew slowly, developing a small collection of books, photographs and maps that Vice President C. B. Gillespie stored in his office vault. In 1933 the Society reached an agreement with Southern Methodist University to store its collections in the university library. Dr. Herbert Gambrell of the history department became curator. Five years later, the Dallas Historical Society accepted an invitation from the city of Dallas to assume management of the magnificent Hall of State Building at Fair Park. Here, for the first time, the Society had the space to collect three-dimensional artifacts as well as manuscripts and to display its holdings in a museum setting.

Today, the Dallas Historical Society, which still occupies the Hall of State, has a library of more than 10,000 volumes, 3 million historic documents, 8,000 photographs, 2 million artifacts and 3,500 garments. In addition to exhibitions, the Society sponsors a series of educational programs for school children and adults. It has recently entered into a contract to curate a new Museum of Dallas County in the "Old Red" courthouse, a venue that will provide expanded exposure for its priceless collections.

Dynamic Dallas: An Illustrated History

DALLAS PUBLIC LIBRARY

CREATING A FREE PUBLIC LIBRARY IN DALLAS was the first project of the Dallas Federation of Women's Clubs, founded in 1898 by Mrs. Henry (May Dickson) Exall. After Dallas citizens contributed $11,000, Mrs. Exall requested and received a $50,000 grant from steel baron Andrew Carnegie to construct the first library building. On October 30, 1901, the original Carnegie library opened at the corner of Harwood and Commerce streets in downtown Dallas with 9,852 volumes and a staff of five. The first floor housed the entire collection, with an auditorium and the art room (the first public art gallery in Dallas) on the second floor.

The first branch library opened in 1914 in Oak Cliff, the recently annexed community on the west side of the Trinity River. Oak Cliff residents took the lead in acquiring a site, and Andrew Carnegie again supported construction with a grant of $25,000. Several more branches opened in the 1930s, but the economic impact of the Great Depression, followed by World War II, halted further development of the library system. In 1948 the Dallas Federation of Women's Clubs donated the first bookmobile, and for the next decade these libraries-on-wheels made weekly stops at shopping centers throughout the rapidly growing city.

In 1954 the badly deteriorating and overcrowded Carnegie facility was torn down and a contemporary six-story facility that held 433,000 books was built in its place. While construction was underway, the library moved to the city's busy train depot, Union Terminal. By the 1970s the second central library was also overloaded and unequipped to handle emerging technology. In 1972 the city designated a site at the corner of Young and Ervay, across from City Hall, as the location for a new central library building. When it opened in 1982 it was one of the first libraries in the country to have an online catalog system and state-of-the-art audiovisual capabilities. In 1986 the library was renamed the J. Erik Jonsson Central Library in honor of the former mayor who played a major role in its development.

Today the Dallas Public Library operates a network of 22 branches in addition to the central library, with 2.5 million holdings, including books, magazines, videos and cassettes. In 2000 the "Library on Wheels" Mobile Learning Center began providing service to several inner-city communities. While marking its centennial in 2001, the library unveiled a master plan outlining a strategy to handle the projected growth and the technological advances required to serve Dallas citizens effectively over the next decade and beyond.

Quality of Life

THE SHELTON SCHOOL AND EVALUATION CENTER

THE SHELTON SCHOOL IS A PRIVATE, NON profit, nonsectarian, co-ed school serving intelligent children with learning differences. Founded in 1976 by Dr. June Shelton, the school has attained a national reputation as a leader in learning disabilities (LD) education and is one of the most cherished of Dallas' institutions.

According to the National Institutes of Health, learning disabilities affect about one person in every seven in the United States. These disabilities, which include dyslexia, attention deficit disorder, attention deficit hyperactivity disorder, and speech and language disorders, are frequently and unfortunately misread as symptoms of below-normal intelligence.

Rather than slow — Thomas Edison and Albert Einstein had learning differences — most learning-different students are bright and expressive children whose brains simply function differently. Their intelligence quotients (IQs) are usually normal or above.

Yet because their inaccurate processing of information prevents them from unlocking the code of written language, they often have a hard time in traditional classrooms. This greatly diminishes their chances for educational success, which can lead to a downward spiral in their lives. Withdrawal, depression, hostile behavior, juvenile delinquency, abuse of drugs and alcohol, even suicide can result when learning differences are left untreated.

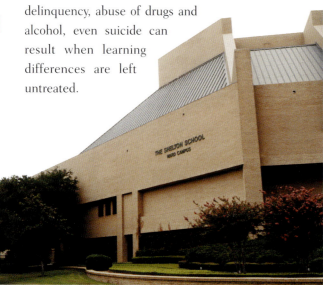

One of Dallas' most cherished institutions
© 2001 Bonneau Photography

Accredited by Southern Association of Colleges and Schools and Southern Association of Independent Schools, Shelton's individualized, structured, multisensory, academic program for learning-different students helps them build the necessary skills to successfully further their education and enjoy their lives.

Since its inception Shelton has also shared information and expertise with individuals and professionals beyond its campus. Its Outreach Program includes teacher training for public and private school teachers. Shelton's Scholars Program serves adults and children, many of whom do not attend the school, who need intensive one-on-one remedial attention. Additionally, Shelton is a national demonstration, training and referral center for educators, parents, physicians, psychologists and student interns.

Shelton's evaluation center offers comprehensive assessment for children and adults through a full clinical battery of tests that determine specific learning problems. The speech/language/hearing clinic conducts in-depth evaluations, screenings and group therapy.

With a teacher to student ratio of 1-to-6, Shelton's four divisions, lower school (early childhood-2); upper elementary school (3-5); middle school (6-8); and upper school (9-12) offer its more than 700 students a wide choice of instructional options beyond academics. These include perceptual-motor training, physical education, typing, study skills, art, crafts, computer education, social skills and creative drama.

In addition, the athletic program offers participation in a variety of sports, including football, basketball, volleyball, softball, track, tennis and golf. Enriching experiences, including museum outings, trips to a TV station, grocery shopping, designing a personal Web page, or participating in a play, help students develop a well-rounded life, packed with learning opportunities and full of fun.

Shelton School's stirring success can be seen in the improved lives of its learning-different students, who become contributing citizens, proud to live up to their potential.

Carolyn Brown Photography

TECHNOLOGY

*N*UMEROUS AND DIVERSE BUSINESSES HAVE GATHERED TO MAKE DALLAS ONE OF THE COUNTRY'S LEADING CENTERS OF TECHNOLOGICAL INNOVATION, DEVELOPMENT, MANUFACTURING AND EMPLOYMENT.

ABBOTT LABORATORIES

OVER THE LAST 100 YEARS ABBOTT Laboratories has created many medical breakthroughs, including: developing the anesthetics Pentothal and Nembutal; introducing the first diagnostic test for AIDS in 1985; developing Novir, one of the first protease inhibitors, to fight HIV in 1996; and in 1941 beginning the early commercial mass production of penicillin, aiding the U.S. war effort in the process. The company's roots trace back to 1888 when 30-year-old Dr. Wallace C. Abbott purchased a medical practice and drugstore in Chicago. He wasn't satisfied with the medicines available at the time, which were largely alcoholic extracts or waters drawn from medicinal plants. Dr. Abbott promoted a new scientific theory of pharmacy based on the alkaloid of a drug plant, allowing for smaller doses in a pill form.

From these beginnings Abbott Laboratories has grown to become a Fortune 150 company, still headquartered in North Chicago, Illinois. The diversity of its health care business makes Abbott a strong and comprehensive provider in a growing number of medical markets throughout the world. The company's three major businesses — pharmaceuticals, nutritionals and medical products — are all focused on the discovery, development and marketing of products that address some of the world's most critical medical conditions.

Abbott's ongoing mission is to deliver breakthrough medical technologies that advance the practice of health care — from prevention and diagnosis to treatment and cure. To achieve this goal, the company combines the core strengths that characterize its diverse business: leading-edge science, extensive manufacturing expertise, well-developed distribution channels and superior sales organizations.

Irving, Texas, is the home of one of Abbott Laboratories' largest facilities dedicated to research, development, manufacture and service of diagnostic instruments used to detect and assess many diseases and medical conditions. In addition to the manufacturing and development operations, the facility also includes a customer training center where health care professionals gain operational skills on Abbott's diagnostic instruments.

In 1976 the soaring growth of the newly formed Abbott Diagnostics, a division of Abbott Laboratories, required a central location for its instrument design center and manufacturing operations. The Dallas high-tech industry and proximity to Dallas/Ft. Worth International Airport made Irving an excellent choice. The site consists of over 600,000 square feet of floor space and employs a diverse work force of more than 1,500 people with professionals in areas such as software and hardware engineering, customer service, finance, manufacturing, quality assurance and human resources. The company provides numerous employee benefits at the site, including annual picnics, achievement celebrations, a fitness center and an active wellness program, cash profit sharing, and reward and recognition programs. Employee pride in the products produced and a commitment to customers and community have all been key factors to the site's success.

The Irving facility produces instrument systems, sub-assemblies, spare parts and accessories providing in excess of 5,000 end items for shipment. These products

Main building

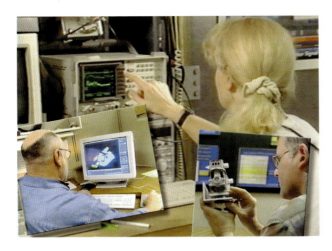

Engineering tools and personnel

serve four primary markets: immunodiagnostics, clinical chemistry, transfusion diagnostics and molecular diagnostics. The immunodiagnostics market includes testing for hepatitis, HIV, sexually transmitted diseases, cancer, pregnancy, drugs of abuse and therapeutic drug monitoring. The clinical chemistry market includes common blood tests (e.g. calcium, cholesterol and glucose) that provide doctors with information on a patient's overall health. The transfusion diagnostics market includes testing of blood for infectious disease prior to using for transfusion and helps to ensure the safety of the world's blood supply. The molecular diagnostics market includes viral, oncology, pharmacogenomic and infectious disease tests that detect at the DNA molecular level, providing superior sensitivity and specificity. Abbott's diagnostic instruments have experienced a constant evolution of innovation that began with manual testing in the early 1970s and moved to highly sophisticated automated systems during the 1980s. Labor-saving instruments with increased capacity, integrated testing on single platforms, and diagnostic tests that provide earlier detection of diseases and medical conditions are leading the way in the 21st century. Reliability, quick turnaround of results, usability, cost containment and automation are all key factors in the development of Abbott products.

A dynamic engineering organization incorporating core research, development and ongoing product support provides innovation and engineering excellence to all products. Abbott's products have been rated by industry experts to be among the most complex development and manufacturing challenges based on the number of unique technologies integrated into a single product. A medical diagnostic instrument system will integrate computer processing, precise fluidics control, chemical reaction temperature control and high-sensitivity optical detection while internally employing the robotics of blood handling automation. Abbott's continuing ability to meet this type of technical challenge has earned the company many awards, including "Concurrent Engineering Company of the Year."

In addition to its commitment to medical care, Abbott plays an active role in supporting the communities in which its employees live and work. Abbott contributes millions of dollars annually to philanthropic organizations in the United States and around the world, from educational initiatives, to cultural institutions, to human health and welfare. Involvement in the Dallas/Ft. Worth Metroplex includes activities with area educational programs, the United Way, blood drives, the Chamber of Commerce, Habitat for Humanity and many other volunteer organizations. The value of goods and services purchased by Abbott's Irving facility exceeds $170 million, with over $50 million supporting the local Dallas/Ft. Worth Metroplex economy.

Dallas is also home to one of Abbott's five national distribution centers. The 62,400-square-foot air conditioned warehouse, built in 1975, employs 30 people and distributes products from several other Abbott divisions. Prime geographical coverage includes the southwest and midwestern states.

More than ever, diagnostic testing is playing an increasingly important role in managing the health of people worldwide — as well as the costs associated with good health care. Abbott's ability to apply sophisticated technologies and life sciences to meet the needs of patients and health care providers continues to strengthen its role as a leader in improving the quality of life for people around the world.

Instrument assembly workstation

Technology

EDS

WHETHER IT'S DESIGNING A NEW APPROACH to health care delivery, ensuring the security of U.S. Naval communications or supporting the postal system in Canada, EDS is clearly established as the leading global services company. Headquartered in Plano, Texas, part of the Dallas metroplex, EDS and its management consulting subsidiary A.T. Kearney provide strategy, implementation and hosting for 9,000 accounts in 60 countries. EDS helps its clients manage the business and technology complexities of the digital economy.

Even people who don't know EDS by name have probably benefited from the company's innovative use of technology. Consider that 13 billion business, consumer and government transactions are made possible daily because of EDS. The company processes 2.5 million ATM transactions alone every day.

With clients that include General Motors, The Dow Chemical Company and Ericsson, EDS offers solutions, integrating hardware and software, and works with alliance partners to enhance revenue and improve efficiency. Rolls-Royce, a client since 1996, reaffirmed its confidence in EDS, extending an existing contract into a new technology, services and consulting contract worth $2.1 billion. A mobile solutions center in Tokyo is helping Japanese companies eliminate boundaries. Cybird, a recognized leader in Java and 3G wireless Internet content provision, has benefited from an EDS designed high-availability Web-hosting architecture as well as information technology strategy to support rapid growth.

It's not just private enterprises that trust EDS; governments also turn to EDS. The U.S. government is looking to EDS to guide its military into the future, awarding the company the largest federal information technology contract in history — valued at $6.9 billion. An EDS-led team is developing a managed Intranet service for the U.S. Navy and Marine Corps that requires integrating 360,000 desktops. EDS e-business solutions are modernizing the United Kingdom's government and the company's work with the South Australian government has been recognized as one of the best government outsourcing relationships.

EDS integrated an award-winning authentication system at Tel Aviv's Ben Gurion International Airport that

EDS Service Management Center at the global headquarters in Plano, Texas

enhances security and efficiency for more than 85,000 Israeli citizens enrolled in the Express Entry system. This system scans an individual's biometric hand geometry characteristics at kiosk checkpoints. Meanwhile, at Las Vegas McCarran Airport, EDS developed a plan for a 21st-century airport with a common IT infrastructure that increases efficiency at ticket counters.

EDS manages more than 50,000 servers worldwide and provides Web hosting to hundreds of clients. Mainframe systems are housed inside 14 service management centers, and 140 data centers around the world help provide support.

The largest of the EDS service centers is near the heart of Dallas at its Plano headquarters. Nearly 10,000 of EDS' 140,000 employees work inside the immense, five-building complex; 250,000 square feet of space is available for hardware.

It's a far cry from the company's humble beginnings in Dallas. When former presidential candidate Ross Perot founded the company in 1962, EDS didn't own any mainframes. Instead, it used idle time on other people's mainframes to process data for EDS clients.

Still, from its inception, EDS understood how to help companies manage their data. EDS established the information technology outsourcing industry by pioneering the system management and integration industries in the 1960s and 1970s. In the 1980s the company built the world's largest private voice and data network by connecting disparate islands of data to create a new world of information that expanded beyond borders. So, when the digital economy roared into the world market like a freight train, there was no panic. EDS was a well-seasoned conductor for its clients who were already on track thanks to the company's foresight.

EDS, like most companies, is full of life experiences built by changes. General Motors acquired the company in 1984; Perot left EDS in 1986. In 1996 the company became independent again, but by 1998 EDS was in trouble. As earnings declined and revenues flattened, EDS brought in an outsider to turn the company around. Dick Brown, a 28-year veteran of the telecommunications industry, did just that. Brown prescribed drastic medicine, instituting major changes and putting the muscle back in a business that had grown pudgy from complacency. The company is now organized into four business divisions and has instituted several operating mechanisms to enhance business and sales effectiveness — a weekly report ranking the top managers and a computerized "service excellence dashboard." By 2000 EDS revenues bounced back, and reached $21.5 billion in 2001. EDS' resurgence has inspired a book, and other companies are using it as a model for success.

The EDS commitment to service excellence reaches past its clients and into the world community. Education and bridging the digital divide are top priorities. Live scientific exploration is viewed by thousands of students worldwide thanks to EDS sponsorship of the JASON project, a premier distance-learning program by Dr. Robert Ballard after the discovery of the RMS Titanic. Ballard wanted to share the experience of expeditions with students. EDS makes that possible with Internet solutions and funding. Meanwhile, EDS employees volunteer time and expertise year-round to community outreach. And on Global Volunteer Day employees enlist family and friends to work with diverse community projects ranging from painting playground equipment and repairing buildings to setting up e-mail networks. Moving into a new era, the company's hope is to expose the world to the possibilities of technology solutions while still preserving the incomparable nature of human interaction.

EDS is the first corporate contributor to the Dallas Performing Arts Center. This is one of the largest and most significant cultural projects in the history of Dallas. EDS is also the only Platinum sponsor of the Science Place in Dallas and from 2003 to 2006 will have the honor of being the title sponsor of the Byron Nelson Golf Tournament.

As EDS leads the way in the digital economy, the company is challenging the industry itself to look beyond e-space and technologies du jour. EDS leaders believe that applying technology and delivering the right strategies and solutions are critical for survival in today's economy. Enterprises today have a renewed focus on business fundamentals like security and privacy, in which EDS is the world leader. They demand products and services from partners they trust. For the founder of the IT services industry, excellence isn't just about delivering a customer's order today; it's about anticipating what clients need to transform their business for the future.

BIBLIOGRAPHY

Bendsen, Kay. "The First Telephones in Dallas: Telecommunicating and Reaching Out to the World," a paper prepared for the Master of Liberal Arts Program, 1993, Southern Methodist University.

Biderman, Rose G. *They Came to Stay: The Story of the Jews of Dallas, 1870-1997.* Austin: Eakin Press, 2002.

Bywaters, Jerry. *Seventy-Five Years of Art in Dallas.* Dallas: Dallas Museum of Fine Arts, 1978.

Carraro, Francine. *Jerry Bywaters: A Life in Art.* Austin: The University of Texas Press, 1994.

Castleberry, Vivian Anderson. *Daughters of Dallas.* Dallas: Odenwald Press, 1994.

Cohn, David. "Dallas," *Atlantic,* October, 1940.

Cristol, Gerry. *A Light in the Prairie: Temple Emanu-El of Dallas, 1872-1997.* Fort Worth: Texas Christian University Press, 1998.

"Dallas in Wonderland," *Fortune,* November, 1937.

Dallas/Fort Worth International Airport. Internet web site, http://www.dfwairport.com/

Enstam, Elizabeth York, ed. *When Dallas Became a City: Letters of John Milton McCoy, 1870-1881.* Dallas: Dallas Historical Society, 1982.

Enstam, Elizabeth York. *Women and the Creation of Urban Life: Dallas, Texas, 1843-1920.* College Station: Texas A&M Press, 1998.

Fairbanks, Robert B. *For the City as a Whole: Planning, Politics, and the Public Interest in Dallas, Texas, 1900-1965.* Columbus: Ohio State University Press, 1998.

Governar, Alan B., and Jay Brakefield. *Deep Ellum and Central Track: Where the Black and White Worlds of Dallas Converged.* Denton: University of North Texas Press, 1998.

Greater Dallas Chamber of Commerce. Internet web site, http://www.gdc.org/

Greater Dallas Illustrated. Dallas. The American Illustrating Co., 1908, reprinted 1992 by the Friends of the Dallas Public Library, Inc.

Greene, A.C., *A Place Called Dallas*: Dallas: Dallas County Heritage Society, 1975.

Hay, Laurie H., "Goals for Dallas and Why It Was Successful," a paper prepared for the Master of Liberal Arts Program, 2001, Southern Methodist University.

Hazel, Michael V. *Dallas: A History of Big D.* Austin: Texas State Historical Association, 1997.

Hazel, Michael V. *The Dallas Public Library: Celebrating a Century of Service, 1901-2001.* Denton: University of North Texas Press, 2001.

Hazel, Michael V., ed., *Dallas Reconsidered: Essays in Local History.* Dallas: Three Forks Press, 1995.

Holmes, Maxine, and Gerald Saxon, eds., *The WPA Dallas Guide and History.* Dallas: Dallas Public Library and University of North Texas Press, 1992.

Kimball, Justin F., *Our City-Dallas*. Dallas: Kessler Plan Association, 1927.

Linden, Glenn M. *Desegregating Schools in Dallas: Four Decades in the Federal Courts*. Dallas: Three Forks Press, 1995.

Liles, Allen. *Oh Thank Heaven! The Story of the Southland Corporation*. Dallas: Southland Corporation, 1977.

Marcus, Stanley. *Minding the Store: A Memoir*. Boston: Little, Brown and Company, 1974.

McElhaney, Jacquelyn Masur. *Pauline Periwinkle and Progressive Reform in Dallas*. College Station: Texas A&M Press, 1998.

McMath, Linda Barber. "Cattle Town Dallas," *Legacies*, Fall 1996.

Memorial and Biographical History of Dallas County, Texas. Chicago: The Lewis Publishing Company, 1892.

Minutaglio, Bill, and Holly Williams. *The Hidden City: Oak Cliff, Texas*. Dallas: Elmwood Press and Old Oak Cliff Conservation League, 1990.

North Central Texas Council of Governments. Internet web site, http://gls.dfwinfo.com/

Payne, Darwin. *As Old As Dallas Itself: A History of the Lawyers of Dallas, the Dallas Bar Associations, and the City They Helped Build*. Dallas: Three Forks Press, 1999.

Payne, Darwin. *Big D: Triumphs and Troubles of an American Supercity in the 20th Century*. Dallas: Three Forks Press, rev. ed., 2000.

Payne, Darwin. *Dallas: An Illustrated History*. Woodland Hills, California: Windsor Publishing Co., 1982.

Payne, Darwin, and Kathy Fitzpatrick, *From Prairie to Planes: How Dallas and Fort Worth Overcame Politics and Personalities to Build One of the World's Biggest and Busiest Airports*. Dallas: Three Forks Press, 1999.

Powers, Charris R., "The Early Days of Dallas' Mass Transit System: Streetcars," a paper prepared for the Master of Liberal Arts Program, 2000, Southern Methodist University.

Ragsdale, Kenneth B., *The Year America Discovered Texas: Centennial '36*. College Station: Texas A&M Press, 1987.

Rogers, John William. *The Lusty Texans of Dallas*. New York: E.P. Dutton and Co., rev. ed., 1960.

Schiebel, Walter J.E. *Education in Dallas: Ninety-two Years of History*. Dallas: Dallas Independent School District, 1966.

Sharpe, Ernest. *G.B. Dealey of the Dallas News*. New York: Henry Holt and Co., 1955.

Simpson, Gwen. "Early Automobiles in Dallas: Heralds of a New Age," *Heritage News* Winter, 1984, 1985.

Starling, Susanne. *Land Is the Cry!: Warren Angus Ferris, Pioneer Texas Surveyor and Founder of Dallas County*. Austin: Texas State Historical Association, 1998.

Sumner, Alan R., ed. *Dallasights: An Anthology of Architecture and Open Spaces*. [Dallas]: American Institute of Architects, Dallas Chapter, 1978.

Thomas, Mary Martha Hosford. *Southern Methodist University: Founding and Early Years*. Dallas: SMU Press, 1974.

Thompson, Kerry. "Central Expressway: The Oldest Continuous Freeway Controversy," a paper prepared for the Master of Liberal Arts Program, 1999, Southern Methodist University.

White, James F. Architecture at *SMU: 50 Years and Buildings*. Dallas: SMU Press, 1966.

White, William W. "The Texas Slave Insurrection of 1860," *Southwestern Historical Quarterly*, January, 1949.

Whiteside, Frances Beall. "The Annual Trade Excursions," a paper prepared for the Master of Liberal Arts Program, 1996, Southern Methodist University.

INDEX

Abilene 38	Belasco, David 85	Carnegie, Andrew 59
Adams, Nathan 92	Bell, Alexander Graham 37	Carpenter, John 98
Adamson, W. H. 81	Belle, Scioto 12	Carter, Amon 97
Adolphus Hotel, The 80	Belo, Alfred H. . .38, 40, 52, 56, 117	Caruth, William W. 72
Adoue, J. B. 53	Billingsley, John B. 11, 13	Cathedral of the Sacred Heart . .56
Aikman, Troy 116	Bird, Jonathan 11	CCC 96
Alamo 9, 92	Black Jack Grove 24	Cedar Hill 26
Alger, Bruce 104, 105	Blaylock, Mayor Louis 82	Cedar Snag 15
American Airlines 114	Bluitt, Dr. Benjamin 49, 51	Cedar Springs 10
American League 116	Bond, Frank S. 38	Cedars 37, 81
American Petroleum Institute . . .77	Bonner, W.A., The 45	Centennial Commission 92
Appomattox 26	Booker T. Washington	Centennial Midway, The 94
Armstrong, John S. 44, 56, 72	High School 81	Centennial, The 91
Army 16, 71	Bossom, Sir Alfred C. 76	Central Dallas Public Library . .114
Arts District, The 114	Bradford, Daisy 77	Chamber of Commerce, The
Associated Advertising	Brodie, Otto 68	. . . . .52, 68, 92, 106
Clubs of America 91	Browder Springs 29	Chance-Vought 98
AT-6 Texan 96	Brown, John Henry 28	Cherokees 11
Atlantic Monthly 93	Bryan High School 81	Chisholm Trail 17
Austin, Stephen F. 10, 22, 37	Bryan, John Neely	Citizens Association 84
Bachman Lake 71	. . . . .11, 21, 37, 48, 106	Citizens Charter Association
Baker Hotel 80	Bunkley, C.B. Jr. 100, 101	. . . . .85, 94
Ballard, Kay 96	Burford, Judge Nat 15, 24	Citizens Council 94, 106
Bar Association of Dallas 33	Burt, R.E. 85	City Council 112
Barnes, Edward Larrabee 114	Busch Building 117	City Directory 32, 67
Barnett, Tom 80	Busch, Adolphus 80	City Hall 112
Bass, Sam 37	Bywaters, Jerry 86, 88, 89	Civil Aeronautics Board 109
Baylor Hospital 56	Cabell, Mayor Earle 106	Civil War 24
Beeman, John 13	Caddos 11	Civilian Conservation Corps, The
Beeman, Margaret 11	Camp Dick 71	96
Belasco Cup 85	Carnegie Library 59	Clay, Henry 25

Dynamic Dallas: An Illustrated History

Cliff Water Supply Co. 44
Cockrell, Alexander 16, 22, 32
Cockrell, Sarah Horton
. . . . . . .16, 18, 19, 22, 26, 32, 33
Coffee, Holland 10
Coit, Catharine 32
Cole Park 40
Cole, J.H. 40
Colquitt, O.B. 83
Commercial Club 52
Committee of Expulsion 23
Connally, John 107
Connor, William O. 53
Cooke, William G. 10
Coppell 112
Corsicana 28, 91
Crane, Martin M. 83
Critic Club 60
Crockett, John M. 15
Crutcher, George W. 43
Crutchfield House, The 19, 22
Cuban, Mark 116
Cullum, Robert B. 98, 106
Curtiss 68
Dahl, George L. 92
Daily Times Herald 56, 69
Dallas Alley 118
Dallas Art Institute 86
Dallas Art Museum 86
Dallas Artists League 86
Dallas Automobile Club 67
Dallas Chamber of Commerce, The
. . . . .68, 109
Dallas City Hall 114
Dallas City Plan and
Improvement League 60
Dallas Cotton Exchange 72, 74
Dallas County Citizens League .83
Dallas County Courthouse 50

Dallas County Treasurer, The . . .24
Dallas County
. . . .10, 22, 34, 48, 68, 80, 94, 104
Dallas Cowboys 116
Dallas Daily Herald 45
Dallas Federation of Women, The
. 56
Dallas Herald, The . .15, 22, 23, 49
Dallas Klan No. 66 Drum and
Bugle Corps 83
Dallas Library Association 58
Dallas Little Theatre 85
Dallas Mavericks 114
Dallas Morning News, The
. . . . .40, 49, 67, 83, 93, 105
Dallas Museum of Art 59, 114
Dallas Museum of Fine Arts
. . . . .59, 89, 92, 104
Dallas Stars 114
Dallas Summer Musicals 97
Dallas Times Herald 105
Dallas Times 105
Dallas, Commodore
James Alexander 15
Dallas, George Mifflin 14
Dallas/Fort Worth Consolidated
Metropolitan Statistical Area . . .112
DART 113
Davis, Governor E.J. 25
Dealey Plaza 12, 95, 106
Dealey, George Bannerman
. . . . .38, 41, 60, 117
Dealey, Joe 107
"Deep Ellum Blues" 88
Deep Ellum District, The
. . . . .86, 88, 117
DeGolyer Library 38, 106
Denison 66
Denton County 11, 81

Denton 11, 37, 81
DFW International Airport
. . . . .97, 109, 112
DISD 112
Dorris, George P. 66
Dorsey, James A. 53
Dowling, Dick 27
Drefuss & Sons 117
Dreyfuss, Sol 54
Duncanville 112
Durham, W.J. 100
Eagle Ford 34
Eakins, J.J. 24
Ellis County 28
Ennis 66
Ervay, Mayor Henry S. 25, 26
Evans, Hiram Wesley 84
Exall, May Dickson 56
Exxon 113
Fair Park Auditorium, The . .80, 97
Fair Park Casino 96
Fair Park 67, 80, 92, 113
Fannin County 23
Feld und Flur 49
Ferber, Edna 37
Ferguson, Miriam 84
Ferris, Warren 10, 23
Flanders, James 36
Flavia, Princess 81
Florence, Fred 92
Ford Motor Co. 67, 98
Ford, Col. John S. "Rip" 40, 56
Forest Avenue High School 81
Fort Inglish 10
Fort King 10
Fort Worth Consolidated Metropolitan
Statistical Area 112
Fort Worth
. . .11, 22, 34, 54, 66, 97, 108, 111

Fourier, Charles 17	Hogg, James S. 91	Kennedy, Robert 106
Frisco 116	Hogue, Alexandre 86	Kessler Plan Association
Galveston Bay 12, 22, 38, 49	Holmes, William A. 108	. . . . .60, 61, 82
Galveston Daily News, The 40	Hord's Ridge 14, 44	Kessler, George 60, 61, 85, 97
Galveston 47	Houston & Texas Central Railroad	Kickapoos 11
Gano, Richard M. 34	. . . . .22, 97	King, B.B. 88
Garland 112	Houston 13, 22, 47, 92, 109	King, Dr. Henry 10
Gaston Avenue Baptist Church	Houston, Sam 13	Kingsboro 10
. . . . .40, 56	Huey and Philp 36	Kirk, Ron 112
Gaston, William H. 40, 41	Hughes, W.E. 56	Kiwanis 82
General Motors 98	Hunt Jarvis 63	Ku Klux Klan 83, 84, 106,
Georgetown 72	Hunt, H.L. 105	La Reunion 17, 23
Gilbert, Mabel 13	Hyatt Regency Dallas 112	*La Tribuna Italiana* 49
Goettinger, Max 54	Hyer, Dr. Robert S. 72	Lake Dallas 81
Good, John J. 22, 33	Inge, William 86	Lakewood Country Club 69
Goodnight, Colonel Charles 28	International Aviators 68	Lancaster 14, 26
Grand Opera House 55	J.C. Penney 113	Landry, Tom 116
Grand Prairie 98	Jackson, Andrew 13	Lane, John W. 28
Grapevine 109, 112	Jackson, Bob 108	Lang and Witchell 53, 74
Great Depression 94	Jackson, Maynard Jr. 99, 100	Latimer, James Wellington 15
Green, Cecil 99	Jefferson Peak 43	Lawrence, Jerome 86
Green, E.H.R. Ned 66	Jefferson 16, 22, 38	Lawther, Joe E. 71
Green, Paul 85	Jefferson, Blind Lemon 88	Ledbetter, Huddy "Leadbelly" . . .88
Green, W.A. 53	Jefferson, John 99	Lee, George T. 84
Grove, Captain D.E. 53	*Job Boat No. 1* 27	Lee, Robert E. 86
Guillot, Maxime 22	John Birch Society 105	Lee, Umphrey 72
Gulf of Mexico 28, 51	Johnson, Andrew 26	Leonard, Silas 24
H&TC Railroad 32, 61, 86	Johnson, Lady Bird 105	Lewisville 38
H.A. Harvey Jr. 51	Johnson, Lyndon B. 96, 105	Lincoln High School 100, 101
Harris, Adolph 53, 54	Joiner, Columbus Marion (Dad) . .77	Lindsley, Philip 36
Hart, District Judge Hardin 33	Jones, Jerry 116	Little Rock 22
Hay, Stephen J. 69	Jones, Margo 86	Little Theater of Dallas 85
Haynes, Sallie 27	Jonsson, J. Erik	Lone Star Cowboys 88
Henderson County 27	. . . . .99, 106, 108, 109, 114	Lone Star Defenders 24
Henry, John L. 36, 43	Kahn, E. M. 36, 54	Long, Ben 17, 18
Hicks, Steve "Texas" 69	Kaufman 10, 22	Love Field 71, 85, 97, 106
Hicks, Tom 69, 116	Keating, Cecil A. 40, 41	Love, Lt. Moss L. 71
Highland Park 72	Kennedy Library 107	Love, Marvin B. 98
Hillsboro 38	Kennedy, Jackie 106	Lynch, Judge 85
Hoblitzelle, Karl 83	Kennedy, John F. . . .105, 106, 107	Maennerchor, Schweitzer 49

Magnolia Building 76, 80, 113
Magnolia Lounge 87
Magnolia Petroleum Building
........................74, 80
Majestic Theater, The 85, 86
Marcus, Herbert 54, 93
Marcus, Minnie 54
Marcus, Stanley 105
Marion, Columbus 77
Marsalis, Thomas L. 40
Mason Refining Co. 77
Mayer's Garden 37
McCommas Bluff 51
McCoy, John Calvin ..13, 14, 26, 43
McCoy, John M. 26
McDermott, Eugene 99
McGarvey, Captain James H. ...27
McKinney 24
Meacham Field 97
Mesquite Championship Rodeo
........................116
Metroplex 112
Meyerson Symphony Center ..114
Milford 24
Military Road Act 10
Miller, Crill 24, 69,
Miller, Lestere 69
Millwood 24
Mineola 38
Mitchell, Billy 71
Moore, Andrew M. 19
Moore, Henry 114
Morton Meyerson Symphony
Center, The 115
Murchison, Clint Jr. 116
Museum of Natural History 92
Mustang Branch 13
NAACP 99
Nacogdoches County 10
Nasher Sculpture Garden 114

Nasher, Raymond 114
National Indignation Conference
........................105
National Youth Administration, The
........................96
Negro Chamber of Commerce ..99
Neiman, Al 54
Neiman, Carrie 54
Neiman-Marcus 54, 93
Netherwood, Major Douglas B. ...71
New Century Cotton Mill Co. ...49
Nichols, Charles H. 37
North American Aviation
of Inglewood 96, 98
North Dallas High School ..40, 81
Norton, Andrew Banning ...25, 26
Norton's Union Intelligencer 26
O.K. Corral 37
Oak Cliff High School 81
Oak Cliff Park 44
Oak Cliff 44, 60, 66, 99, 107
Ochiltree, Judge William Beck ..15
Old Red Courthouse 48, 106
Oliver, F.N. 45
Orlopp, M.A. 50
Oswald, Lee Harvey 107
P-51 Mustangs 96
Padgitt, Tom 53
Parkinson, E. 13
Partee, Cecil J. 101
Peak, W.W. 23
Pearl Harbor 96
Pegasus 77, 114
Pei, I.M. 114
Periwinkle, Pauline 56
Peters Company, The 12
Peters, William C. 12
Peyton, Harry L. 69
Picasso, Pablo 104
Pilot Point 24, 45

Pioneer Plaza 119
Pittman, Portia Washington 81
Plano 98, 112
Plaza Hotel 80
Polk, James K. 14
Praetorian Building 55
Progressive Voters League 99
Prohibition 79
Pryor, Dr. Samuel 16
Public Art Gallery, The 59
Ragsdale, Kenneth 93
Rattan, Wade (Hamp) 12
Reardon, E.M. 40
Reaugh, Frank 59
Red River 10, 22
Register of Motor Vehicles, The ..67
Republic of Texas Congress 10
Reunion Tower 112
Richardson 98, 112
Rivera, Diego 104
Robertson, Felix 84
Rodgers, Woodall 97
Rodriguez, Alex 116
Rogers, John William Jr. 85
Romberg, Sigmund 81
Roosevelt, Franklin D. 93, 96
Round Rock 37
Ruby, Jack 107
Rusk County 77
Ruth, Babe 79
San Antonio 22, 47, 92, 109
San Jacinto 9, 40, 92
Sanger Brothers 34, 37, 53, 54
Sanger, Alexander ...36, 37, 53, 83
Sanger, Philip 36, 37, 54
Sanger-Harris 117
Sanguinet and Staats 55
Santa Anna 40, 92
Santa Fe Building 117
Savin, Ollie 67

Schoellkopf, G. H. 53
Schramm, Tex 116
Scott, Sam H. 49
Scyene 26, 37
Seagoville 96
Seay, Robert 28
Seegar, Dr. John A. 36
Shahn, Ben 104
Shawnee Trail 17, 119
Shawnees 11
Shelton, Joe 88
Sherman 38
Shirley, Myra Belle
  (see also Starr, Belle) 37
Silkwood, Solomon 12
Simpson, J.B. 40
Sisters of St. Vincent, The 57
Slaughter, C.C. 43, 59
Sloan, Robert 10
Smith v. Allwright 88
Smith, A. Maceo 99
Smith, Henry "Buster" 67, 88
Smith, Sydney 40
Smithsonian Institution 15
Snag Boat Dallas 51
Societa Roma Mutuo Soccorso . .49
Southern Methodist University
  . . . . .38, 72, 73, 106
Southland Corporation, The 99
Southwestern Medical School . .96
St. Nicholas Hotel 19, 22
Stanley Cup 116
Starlight Ballet 96
Starlight Operetta 97
Starr, Belle ("Bandit Queen") . . .37
State Fair Music Hall 80
State Fair of Texas
  . . . . .40, 41, 67, 80, 81, 116
State-Thomas Historic District . .117
Staubach, Roger 116

Stevenson, Adlai E. 105, 106
Sunset High 82
Super Bowl 116
Swindells, John W. 26
Tannehill Masonic Lodge 14
Tarrant County 11
Tarrant, Edward H. 11
Tejas Warrior 113
Temple Emanu-El 56
Tenison, A. P. 53
Tennant, Allie 86, 113
Terrell .66
Texan Land and Emigration
  Company 12
Texas & Pacific Railway . .29, 38, 60
Texas Almanac 38
Texas Baptist Memorial
  Sanitarium 56
Texas Centennial Exposition . .87, 92
Texas Instruments 98
Texas Press Association 91
Texas Rangers (baseball team) . .116
Texas Rangers 24, 37
Texas School of Aviation 69
Texas Schoolbook Depository . .107
Texas State Fair 40
Thornton, Robert L.
  . . . . .92, 94, 98, 108
Three Forks 9
Titche, Edward 54
Titche-Goettinger 54, 117
Travis, Olin 86
Tri-Centennial Exposition 49
Trinity Play Park 60
Trinity Railway Express 113
Trinity River Navigation Company
 51
Trinity River, The
  . . . . .9, 22, 32, 51, 66, 82
Trinity 21, 31, 49, 81, 94

Turner, E.P. 83
Turtle Creek 60
U.S. Supreme Court, The 100
Ulrickson Committee 85
Ulrickson, Charles E. 82
Union Station 96
Union Terminal 61
United Nations Association . . .105
United Nations 104
University of Texas Southwestern
  Medical Center 97
University Park 72
Village Creek 11
W.A.F. .13
Waco 10, 11, 38, 66
Wahoo Park 100
Walker, Aaron "T-Bone" 88
Walker, Edwin A. 105
Walker, Landen 13
Wallace, Capt. W.A.A.
  "Big Foot" 40
Warwick 10
Waxahachie 24
Weichsel, C. 53
Welch, Carie 109
Welch, Robert 105
White Rock Creek 10
White Rock Lake 81, 96
White Rock 10
Wiley, Joseph E. 49
Williams, Tennessee 86
Wilson Building 54, 117
Woodrow Wilson High 82
World War I 52, 66, 67, 71
World War II 61, 86, 98
Wright, S. M. 98
Yahoo Inc. 116
Younger, John 37

INDEX OF PARTNERS AND WEB SITES

7-ELEVEN, INC. 178
www.7-11.com

ABBOTT LABORATORIES ..268
abbottlaboratories.com

ADLETA & POSTON,
REALTORS 140
adletaposton.com

AGUIRRECORPORATION 198
www.aguirre.com

AMERICAN AIRLINES 190
www.aa.com

AMERICAN GOLF
CORPORATION 224
www.americangolf.com

ASSOCIATED
AIR CENTER 192
www.associatedaircenter.com

ATI CAREER TRAINING 226
www.ATICareertraining.com

BARON & BUDD, P.C. 200
www.baronbudd.com

BAYLOR HEALTH
CARE SYSTEM 216
www.baylorhealth.com

BILL PRIEST INSTITUTE,
THE 261
www.billpriestinstitute.org

BORDEN 160
www.elsie.com

BRIGGS-FREEMAN REAL ESTATE
BROKERAGE 124
www.briggs-freeman.com

BUCKNER
BENEVOLENCES 228
www.buckner.org

CANDLEWOOD SUITES 230
www.candlewoodsuites.com

CAPITAL ALLIANCE 146
www.cadallas.com

CAROLYN BROWN,
PHOTOGRAPHER 186
www.carolynbrownphotographer.com

CATHOLIC DIOCESE
OF DALLAS 250
www.cathdal.org

CATHOLIC EDUCATION
OF DALLAS 251
www.cathdal.org

CERAMIC TILE
INTERNATIONAL 168
www.interceramicusa.com

CITY OF PLANO 252
www.plano.gov

COURIERGUY.COM 187
www.courierguy.com

CROWN COMPUTER
SUPPLIES, INC. 169
www.crowncomputer.com

DALLAS CAN! ACADEMY ...232
www.dallascan.org

DALLAS CHRISTIAN
SCHOOL 253
www.dallaschristian.com

DALLAS COUNTY COMMUNITY
COLLEGE DISTRICT 220
www.dcccd.edu

DALLAS HISTORICAL
SOCIETY 262
www.hallofstate.com/www.dallashistory.org

DALLAS PUBLIC LIBRARY ...263
www.dallaslibrary.org

DALLAS THEOLOGICAL
SEMINARY 254
www.dts.edu

DALLAS VA
MEDICAL CENTER 234

DIKITA ENTERPRISES 126
www.dikita.com

EDS 270
www.eds.com

EPISCOPAL DIOCESE
OF DALLAS 236
www.episcopal-dallas.org

FRISCO SQUARE 128
www.friscosquare.com

FRISCO, TEXAS 255
www.friscoedc.com

GARRETT METAL DETECTORS 162
www.garrett.com

GOODMAN FAMILY OF BUILDERS 130
www.goodmanfamily.com

HALFF ASSOCIATES, INC. 212
www.halff.com

HARWOOD INTERNATIONAL 132
www.harwoodinternational.com

HUGHES & LUCE, LLP 202
www.hughesluce.com

HUITT-ZOLLARS, INC. 204
www.huitt-zollars.com

INTERNATIONAL LINGUISTICS CENTER 256
www.sil.org

INTERVEST COMPANIES 180
www.bradfordsuites.com

JR MORTGAGE CORP. 156
www.aragnauth@yahoo.com

KINDRED HOSPITAL 238
www.kindredhealthcare.com

KPMG LLP 148
www.us.kpmg.com

MANHATTAN CONSTRUCTION COMPANY 141

MARY KAY INC. 164
www.marykay.com

McSHAN FLORIST 182
www.mcshan.com

MEDICAL CITY DALLAS HOSPITAL 257
www.lonestarhealth.com

MILLS ELECTRICAL CONTRACTORS 134
www.millselectrical.com

MRS BAIRD'S 184
www.mrsbairds.com

OCCIDENTAL CHEMICAL CORPORATION 166
www.oxychem.com

OLD CITY PARK: THE HISTORICAL VILLAGE OF DALLAS 258

PARKLAND HEALTH & HOSPITAL SYSTEM 240
www.pmh.org

PILGRIM'S PRIDE 174
www.pilgrimspride.com

PRESBYTERIAN HOSPITAL OF DALLAS 242
www.phscare.org

PRESERVATION DALLAS ...259
www.preservationdallas.org

PULTE HOMES 142
www.pulte.com

REPUBLIC GROUP OF INSURANCE COMPANIES ..150
www.republink.com

RICHARDSON CHAMBER OF COMMERCE 260
www.telecomcorridor.com

RTKL 206
www.rtkl.com

RYLAND HOMES 136
www.ryland.com

SHARIF & MUNIR 138
www.sharif-munir.com

SNELLING AND SNELLING INC. 208
www.snelling.com

STATE FARM® INSURANCE 152
www.statefarm.com

STRASBURGER & PRICE 210
www.strasburger.com

SALVATION ARMY, THE ..244
www.salvationarmytexas.org

SHELTON SCHOOL AND EVALUATION CENTER, THE 264
www.shelton.org

STANLEY WORKS, THE 170
www.stanley.com

UNIVERSITY OF TEXAS AT DALLAS, THE 246
www.utdallas.edu

URSULINE ACADEMY OF DALLAS 248
www.ursuline.pvt.k12.tx.us

WASHINGTON MUTUAL ..154
www.wamu.net

WRR CLASSICAL 101.1 FM ..194
www.wrr101.com

Dynamic Dallas: An Illustrated History